Security Strategy and Transatlantic Relations

Security Strategy and Transatlantic Relations is the first major assessment of the impact on transatlantic relations of the US National Security Strategy of 2002 and the European Security Strategy of 2003.

The book argues that the US and EU security strategies have an enduring relevance, representing critical efforts to reconceptualise the radically changed nature of post-9/11 international security and to define new post-Cold War security doctrines. These strategies provide insights into the strains and tensions in the transatlantic relationship, particularly during and after the 2003 Iraq war, but also reveal how both the United States and the European Union have become 'revolutionary', not status quo, powers.

The contributors to this volume address three key questions. The first is the degree to which these new security strategies signal convergence or divergence in US and EU foreign and security policy. Second, what tangible political and policy impacts can be attributed to the new security strategies, particularly in the 'war on terror' and on the role of NATO? Third, what are the implications for US and EU policies towards specific regions, particularly the Middle East, Russia and China?

Offering wide-ranging perspectives on transatlantic security policies, this new text will appeal to students and scholars of international relations, European politics, American politics and security studies.

Roland Dannreuther is a Senior Lecturer in Politics at the University of Edinburgh. **John Peterson** is Professor of International Politics at the University of Edinburgh.

Security Strategy and Transatlantic Relations

Edited by
Roland Dannreuther and
John Peterson

LONDON AND NEW YORK

First published 2006
by Routledge
2 Park Square, Milton Park, Abingdon, Oxon OX14 4RN

Simultaneously published in the USA and Canada
by Routledge
270 Madison Ave, New York, NY 10016

Routledge is an imprint of the Taylor & Francis Group, an informa business

Typeset in Times by
Book Now Ltd
Printed and bound in Great Britain by
MPG Books Ltd, Bodmin, Cornwall

British Library Cataloguing in Publication Data
A catalogue record for this book is available from the British Library

Library of Congress Cataloging in Publication Data
Security strategy and transatlantic relations/edited by Roland Dannreuther
and John Peterson.
    p. cm.
  Includes bibliographical references and index.
  1. National security–United States. 2. National security–Europe.
3. United States–Military policy. 4. Europe–Military policy. 5. United States–
Relations–Europe. 6. Europe–Relations–United States. 7. World politics–
21st century. I. Dannreuther, Roland. II. Peterson, John, 1958– .

UA23.S415 2006
355'.03351821–dc22   2006001551

ISBN10: 0–415–40190–9 (hbk)
ISBN10: 0–415–40189–5 (pbk)

ISBN13: 978–0–415–40190–6 (hbk)
ISBN13: 978–0–415–40189–0 (pbk)

Contents

Contributors

Ronald D. Asmus	German Marshall Fund
Alyson J. K. Bailes	Stockholm International Peace Research Institute
Annika Bergman	University of Edinburgh
Fraser Cameron	European Policy Centre
Chad Damro	University of Edinburgh
Roland Dannreuther	University of Edinburgh
Anoushiravan Ehteshami	University of Durham
Jolyon Howorth	Yale University
Luke March	University of Edinburgh
Seán Molloy	University of Glasgow
John Peterson	University of Edinburgh
James H. Wyllie	University of Aberdeen

Preface and acknowledgements

This volume is the product of one of those projects that never, ever lacked setbacks. It has been seen through to completion only through a combination of very hard work and good humour. Its first seeds were sown in early 2005 when Robert Cooper – Director of Politico-Military Affairs in the European Union Council and former foreign policy advisor to the British Prime Minister – delivered the first annual John Erickson Lecture at the University of Edinburgh as part of Edinburgh Politics' Transatlantic Seminar series. As one of the authors of the European Security Strategy, Cooper's reflections on the state of relations between Europe and America after the transatlantic crisis over Iraq inspired us to gather together a group of leading analysts to interrogate the meaning of the appearance of the European Union's first ever security strategy the year after the publication of the 2002 US National Security Strategy. At a defining 'Trumanesque' moment in the history of international relations, we saw an opportunity to use the security strategies as lenses through which to view the future of the transatlantic alliance.

We had hoped to include a revised version of Cooper's lecture as a sort of keynote chapter to this volume. However, events conspired – recalling our earlier allusion to 'setbacks' – to make this aspiration one that remained unrealised. Still, references to the original lecture (see Cooper 2005b), delivered the week that George W. Bush and other top American officials had visited Brussels and demonstrated both a will to move on from Iraq *and* a recognition of the primacy of the European Union itself in transatlantic relations, appear repeatedly throughout the book.

Will to get beyond Iraq and recognise Europe's importance (as 'home to some of our oldest and closest allies') was also evident in a revised US National Security Strategy, which appeared in March 2006 at the last minute (literally) before this book went to press. Its appearance seemed, at first, to be yet another setback to this project. However, upon investigation, the 2006 NSS reflects considerably more continuity than change with the 2002 version on which this book focuses. In fact, each chapter of the 2006 version begins with a summary of what NSS 2002 decreed about 'ending tyranny', 'defeating terrorism', 'defusing regional conflict', and so on. Of course, the claim of the 2006 NSS to be 'founded on two pillars' – 'promoting freedom, justice, and human dignity' and 'leading a growing community of democracies' – reflected a subtle course correction and change of foreign policy style in the second George W. Bush administration (see Chapter 12 of this volume). But Bush's own prelude to the 2006 NSS revealed starkly that the underlying conditions that prompted the radical strategic shift of the 2002 version still obtained: 'America is at war. This is a wartime national security strategy.'

And this is a book whose editors are indebted to a long list of institutions and individuals. The University Association of Contemporary European Studies (UACES), the University of Edinburgh Development Trust, and the School of Social and Political Studies of the University of Edinburgh provided funding that made possible two workshops that brought together contributors in Edinburgh and Brussels in February and September 2005, respectively. We are grateful to Margaret Beechey, Sir David Edward, Drew Scott, and (especially) Andrea Birdsall for their efforts in organising the Edinburgh event, and Fraser and Margaret Cameron and Stéphanie Danis for all they did to make us feel welcome in Brussels. We also owe vociferous votes of thanks to Sven Biscop, Kori Schake and William Walker for reading and commenting on various parts of earlier drafts of the book's manuscript. Perhaps above all, we were provided with absolutely professional and essential research assistance by three University of Edinburgh postgraduate students, Travis Elliott, Emily Rueb and Natasa Zambelli, whose futures are so bright we have to wear our proverbial shades.

As is so often the case when edited books succeed in being both coherent and greater than the sum of their parts, as we hope this one is, we owe the biggest vote of thanks to our contributors. All were unfaltering and undaunted in responding to our (hopefully) constructive criticisms and injunctions to meet the next deadline. All delivered analyses that are a credit to the collective analytical enterprise. It has been our pleasure and privilege to work with them.

Roland Dannreuther and John Peterson
Edinburgh, March 2006

Abbreviations

ASC	Alliance Strategic Concept
ASEAN	Association of South East Asian Nations
CFR	Council on Foreign Relations
CFSP	Common Foreign and Security Policy
CIA	Central Intelligence Agency
CIS	Commonwealth of Independent States
CoE	Council of Europe
CSIS	Center for Strategic and International Studies
EAS	External Action Service
ECAP	European Capabilities Action Plan
EDA	European Defence Agency
ENP	European Neighbourhood Policy
ESDP	European Security and Defence Policy
ESS	European Security Strategy
EU-ISS	European Union Institute for Security Studies
FRY	Federal Republic of Yugoslavia
GCC	Gulf Cooperation Council
GDP	gross domestic product
GMEI	Greater Middle East Initiative
GWOT	'global war on terror(ism)'
IAEA	International Atomic Energy Authority
ICC	International Criminal Court
ICI	Istanbul Cooperation Initiative (NATO)
IFC	International Finance Corporation
IGC	Intergovernmental Conference
IISS	Institute for International Strategic Studies
ISAF	International Security Assistance Force
LoI	Letter of Intent
MENA	Middle East and North Africa
MERCOSUR	Mercado Común del Sur
NATO	North Atlantic Treaty Organisation
NIC	National Intelligence Council
NSC	National Security Council

NSD	National Security Directive
NSS	National Security Strategy
NTA	New Transatlantic Agenda
OCCAR	Organisation Conjointe de Coopération en matière d'Armement
ODA	overseas development assistance
OSCE	Organisation for Security and Cooperation in Europe
R&D	research and development
RIIA	Royal Institute of International Affairs
RRF	(European) Rapid Reaction Force
SIPRI	Stockholm International Peace Research Institute
UAE	United Arab Emirates
UNSC	United Nations Security Council
SAVE	Strategy Against Violent Extremism
SORT	Strategic Offensive Reductions Treaty
WEU	Western European Union
WMD	weapons of mass destruction

1 Introduction

Security strategy as doctrine

Roland Dannreuther and John Peterson

In September 2004, the appointment of John Bruton as head of the European Commission's delegation in Washington was a signal of genuine will on the part of the European Union to heal relations with the United States after the previous year's trauma over Iraq. A former Prime Minister (Taoiseach) of Ireland, a state with a massive American diaspora and strength beyond its size in the US political class, Bruton was a political heavyweight. As a delegate to the Convention on the Future of Europe (2002–3), Bruton had helped draft the European Union's 'Constitutional Treaty', which promised a major overhaul of its rules and institutions. Specifically, it pledged to endow the Union with its own powerful Minister of Foreign Affairs as well as a new External Action Service (EAS), with the potential to transform the already large (80-member) Commission delegation in Washington into a 'real' embassy, with genuine resources and clout. An important reason to think these institutional changes might make a difference was that the European Union had earlier (in 2003) agreed a European Security Strategy[1] (ESS), moving it closer than ever before to a *doctrine* for its foreign policy.

One of Bruton's first moves in Washington was to launch a public awareness campaign focused on the Constitutional Treaty in the United States.[2] A central theme was 'European Union foreign policy under the Constitution'.[3] The basic argument was that a 'stronger and more unified Europe' would lead to a stronger and more unified transatlantic alliance.

Within months, the Constitutional Treaty appeared dead. Referendums in May/June 2005 in France and the Netherlands saw voters reject it by large majorities. Work on forming the External Action Service was halted amidst concerns that it was illegal under existing EU treaties. One effect was to deal a major blow to the EU Commission, which stood to be empowered by its creation and which had suffered through years of neglect and even bullying by EU member states (see Peterson 2006). Europe seemed a very long way away from its ambition – stated in the ESS – to 'share in the responsibility for global security and in building a better world'.

At this point, the United States under George W. Bush appeared to have little incentive to share responsibility for global security with Europe. Three years earlier, its own US National Security Strategy (NSS) had begun with a pledge to 'strengthen alliances to defeat global terrorism'. Even some of the Bush administration's harshest critics conceded that the NSS 'correctly iden- tified the challenges growing out of the deep changes to the political world that were illuminated on September 11' (Nye 2003: 72): specifically, inter- national terrorism, failed states and the proliferation of weapons of mass destruction (WMD). In meeting them, the NSS affirmed that there was 'little of lasting consequence that the United States can accomplish in the world without the sustained cooperation of its allies and friends in ... Europe'. The NSS (in somewhat awkward language) 'welcome[d] our European allies' efforts to forge a greater foreign policy and defence identity with the EU'.

Yet the National Security Strategy also portrayed alliances and inter- national institutions as almost entirely instrumental to a global war on terrorism. No alliance, with Europe or anyone else, would qualify America's right to take 'pre-emptive' (military) action against emergent new threats. As such, the NSS seemed to mark a radical doctrinal shift. It asserted US primacy and a willingness to use all instruments of power, but particularly military ones, to deal with new security threats. Its publication – in September 2002 – could plausibly be viewed as a first step towards the transatlantic crisis over a pre-emptive war in Iraq. From a European perspective, the European Security Strategy – published in draft form only a few months after US-led invasion of Iraq in early 2003 – was a necessary counterpart or Hegelian anti- thesis, extolling the need for 'effective multilateralism' and rejecting the notion that new security threats could 'be tackled by purely military means'.

Agreed on the cusps of one of the worst schisms ever in transatlantic rela- tions, the US and European Security Strategies might seem to merit little reflection beyond an assessment of where and how much they clash. In fact, the NSS and ESS share a generally common view of the nature of new security threats, a refusal to accept the international status quo, and a deter- mination to change it. In effect, they signalled that both the United States and the European Union were now *revolutionary* powers, pursuing strat- egies that sought to change the world essentially in their own images.

We begin here by considering the views of different theoretical perspec- tives on where transatlantic relations stand, and where they are headed. We then consider how to define 'doctrine' and 'strategy'. Our third section offers a short history of security strategy during the Cold War and after. Finally, we consider where the NSS and ESS have 'come from': how they were written and for what purposes.

Theory, practice, and security strategy

Do the United States and European security strategies really matter? All official government statements are best approached with caution and even suspicion. There is always and inevitably 'a long way from declaration to action' (Hunter 2004: 44). Nevertheless, both the ESS and the NSS can be interpreted as marking the adoption of new *doctrines* after a period of tumultuous change in the international order. They arrived after a lengthy period – more than a decade – when both sides often appeared bereft of any settled doctrine to replace containment. We begin with the assumption that the security strategies are guides to potential foreign policy futures. They are also regulators of expectations in transatlantic relations, with the potential to shape policy choices.

Of course, ours is only one interpretation. Another, broadly 'realist' one holds that whatever the security strategies say is far less important than the vast disparities in power and outlook that now divide Europe and America. By the mid-2000s it was plausible to dismiss the EU Security Strategy as a mere statement of what seemed to unite the expanded EU-25 in analytical and policy terms (see Heisbourg 2004), but one with little or no impact without the institutional changes envisaged in the (now doomed) Constitutional Treaty. As one of the contributors to this volume put it (before the 2005 French and Dutch referendums), 'it seems clear that the aspirations of the ESS for greater ... coherence will never be realized until and unless such provisions of the Constitution as the fusion of EU external services and ... "foreign minister" come into force' (Bailes 2005: 25). Lacking these innovations, a European Union of 25 member states (after its 2004 enlargement) could never hope for more coherence than the European Union of 15 it replaced, which was never very coherent in the first place (see Smith 2005). Meanwhile, a fundamentally unilateralist and overwhelmingly powerful America had little inclination to compromise its foreign and security policy agenda for the sake of transatlantic harmony. By this view, the US–European alliance was dead.

By another, broadly liberal interpretation, neither side had much alternative but to partner with the other. As European diplomats sought in 2005 to interest the United States in an overhaul of the decade-old institutional framework for US–EU relations, the New Transatlantic Agenda (see Steffenson 2005), they were told by the Americans: 'just focus on the jobs'.[4] Specifically, the United States pushed the European Union to back its new brand of *transformational diplomacy*, particularly in the Middle East, and to pressure autocratic states to democratise, liberalise and root out terrorism. Despite the high costs of the US military presence in Iraq, and a decisive domestic opinion shift in 2005 against the decision to go to war, the Bush administration could point to tangible progress towards democratisation in Lebanon, Egypt and Saudi Arabia as well as Georgia and Ukraine. In all of these states, plus others (including Turkey), EU states either worked together with the Bush administration, or at least did not undermine US policy. Besides, the enlarged Union was more Atlanticist with the addition of central and eastern European states (especially Poland). It also wielded more clout internationally, sometimes via coordinated actions between national capitals that appeared to bypass Brussels. An illustrative example was European input into work in summer 2005 on the design of a (potentially) new US security strategy that promised to be more multilateralist, less militarist, and supersede, terminologically, the 'global war on terrorism' with a 'strategy against violent extremism' (SAVE). A State Department committee worked on the strategy in close consultation with British and French officials, who spoke of the opening of a true 'strategic dialogue on terrorism'.[5]

If nothing else, the security strategies help frame interesting theoretical questions. Do they, for instance, mark a definitive end to the 'unipolar moment' of overwhelming American power and relative European weakness? Specifically, will the pattern be broken whereby other great powers, including those in Europe, stop 'bandwagoning' with the United States, a phenomenon always surprising from a realist perspective (see Mastanduno 1997; Smith 2002), and instead adopt a strategy of 'balancing' against the United States? Put somewhat differently, does the arrival of a European Union with high ambitions in foreign and security policy (as revealed by the ESS) coincide with an inevitable slide in American soft power post-Iraq (see Nye 2004)?[6]

Alternatively, as William Wohlforth (2004: 186–7) has argued, perhaps 'elite anxiety over US–EU relations is ... driven more by expectations than by current events'. That is, each 'side' (simplifying considerably to make Europe one 'side') is concerned less with the other's response to current international developments than with a sense that a fraying of the transatlantic alliance is inevitable. A long-term drift towards rivalry thus may become a self-fulfilling prophecy. Investing in the alliance – 'this policy choice is hard, but we've got to do it for the Americans/Europeans' – seems a waste of political capital.

Another different, broadly constructivist, view holds that the security strategies augur an era in which the transatlantic alliance can be modernised and 'reconstructed' through dialogue and exchange. Regardless of differences of tone and emphasis in the ESS and NSS, Europe has moved closer to the United States insofar as its normative emphasis on non-military methods is now tempered by its moves towards a European Security and Defence Policy (ESDP) with teeth (see Cornish and Edwards 2005). Whether or not the ESS really qualifies as 'strategy' (see Chapter 11 in this volume; see also Heisbourg 2004), it converges considerably in both doctrine and outlook with the NSS, particularly on the need for proactive policies to counter new security threats.[7] It also marks a turn away from Europe's past disavowal of grand strategy.

Meanwhile, the second George W. Bush administration showed fresh interest in cooperative engagement, particularly with the European Union, after its re-election in 2004. American responsibilities in post-war Afghanistan and Iraq and US focus on democratisation in the Middle East naturally gave rise to fresh interest in non-military strategies for conflict resolution. Given that these were the main 'jobs' of US foreign policy, European values and methods suddenly may have appeared more attractive than before.

Of course, many in the American political class found it impossible to say so. The comment of Senator John McCain, a likely presidential candidate in the post-Bush election of 2008, on how Iraq changed the political equation in the Middle East was: 'The Europeans will have been on the wrong side of history. Again.'[8] Yet Iraq also had a sobering demonstration effect: it revealed to Americans that democracy could not be 'imposed' by an outside power.

Theorists of different stripes disagree about much besides whether sustained, collective effort by the world's richest and oldest democracies is possible in a 'strategy against violent extremism', or more generally. Very few would try to deny that democratisation of the world's remaining autocracies is impossible without both that kind of collective action, and some kind of collective strategy to facilitate it.

Defining 'doctrine' and 'strategy'

'Doctrine' is a term that fits in a special category. Much like 'national interest' or 'globalisation', it is often tossed around loosely. Terms in this category are slippery to start with, defined differently in different contexts. A basic 'define: doctrine' Google search yields 18 different definitions, most connected somehow to religion.[9] Nearly all build on the notion of a 'belief' or 'system of beliefs' accepted as authoritative. Definitions that specifically relate to foreign or security policy include a 'guide to action in support of national objectives', but also stress its contingent nature: 'it is authoritative but requires judgement in application' – a doctrine helps 'decide what to do' and 'fill[s] in details that are not specified explicitly by orders'.[10]

'Strategy' is a more straightforward term: the art or science of planning for success. Usually, it involves thinking about what goals are achievable, and how, given available resources and capabilities and in a chosen timeframe. Strategies are endemic to politics or business, but having a strategy is seen as a Good Thing in all walks of life. It is especially crucial in the conduct of war to have a strategy designed to achieve military victory (hence the academic sub-discipline of 'strategic studies'). The US Department of Defense defines security strategy as 'the art and science of developing, applying, and coordinating the instruments of national power (diplomatic, economic, military, and informational) to achieve objectives that contribute to national security'.[11]

The most important definitional point for our purposes is that security strategies, by nature, contain principles of *doctrine*. They reflect a series of core beliefs about how to achieve security, what threatens it, and how threats to it are best countered. Revealingly, the NSS states early on that US security strategy must 'start from ... core beliefs and look outwards for possibilities to expand liberty'. At a similar stage in the ESS, it is claimed that 'development is a precondition of security'.

Doctrine and security strategy during the Cold War

In retrospect, what was notable about the Cold War was how Western policy seemed guided by a superfluity of doctrines but which, in practice, were all reducible to one. During the Cold War, virtually every US president became identified with their own doctrine. Yet all were directed mainly at containing communism and usually in specific regions: Eisenhower in the Middle East, Kennedy in Latin America, Nixon in south-east Asia, Carter in the Persian Gulf, and Reagan in Nicaragua, Afghanistan and Angola.

In the post-9/11 security environment, where the threat is more from shadowy terrorist networks than other states, it is easy to lapse into nostalgia for the predictability of the Cold War. The NSS does just that in declaring that 'in the Cold War, especially following the Cuban missile crisis, we faced a generally status quo, risk-averse adversary'. Or witness the claim by Democratic presidential candidate Bill Bradley in 2000 that: 'For fifty years after the end of World War II and until the fall of the Berlin Wall in 1989, we were sure about one thing: We knew where we stood on foreign policy' (quoted in Mann 2004: 330).

To the extent that the United States and Western European states 'knew where they stood' during the Cold War, it was largely because the United States under the Truman administration developed a set of ideas and institutions in the early post-war period based on containment of the Soviet threat. The Truman doctrine, unveiled in 1947, committed the United States to (in the president's own words) 'support free peoples who are resisting attempted subjugation by armed minorities or by outside pressures'. For the first time in history, American power would be deployed actively in peacetime outside of the Americas (see Cameron 2002: 8). Over the next few years, the institutional and material underpinnings for containment and extended deterrence as the bases for security strategy were rapidly constructed. The 1947 US National Security Act consolidated the Pentagon into a single monolith, created the Joint Chiefs of Staff, the National Security Council (NSC), and Central Intelligence Agency (CIA). Its section 108 (later amended) required the US president to submit to Congress each year 'a comprehensive report on the national security strategy of the United States'.[12]

Two years later (in 1949), NATO was born. Then arguably the single most important statement of Western security strategy ever, National Security Council (NSC) document 68, was unveiled in April 1950. It stressed the importance of a global US military presence and defined the American national interest in terms of a moral imperative to prevent the spread of communism: 'a defeat of free institutions anywhere is a defeat everywhere'.

The early post-war period was, to an extent often unappreciated today, another unipolar moment. America's hegemony in Europe was, in Lundestad's (2003) words, an 'empire by invitation', or one which most Europeans were pleased to accept. Effectively, the United States defined security doctrine for its European allies. It also provided most of the material resources needed to deter the Soviet threat to West European security. There is consensus, at least amongst American conservatives, that Western security strategy was unusually high-minded and sourced in Washington:

> America's leaders made exertions and sacrifices unprecedented in peacetime coalitions on behalf of appeals to fundamental values and comprehensive solutions, instead of calculations of national security and equilibrium that had characterised European diplomacy.
>
> (Kissinger 1994: 461; see also Mead 2002)

The apparent doctrinal purity of deterrence, and the appearance of consensus on its merits, masked considerable tensions. Debates over 'burden-sharing' flared repeatedly. France's disengagement from NATO's military command sparked an outright crisis in the 1960s, which persisted in a slow burn for decades. The credibility of US commitments to defend Europe as if it were an extension of American territory was debated repeatedly and intensely.

What was clear was the emphasis of Cold War security strategy on *defence* – particularly territorial defence of the NATO area. It was not on *security*, in the considerably wider sense of threats of all kinds, military or non-military, from all sources, state or non-state. Security strategy was mainly *military* strategy, overwhelmingly determined in Washington and focused on Moscow. In fact, only in the Reagan years did the United States get into the business of explicitly developing and issuing a genuine 'security strategy'.

Even then, the main impetus was internal (to the US military), in the form of the Goldwater–Nichols Act of 1986, and not international. Amidst concerns about inter-service rivalries that hampered US military efforts in Vietnam (and Grenada), and even whether each branch of the military operated according to their own 'doctrine', Goldwater–Nichols mandated the most fundamental reorganisation of the US military since the 1947 National Security Act. Its primary purpose was to put all US forces under the central operational command of the Chairman of the Joint Chiefs of Staff. It also reiterated the requirement that every US administration should produce (approximately once per year) an overview of its national security strategy.

Security strategy in the post-Cold War period

The democratic revolutions of 1989–91 in central and eastern Europe brought an abrupt end to the doctrinal simplicities of the Cold War. They also opened up new opportunities for Europe – especially the newly, grandly named 'European Union' – to assert its independence and define a distinctively European security strategy. Yet, before 2003, the closest that the European Union came to a strategy was the colourless 1991 Asolo list, unveiled as the Union was about to launch (in name anyway) a new Common Foreign and Security Policy. The Asolo list identified four areas – the

Conference (later Organisation) for Security and Cooperation Europe, disarmament, nuclear non-proliferation, and economic security – where it contended (vaguely) that EU member states shared security interests and thus might consider joint action (Duke 2004: 459–60). More than anything else, the Asolo list showed how very far the European Union remained from either a common security policy or strategy.

Meanwhile, US security strategies during this period were mostly anodyne documents, long on platitudes and short on 'doctrine' (Mann 2004: 329).[13] The 1991 National Security Strategy was notable for being the first to contemplate the radically different international landscape left at the end of the Cold War. It signalled a shift of preoccupation from 'defence' to 'security', and acknowledged a 'new agenda of new kinds of [non-military] security issue'. It also conceded that 'international relations promise to be more complicated, more volatile and less predictable'. Still, it seemed to cling to past certainties in stressing, in an early paragraph, that 'the Soviet Union remains the only state possessing the physical military capability to destroy American society with a single, cataclysmic attack'.[14]

The end of the Cold War also induced a rethink of NATO strategy, as manifest in its 1991 Alliance Strategic Concept (ASC). The ASC was more a 'concept' – an abstract attempt to clarify the new security environment – than a strategy. In particular, it focused on developing a framework for coordination between NATO's member states, as well as between NATO and the Western European Union, the exclusively European (and largely moribund) military alliance. Like the American NSS of the same year, it embraced a broader approach to security, extending to dialogue between all European states, including those formerly of the Warsaw Pact. The ASC acknowledged that NATO had to refocus on crisis management, rather than territorial defence. In a sign that the burden-sharing debate was far from over, it asserted European members had to take more responsibility for their own security. The 1991 Strategic Concept gave an early indication, later re-emphasised in a revised ASC of 1999, of the need for collective action to counter the proliferation of WMD. In practice, however, 'the [NATO] alliance did little in real terms to respond to the terrorist challenge prior to [9/11]' (Sloan 2003: 92) or, for that matter, afterwards.

A new ASC was endorsed at the Washington summit by NATO Heads of State and Government in April 1999.[15] At the time, the alliance was celebrating its 50th anniversary while also preparing to launch Operation Allied Force against Serb forces operating in Kosovo and Serbia. By the end of the year, the Clinton administration had absorbed the lessons of Kosovo sufficiently to issue its final NSS (and the last before George W. Bush's administration in 2002). The 1999 document was striking in its basic assumption of international peace. While allowing that civil and ethnic wars were still scars on the international order, it seemed to assume that powerful states – led by the United States as in Kosovo – could end or manage them. Its long-winded, discursive (very Clintonite) style obscured its basic lack of clear doctrine.

To view it charitably, its singling out of three essential goals – enhancing American security (broadly defined, but with terrorism one threat in a very long list), bolstering economic prosperity, and promoting democracy and human rights – pointed to a new era in US security strategy. By another view, the 1999 National Security Strategy was symptomatic of a general lack of consensus, on both sides of the Atlantic, on what the new doctrinal imperatives of the post-Cold War age were.

Very broadly, the general presumption was of a single, dominant great power and by extension a prevailing 'democratic peace', where traditional military defence was essentially redundant (Jervis 2002). One consequence was a new, wider security agenda, consisting of a list of environmental ills, infectious diseases and the proliferation of civil wars in far distant places, most notably in Sub-Saharan Africa (Mathews 1989; Hironaka 2005). The European Union, while willing to acknowledge the widening of the security agenda, remained primarily focused on internal challenges, such as European Monetary Union, or enlargement in its immediate neighbourhood. For its part, the United States equivocated about whether it should be engaged in 'assertive multilateralism', as in the first Clinton administration, or in more traditional 'selective engagement' after the loss of 18 marines in the 1993 Somali fiasco forced a shift in thinking.

The security strategies of this period are, therefore, not the place to understand the dynamics of current European and US strategic thinking. Developments on the ground tell us more: particularly the difficult negotiations on joint transatlantic action to try to bring to an end the wars of secession in the former Yugoslavia. European and US responses to the conflicts in the former Yugoslavia provide a prism for identifying patterns of convergence and divergence in transatlantic relations, not least because it was always unclear whether the United States and the European Union were strategically marginal or central to conflicts in the Balkans.

The first crisis was, of course, over Bosnia. The earlier outbreak of war in the Balkans in 1991 exposed as empty the European Union's (then) new claims to be able to wield its collective power effectively in its own backyard. Bosnia then tested NATO as an alliance nearly to breaking point. First, the Clinton administration refused to support the best hope for an early resolution, the Vance–Owen peace plan (see Owen 1995). Then, under pressure after a domestic Republican resurgence in 1994, Clinton's White House effectively did nothing beyond rejecting presidential hopeful Robert Dole's myopic policy of 'lift and strike': that is, lifting the arms embargo on Bosnia's embattled Muslims and using air strikes against ascendant Serb forces. Eventually, in response to international outrage over Serbian atrocities and with Clinton apparently surprised to learn of a US commitment to use its forces to extricate European troops delivering humanitarian aid (see Holbrooke 1999), the United States backed NATO air strikes to bomb Slobodan Milosevic's Serbia to the negotiating table. The result was the Dayton Peace Accord, agreed by the United States with the combatants while European diplomats were literally locked out of negotiations (see Bildt 1998).

As traumatic as Bosnia was, the effect of NATO's first 'out-of-area' (that is, beyond NATO's own territory) engagement was to rejuvenate the alliance. Moreover, Clinton took genuine political risks ahead of his 1996 re-election campaign and convinced Congress to enforce Dayton with American boots on the ground. In the background, NATO was considerably 'Europeanised', on paper at least, via the European Union's European Security and Defence Identity initiative (see Sloan 2003: 164–71). It was also enlarged, with little enthusiasm from EU members of NATO (see Asmus 2002), but with the effect of relieving the European Union itself of pressures to enlarge before it could get its own foreign and security policy act together.

The interlude between the Bosnian crisis and 9/11 revealed that the repair of the Atlantic Alliance had been superficial. It also sowed seeds that sprouted during the Iraq crisis. With humanitarian disaster looming in Kosovo in 1999, the Clinton administration again sought a negotiated solution via the Rambouillet Accords, but according to terms that were widely considered in European circles to be impossible for Milosevic to accept (see MccGwire 2000). This time, it took less time for NATO to undertake a bombing campaign against Serbia, although the Clinton administration nearly opted for the ludicrous alternative of arming the Muslim Kosovo Liberation Army (KLA), which the chief US negotiator in the region had called a 'small, irrelevant terrorist organisation' a few months before (quoted in Peterson 2003: 91). This time, the European Union led efforts to find a diplomatic solution. Eventually – via its special envoy, Marti Ahtisaari, the former Finnish president, supported by former Russian prime minister, Viktor Chernomyrdin – a ceasefire was brokered.

Kosovo could be interpreted either as a revolutionary triumph of humanitarian principles over inflexible respect for sovereignty (Havel 1999) or a blind, incompetent stumble towards a solution through sheer luck (Daalder and O'Hanlon 2001). Perhaps its deepest legacy was that it exposed Europe's militaries as woefully weak and the opposite of helpful to American forces in actual combat. It also revealed NATO's own decision-making structures to be heavily biased towards inaction. The experience of Kosovo cemented a strong distrust in the Pentagon for alliance-led multilateral engagement or 'wars by committee' which institutionalised the interference of other countries (see Clark 2001). Meanwhile, the European Union's own defence policy began to blossom in the background, particularly when the 1999 Helsinki EU summit agreed to mount a potent (on paper at least) rapid reaction force as a way to repent for past sins of military atrophy. One effect was to rekindle fears in Washington that the European Union was determined to eclipse NATO as Europe's primary collective security organisation.

Thus, when 9/11 came, the conditions were right for a Perfect Storm in the transatlantic alliance. European expressions of solidarity – as in *Le Monde*, which declared 'we are all Americans now' on 12 September – appeared to count for little in Washington. When NATO invoked its Article V commitment under its founding Washington Treaty to treat the attack on the United States as an attack on all its members, and European states offered military assets to the October 2001 United States attack on Afghanistan, both were refused. Fortunately for the alliance, the Taliban regime in Afghanistan collapsed even more quickly than European support for the war. However, Bush's State of the Union address in January 2002, which declared that Iraq, Iran and North Korea formed an 'axis of evil', ratcheted up tensions to a new high. The release nine months later of the NSS, and the subsequent build-up of US forces on the Iraqi border, set the scene for putting (certain amongst) the transatlantic 'allies at war' (Gordon and Shapiro 2004).

The dust had settled somewhat when the European Union agreed the final draft of its security strategy in December 2003, approximately eight months after Baghdad had fallen to US–UK forces. That the European Union now had something like a doctrine to guide its foreign policy had the potential either to exacerbate or help heal the rift over Iraq, depending on the precise content of the ESS. We consider it alongside the NSS in the section that follows.

The NSS and ESS: convergence or divergence?

Three broad fundamental comparative observations about the NSS and ESS are worth making at the outset. First, and most generally, they were created to serve essentially different purposes. The NSS was intended to signal to the world America's outrage over 9/11 and to Americans the Bush administration's determination to do whatever was necessary to root out potential sources of catastrophic terrorism. It thus emphasised how the Cold War had ended to yield a new American hegemony while also imposing 'unique responsibilities' on the world's only superpower. Equally, it stressed that the potentially deadly combination of international terrorism, rogue states and WMD proliferation created a 'new condition of life'.

However, the NSS contained no genuine analysis of threats, essentially taking them as self-evident. It jumped at an early stage to detailed action and tactics. It is impossible to read the NSS without feeling a sense of the 'righteous entitlement that underpins America's distinct internationalism' (Duke 2004: 463). Its *fin-de-siècle* overtones are powerful. The NSS reveals that 9/11 profoundly changed America, putting it on a war footing that would continue, if not indefinitely, then at least for an 'extended period of time'.

In contrast, the basic purposes of the ESS were to turn the page after the sharp, internal European split over Iraq, *and* to show doubters that 'a semi-supranational, legalistic and consent-based community like the EU could cope … with the realities of power and responsibility in a world where the "bad guys" were so remote from and contemptuous of anything like European norms' (Bailes 2005: 9). The European Union's security strategy offered a chance to give a fresh policy framework to the ESDP, something that was overdue given that the European Union had already undertaken its first military operations in Bunia (Democratic Republic of the Congo) and Macedonia. Arguably, however, the ESS was created mostly for internal reasons: to agree a set of principles around which all EU states could rally after Europe's apparent impotence over Iraq. In contrast to the NSS, the European Security Strategy barely mentions the Cold War. Its point of departure is European integration, and all of its virtues and past accomplishments. There is a powerful sense of self-satisfaction in its opening line: 'Europe has never been so prosperous, so secure nor so free.' It also waxes optimistic about whether European habits can be exported to other parts of the world.

However it may be criticised, there is no denying that the ESS is distinctively innovative in that it prioritises external threats to the European Union for the first time in its 50-year history (see Biscop 2005). Strikingly, they are essentially the same as those prioritised in the NSS: terrorism, the proliferation of WMD, regional conflicts and state failure. The ESS differs only in the prominence it gives to organised crime.

There is far less sense in the ESS, compared to its American counterpart, that 9/11 ushered in a new international order. Rather, it asserts the need for an 'international order based on effective multilateralism', in particular on the time-honoured rationalist principles of international law. The ESS differs from the NSS not only on appropriate means but also underlying causes: new threats are less a product of radicalism itself than the injustices of a global system where 'half of the world's population live on less than 2 euros a day'. As such, the ESS does not presume that transnational challenges such as poverty, environmental degradation and AIDS are any less acute after 9/11 than they were before.

A second observation flows from the way in which the processes of writing the two strategies differed, and how these differences matter. The NSS was published a few months after Bush unveiled the essence of America's new strategy in a speech at West Point (the elite US military academy) in June 2003. Bush had warned that the United States could resort to 'pre-emptive action' to protect its national security. He had already signalled America's intention to 'keep military strengths beyond challenge, thereby making the destabilizing arms races of other eras pointless'. Even before the West Point speech, Bush's National Security Advisor, Condoleezza Rice, had revealed that the White House staff – particularly veteran analyst Philip Zelikow – was working on a comprehensive new strategy document.

By most accounts, the NSS was drafted almost entirely in the back offices of the National Security Council, primarily by Rice and Zelikow, along with Rice's deputy, Stephen Hadley (see Mann 2004: 329–31). Rice's own hard-headed realism and past background as a Soviet specialist seem evident in the NSS's repeated use of the phrase 'balance of power that favours freedom'. At the same time, the NSS had to please multiple constituencies within the administration (especially the Pentagon), the Republican party and beyond. This political fact helps explain why the NSS is so breathtaking in scope and ambition.

In contrast, the drafting of the ESS was done publicly and in the style of an academic workshop (see Biscop 2005). A first draft was submitted to the Thessaloniki EU summit in June 2003. European leaders gave it *no* substantive discussion at the summit but did direct its ostensible author, the High Representative for the Common Foreign and Security Policy, Javier Solana, to work with 'member states and the Commission' to refine the text, which was deemed 'a living document subject to public debate and to review as necessary' (Bailes 2005: 11).

The text was then debated and revised at three 'research conferences', involving academics and other experts, as well as at several non-public meetings with member states and the Commission. Formally, Solana and his team controlled the drafting of the ESS much as Rice and her team kept a grip on the shaping of the NSS. However, the ESS was the product of a very European process of consensus-building. One consequence is that the ESS is a very broad-spectrum, sometimes discursive, document. It is far less sharp or specific in its policy prescriptions than is the NSS. Officials who worked on the ESS confessed to being opposed even to calling it a 'security strategy'.

A third and final observation is that the NSS was clearly 'a major "source" document' for the ESS (Bailes 2005: 13). It thus (in a sense) continues the post-war tradition of Europeans reacting to security doctrines drafted and published, without their input, across the Atlantic. Yet the ESS evolved during its redrafting in the direction of a text that stressed Europe's distinctive and more reflective view on the nature of threats to security. Most changes made to the Thessaloniki draft, before a final version was agreed at the December 2003 Brussels EU summit, made the ESS 'look less like a toned-down *précis* of the NSS' (Bailes 2005: 13). The final draft contained earlier and more considered analysis of threats (in contrast to its American counterpart), more on the interplay of threats (including the causes of terrorism), and a stronger emphasis on 'effective multilateralism'.

A particularly sensitive issue for the ESS was pre-emption. Much was made of an early draft's inclusion of the term 'pre-emptive engagement' in a paragraph focused on trade, development and justice (that is, a context entirely different from that in which the NSS placed pre-emption). The phrase was changed to 'preventive engagement' in the final draft, particularly after several EU states cited translation problems with the first construction. The European Union was accused, implausibly, of softening its security strategy in the process.[16] In its final draft, the ESS speaks repeatedly of the need for the European Union to develop a 'strategic culture' (see Cornish and Edwards 2005) that 'fosters early, rapid, and when necessary, robust intervention'. But it also takes pains to emphasise the desirability of a 'rules-based international order', as opposed to one in which a hegemon arrogates to itself the right to pre-empt future threats.

The ESS endorses the view that the European Union needs its own military capability but firmly rejects unilateralism in favour of 'effective multilateralism'. The NSS urges that 'it is time to reaffirm the essential role of American military strength'. It unapologetically celebrates how the 'forward presence' of US armed forces has 'maintained the vital peace in some of the world's most strategically vital regions' and promises action to 'dissuade future military competition'. In contrast, the ESS repeatedly stresses that military force alone can solve no major international security problem and insists that 'no single country is able to tackle today's complex problems on its own'.

In some respects, the NSS and the ESS are very different beasts. One obvious reason for this is that the United States and European Union are very different actors in international relations. One is a nation-state with (more or less) centralised control and a traditional commitment to West-phalian sovereignty. The other is a union of nation-states with a post-modern conception of sovereignty as something to be pooled rather than concen-trated (Keohane 2002). Yet there are clear lines of both divergence *and* convergence in the two security strategies. They diverge in their analysis of new threats, why they arise, and appropriate means for meeting them. Whether or not these differences are trumped in importance by the urgent need, fully acknowledged and shared by both security strategies, for more *proactive* policies as a response to a new, radically different security environ-ment is for our authors, and ultimately our readers, to judge.

Conclusion

This book has multiple purposes, none of which is to make more of the United States and EU security strategies than they deserve. In and of themselves, they are mere pieces of paper. At most, they are statements of intention. The chapters that follow explore in detail and practice the impact of the two security strategies on specific issue areas. All of our authors operate without illusions about what can be determined about US–EU relations based on the semiotics of the textual analysis of official doctrinal statements.

All at once, the security strategies are reflections of crucially important dynamics, ideological shifts and differing security perceptions in transatlan-tic relations. We have argued that the security strategies matter in two ways above all: they shape expectations each side has about the other's future behaviour, and they imply that both the United States and the European Union are no longer 'status quo' powers. If the United States and the European Union were not, each in its own way, now in the business of pursu-ing new brands of transformational diplomacy, their security strategies of 2002–3 would have differed radically from those agreed. Close analysis of the security strategies reveals a shared determination to transform the world – individually but also *jointly* – so that Americans and Europeans are spared future atrocities of the kind seen on 9/11 or 3/11 (2004) in Madrid or 7/7 (2005) in London.

As we have seen, the security strategies also reveal that the United States and the European Union diverge fundamentally on some fundamentals. What is more, as the Bush administration's revisiting of the NSS in 2005 shows, the documents do not express unchanging dogmas or eternal verities. Their significance and continuing relevance are dependent on changing circumstances and the inherent unpredictability of international politics.

To illustrate the point, the ESS was born at a time when ratification of the European Union's Constitutional Treaty appeared to be a foregone conclusion. American eurosceptics, mindful of the Constitutional Treaty's ambitious, even radical changes to EU foreign policy institutions, warned that 'not since the European Union's founding in 1957 has the velocity of European integration been as high as it is today' (Cimbalo 2004: 112). By mid 2005, the Constitutional Treaty appeared all but dead, with a new era of 'euro-paralysis' in prospect. At this point, it was easy to revert to the (realist) assumption that the basic disparity in power between Europe and America was growing and thus the alliance between them was doomed.

It was just as easy to forget that the NSS was born in a period before the invasion of Iraq when confidence in the power of military pre-emption meant that George Bush could ignore Colin Powell's warning that 'if you invade Iraq you inherit the problem of Iraq' (Woodward 2004). As Robert Cooper has argued (2005a), democracy cannot be imposed with military force. The experience of Iraq (especially) and the apparent affinity of the second George W. Bush administration for transformational diplomacy might have the effect of enhancing the appeal of change through persuasion rather than coercion, fighting terrorism by emphasising human rights, poverty reduction, disease eradication and so on, and conflict resolution via multilateral diplomacy rather than unilateral force. Or so it might be imagined.

The ESS begins (in its third paragraph) by acknowledging the 'critical role' of the United States in promoting European integration. It ends (three paragraphs from its end) by bluntly asserting:

> The transatlantic relationship is irreplaceable. Acting together, the European Union and the United States can be a formidable force for good in the world. Our aim should be an effective and balanced partnership with the USA. This is an additional reason for the European Union to build up further its capabilities and increase its coherence.

Or so it might be argued.

Notes

1 All quotations from the two security strategies are from the pdf versions of 'The National Security Strategy of the United States of America' (12 September 2002; available from http://www.whitehouse.gov/nsc/nss.html) and 'A Secure Europe in a Better World: European Security Strategy' (12 December 2003; available from http://ue.eu.int/uedocs/cmsUpload/78367.pdf), which are both included as appendices to this volume.

2 One of us led a study for the European Commission in early 2005 on US–EU relations, which was mandated to include prescriptions for EU policy towards the United States. One of the study's recommendations was that the European Union undertake a public relations campaign in the United States to increase awareness of the European Union amongst ordinary (as well as elite) Americans. To our knowledge, there has never been an opinion poll that suggests that a majority of Americans have even *heard* of the European Union. To our surprise, the Commission subsequently launched a follow-on study of how such a campaign might be focused, how much it would cost, its possible effects and so on (see European Commission 2005).

3 One tangible outcome from the campaign was a publication called *EU Focus*, which was distributed as a pull-out section of leading US journals (such as the March/April issue of *Foreign Policy*) in spring 2005. Although clearly a 'treaty' in the legal, definitional sense, the Constitutional Treaty was intended to be more permanent than any of the European Union's previous treaties.

4 Interview with senior European Commission official, 7 June 2005.

5 Anonymous French official quoted in *Financial Times*, 1 August 2005, p.1. It appeared that the 2006 US National Security Strategy was, at least in part, an outcome of this exercise. However, the phrase (or acronym) SAVE was nowhere to be found in the 2006 NSS, thus suggesting Jolyon Howorth (see Chapter 3 of this volume) was right to conclude that this 'rebranding exercise' was 'soon dropped as too blatant a form of PR'.

6 One 25-country poll in 2005 found that in only two states – the Philippines and the United States itself – did a majority have a negative view of a 'Europe that was more influential than the US in world affairs'. More than one-third of *Americans* viewed such a scenario positively. Findings from the poll, conducted by the Program on International Public Opinion at the University of Maryland, are available at http://www.globescan.com/news_archives/GS_PIPA_EU.html (accessed 9 August 2005).

7 Indicative is language in the ESS on new security threats: 'we should be ready to act before a crisis occurs … Conflict prevention and threat prevention cannot start too early … With the new threats, the first line of defense will often be abroad.' For its part, the NSS asserts that the United States 'can no longer rely on a reactive posture as we have in the past'.

8 Quoted in *The New Yorker*, 30 May 2005: 73.

9 In an earlier age, of course, the Oxford English Dictionary was the definitive magic bullet solution. However, the OED (2005) actually contained considerably fewer definitions than a Google search (conducted mid 2005) did.

10 These definitions found at www.rotc.monroe.army.mil/helpdesk/definitions-1/terms.htm and sources.redhat.com/xconq/manual/xcdesign_60.html (accessed 29 January 2006).

11 http://usmilitary.about.com/od/glossarytermsn/g/n4212.htm (accessed 29 January 2006).

12 These provisions appear to have been interpreted loosely by subsequent administrations, none of which submitted a new 'security strategy' (as opposed to defence posture reviews) each and every year.

13 A useful historical archive of US security strategies, and commentary on them, is http://www.wws.princeton.edu/ppns/rr/history.html (accessed 2 February 2006).

14 The full text of the 1991(–2) security strategy is available at http://www.fas.org/man/docs/918015-nss.htm (accessed 2 February 2006).

15 The ASC was subsequently revised at the 2002 Prague NATO summit (see Chapter 4).

16 See, for example, Tomas Valasek, 'Pre-emptively Soft', *Wall Street Journal Europe*, 11 December 2003: 11.

2 The European Security Strategy
An American view

Ronald D. Asmus

This chapter explores American views on the European Union's Security Strategy (ESS), officially adopted in December 2003. Summarizing what official Washington, as well as American commentators, thought of the ESS is easy at one level but difficult at another. While the ESS hardly made headlines in the United States, it is tempting to conclude that it was widely welcomed both by the Bush administration and the vast majority of American experts who follow US–European relations, and leave it at that. The more interesting yet difficult question is how important that reaction was and what it tells us about the shifting American strategic debate after 9/11, as well as Europe's new relevance (or lack thereof) to future US strategic thinking.

The answer to that question is more complicated. This chapter seeks to provide it. It does so by looking briefly at the Bush administration's own National Security Strategy (NSS), not least in terms of what it meant for Europe. It then examines the American response to the European Union's own security strategy by placing that reaction in the context of the debate in Washington over Europe's future relevance as a key strategic partner in a post-9/11 world. It concludes by exploring what these two documents and the debates they produced suggest about the prospects for future US–European strategic convergence or divergence.

Before proceeding, however, it is important to add two caveats to the analysis in this chapter. One is that we are currently living through a moment of remarkable intellectual and strategic fluidity. More conventional wisdom was probably discarded in the Western strategic community in four years after 9/11 than in previous decades. We are still in the midst of this strategic redefinition. It is not always easy to step back and discern the forest from the trees, and particularly to identify what features of the current debate will prove to be enduring and harbingers of new trends and which will be transitory and fall by the wayside. A note of humility and caution in rendering historic judgments or drawing sweeping conclusions is perhaps in order.

The other caveat is a simple reminder that the focus of the American NSS is not Europe. Nor is the United States the primary focus of the ESS. Both were written as responses to the world after 9/11 and were intended for different purposes and audiences. At the same time, both are profoundly important statements on how the Bush administration and the current European Union see the world. Both are revealing in what they say – either implicitly or explicitly – about the transatlantic relationship. Few issues have elicited more *Sturm und Drang* across the Atlantic in recent years than the debate about whether the United States and Europe can and will remain close strategic partners or whether they will inevitably drift apart. Examining these two documents and the debate surrounding them provides us with a window into this central question at the dawn of a new century and strategic era.

The origins of the NSS

In a formal sense, the George W. Bush administration's 2002 National Security Strategy was a response to a slightly obscure bureaucratic mandate in the Goldwater–Nichols Department of Defense Reorganization Act of 1986. It requires every administration to issue an annual national security strategy which, in turn, is supposed to serve as a guide for the development and modernization of the American armed forces (see Chapter 1).[1] One wonders whether the authors of that legislation ever expected that their handiwork would help produce a document as far-reaching and a debate as controversial as the one sparked by the Bush administration's NSS. The Bush administration's predecessors, both Republican and Democratic, tended to view this exercise – one of a number of congressionally mandated official reviews of policy every administration faces – as a check-the-box exercise. Typically, senior civil servants labored to hammer out inter-agency differences yet avoid controversy, as such documents were rarely seen as opportunities for launching major policy initiatives let alone remaking American strategic thinking. Prior to September 2002, success was often defined in terms of avoiding headlines or attracting public attention.

The Bush administration chose a different approach for reasons that were both intellectual and political. It took this exercise more seriously and delib-erately chose it as the venue to lay out to the American people and the world a radically different strategy as its intellectual and strategic response to the terrorist attacks of 9/11. There is little doubt that 9/11 catalyzed a profound strategic rethink in the United States – one that is still underway and whose final contours and outcome are still being shaped. It was not just the signifi-cance of the attacks as such, as important as they were in jolting Americans into confronting the reality of a new terrorist threat. There was also a pal-pable sense that the United States had been asleep at the wheel. And as horrible as these attacks were, there was also a recognition that much worse could and probably would lie in the future. In the minds of many, there was little doubt that terrorist groups who were willing to fly airplanes into the World Trade Center would also be willing to use far more destructive weapons, including weapons of mass destruction, if and when they were capable of doing so.[2]

The Bush administration was convinced that the United States was at the beginning of a new strategic era. It was the end of the decade of peace and prosperity ushered in by the collapse of communism and the Soviet Union and the dawn of a new and potentially very dangerous era in international relations. Then Secretary of State, Colin Powell, captured this perceived turning point when he remarked that we were entering the 'post-post-Cold War era'. Such a sense was not limited to the Bush administration and indeed extended to both sides of the political aisle. The Bush administration's NSS was written against this backdrop and with a sense that the nation faced a new and decisive threat. Philip Zelikow (2003: 17), a former colleague of Condoleezza Rice who was brought in as a consultant to the National Security Council to work on the NSS, captured that mood when he subsequently wrote:

> The attacks of September 2001 did not create the new era, but they were a catalytic moment in our recognition of it. Like previous shocks to the United States in 1940, December 1941 or June 1950, their shock gave emerging trends a form, brought them into mass consciousness, and forced upon us the task of defining a comprehensive national response.

There was also a political motivation. It was a time of strategic fluidity and political opportunity – a Trumanesque moment requiring and in a sense asking for an appropriate historical response. The administration was looking for the successor or modern-day equivalent of containment. And many in the administration perceived an opportunity for George W. Bush to be a modern-day Harry Truman – in other words, to become the leader who would define that new strategy and lead the course correction that was required for the United States and the Western world more generally. As it drafted the document that would become the NSS, it was understood that what the administration was about to launch would elicit controversy. It saw that debate as inevitable and a by-product of exerting leadership in this new era. It recalled that Harry Truman, too, had been fiercely opposed at the time yet would go down in history as one of the century's great presidents. Again, in the words of Zelikow (2003: 22):

> The new strategy is somewhat provocative, but it is deliberately so. It must be provocative if it is to foster the painful worldwide debate that must occur in order to condition the international community to think hard about these new dangers, and about how the cadence of security threats has changed.

The core tenets of the NSS are discussed at length elsewhere in this volume. For the purposes of this chapter, suffice it to recall several key arguments that also set the context for evaluating the American reaction to the European Security Strategy, which was officially adopted by the European Union just over one year later. The first and perhaps most important premise of the NSS is the primacy given to the set of new threats: above all the advent of terrorism with a global reach and the risk of a catastrophic terrorist attack involving weapons of mass destruction. Unlike in the past, such threats were not rooted in geopolitical competition between major nation-states but within societies and civilizations. The corollary of this analysis is that US policy must therefore be much more concerned about and focused on the internal order in these societies and civilizations as a matter of national security policy. This in turn helps explain the focus in this and other core Bush administration statements on the importance of pursuing universalist principles and values – and the president's rejection of past Republican realist policies and embrace of a modern day neo-Wilsonianism focused on expanding liberty and democracy.

The second core argument of the NSS was the assertion that the key strategic doctrines that shaped Western strategic thinking in the twentieth century were no longer adequate in the twenty-first. The major national security threats the United States had previously faced had emanated from large countries and evolved slowly, often visibly, as armies were built and weapons forged. In the modern world, so the authors of the NSS argued, the United States could face a situation where a weak actor could acquire the capability to wage a devastating attack with little if any advance warning. Doctrines developed to meet the threats of a previous era, initially in a pre-nuclear age and subsequently during the Cold War, were anachronistic in an age where the greatest threats to our societies were not deferrable in the traditional sense. If weapons of mass destruction were now the weapons of choice by terrorist groups, the strategic doctrines of the West had to be updated and modernized to meet that threat.

This is why the United States, according to the NSS, had to be prepared to act preemptively if needed. While preemption was certainly not new in American strategic thinking, it had never before been placed center stage in official US strategy – let alone elevated to the position of a doctrine. It had always been considered an option of last resort, one best not discussed openly and instead held quietly in reserve for extraordinary circumstances. In an age where the enemies of the West were openly and actively seeking weapons of mass destruction, the authors of the NSS insisted, it would be irresponsible to wait until such a threat was so universally apparent that an international consensus could be fully formed and the case for action be made. As a result, preemptive action needed to move into the forefront of a strategy to confront these new threats. While critics would claim the US administration had arrogated itself the right to attack anyone it felt it should pursue, the NSS does list five criteria that should be met for a state or organization to claim the right to act. Moreover, it argues that there is a strong case under international law to adapt the concept of imminent threat to meet the realities of a new era (see Appendix 1).

Third, the NSS lays out what might generously be called a very utilitarian approach to multilateral cooperation. Indeed, there is no document that has since become more associated with American 'unilateralism' than the NSS. To be fair, a close reading of the strategy reveals repeated references to the need for international cooperation with partners and allies to achieve the document's goals. But the key point – to return to the Truman analogy – was that striking in its absence was the commitment to use American power to strengthen and build new institutions to meet these challenges or to uphold and modernize core principles of international order and law. A sense that the administration was walking away from decades of traditional American leadership and commitments was reinforced by specific policy decisions with regard to NATO, the European Union and the United Nations in the same period.

The NSS provoked controversy from the second it was publicly released, not least of all in the United States (although less, at least initially, in Europe than might have been expected; see Chapter 3). Critics accused the administration of being too quick to cast aside traditional notions of strategy or the organizing principles of international order that had existed for the past half a century. They warned that both the rhetoric and action of the Bush administration ran the risk of projecting 'a neo-imperial vision in which the United States arrogates to itself the global role of setting standards, determining threats, using force and meting out justice' (Ikenberry 2002b: 44). They warned that such a policy would be politically and financially unsustainable at home; unacceptable to key allies and friends abroad; would not generate the long-term international cooperation needed ultimately to prevail in the war on terrorism; would encourage copycat behavior by other less benign nations who would invoke the right of preemption for their own purposes; and that, at the end of the day, it could isolate the United States and expose it to the danger of self-encirclement precisely at a time when it was most in need of international cooperation (see Ikenberry 2002b).

The NSS was noteworthy in one additional respect, which is especially important for the subject of this chapter. Neither Europe as a region nor the transatlantic relationship as an alliance played critical roles. In many ways, this document marked the culmination of a shift in American strategic attention east and south and away from the old continent and into regions such as the broader Middle East from which these new threats were viewed as emanating. In the United States, it both accentuated and accelerated the debate over what role Europe could and should play in American foreign policy. That debate was, of course, not new. It had been raging from the day communism collapsed. It had produced some of the most dramatic foreign policy battles in the previous decades over issues such as military intervention in the Balkans as well as NATO enlargement.

There were two core issues in this debate (see Asmus 2002). One was the degree to which the United States should be engaged with its own resources and commitments to assist Europe in building a new post-Cold War order on the continent and putting itself back together again – or whether that was a task that should be left to the Europeans themselves. The other was over the long-term goals of US policy. Was the American goal simply to help Europe resolve its residual demons in the Balkans and to anchor Central and Eastern Europe to the West – so that future American presidents would (hopefully) never again have to worry about conflict on the continent? Or was it something even more ambitious, namely to encourage a Europe that was increasingly democratic and secure to broaden its geopolitical horizons and assume more global responsibility, ideally in close partnership with the United States?

This debate was percolating behind the scenes in the US government and in think tanks in Washington in the late 1990s. Yet talk of a new US–European global agenda or partnership seemed largely theoretical and abstract so long as Washington and its European allies had their hands full dealing with day-to-day crises in Kosovo and finalizing plans for NATO and European Union enlargement. What both the US and EU security strategies refer to as 'new threats' were very much beyond the horizon.

The combination of the so-called 'big bang' round of EU enlargement to Central and Eastern Europe and the 9/11 terrorist attacks changed that. In a sense, America's own 'European project' of the 1990s had been brought to a successful close. And the new threats to the United States from beyond the continent had been graphically illustrated by Al Qaeda's attacks on New York and Washington. Thus, in American eyes the question of whether Europe was willing and able to step out onto the global stage and become a more active player, and whether the United States should pursue a set of policies to encourage such an evolution, was increasingly moving from theory to reality. The American NSS did not provide an answer to the question of what role Americans now saw for Europe on a global stage. Indeed, if anything many of the Bush team came to power already skeptical about Europe's future and the transatlantic relationship – which helps explain the reticence to move on NATO's invocation of Article 5 after 9/11, or the administration's downgrading of traditional alliances and its emphasis on 'coalitions of the willing'. But those views would evolve under the pressure of real world events.

The ESS: the American response

The European Union's Security Strategy (ESS) was officially accepted at the Brussels European Council of December 2003. It too was a response to the events of 9/11. Yet it also was in many ways a European response to the American response – that is, a reaction to the Bush administration's National Security Strategy and the debate it had provoked on both sides of the Atlantic. It was also very much part of an effort to overcome the divisive debate within the European Union over the Bush administration's course on Iraq.

To be sure, the European Union would have undoubtedly issued a security strategy at some point. But the fact that it issued this strategy at this point in time was undoubtedly shaped by the United States and the American debate. In private, a number of EU officials admitted that the debate over the American NSS was one factor that had led Javier Solana to ask why the European Union could not issue its own strategy, and which provided the impetus for him seeking and receiving a mandate from member states for one.[3]

The core features of the ESS are discussed in great detail elsewhere in this volume. What is important here is to highlight those features that attracted American attention and which help explain Washington's reaction. First, if one reads the document closely, as well as the key statements by European leaders explaining it, it is clear that this strategy too recognizes the advent of a new strategic era. To be sure, stylistically this document is much more subdued and it does not convey the same sense of urgency about confronting the challenges of a new era that the NSS does. Nevertheless, it does posit that Europe faces new threats that are more diverse, less visible and less predictable than in the past. It acknowledges that terrorism is a primary threat and that it is global in its scope (with Europe being both a target and a base for operations). And the ESS highlights the dangers of terrorists acquiring weapons of mass destruction and producing a unique and potentially radical new threat. As Javier Solana (2003) put it in a speech to European think tank experts a few weeks before the ESS was officially adopted, 9/11 had 'revealed a world more complex and more dangerous' than previously imagined – and the EU Security Strategy reflects this new complexity and danger.

Second, the ESS calls for a strategic response to this new threat environment that is similar in its thrust while softer in tone than its American counterpart. The European Union, the authors concluded, had to address these new threats earlier and at greater distance than had previously been the norm in European strategic thinking. 'The first line of defence will often be abroad,' the document notes, implying that it is no longer sufficient to wait for the threat to manifest itself on one's borders. Instead, in a globalizing world in which threats could strike from afar with little warning and potentially tremendous destruction, the priority had to be on addressing those threats before they became full-blown. As a result, the European Union must develop 'a strategic culture that fosters early, rapid and when necessary, robust intervention' to try to head off or defuse crises. While the phrase 'preemptive engagement' from the Thessaloniki draft was replaced in the final ESS draft by the less-threatening phrase 'preventive action', the document still ended up being very forward-leaning in calling for the European Union to shift strategic gears and to address threats before they reached European soil. In the words of Mark Leonard and Richard Gowan (2004: 7), 'the document remains almost Rumsfeldian in its warning about terrorism and rogue states'. Some conservative American commentators even claimed that Europe was 'starting to dance to the Bush tune' (see Pletka 2005).

Such rhetorical flourishes by commentators were undoubtedly embellished. But they underscored a key point often lost in the growing transatlantic acrimony over the war in Iraq. When Americans and Europeans looked out at the world after 9/11, they did not necessarily have fundamentally different world views. That is not where the differences lay. On the contrary, publics on both sides of the Atlantic saw very similar threats and drew conclusions that pushed policymakers in Washington and European capitals in similar strategic directions. Indeed, it was striking after 9/11 just how similar public threat perceptions became – even if it was also clear that the saliency and personal intensity of these perceptions was at times greater in the United States.[4]

Americans and Europeans were also, for the most part, in agreement on what part of the world accounted for the lion's share of the problem: namely, the broader Middle East. For it is indeed in that region that they were most likely to find this new combination of the world's deadliest ideologies along with some of its deadliest weapons. While the Bush administration's NSS is cast in terms of combating terrorism with a global reach and the ESS also speaks about terrorism's global scope, one hardly needed to read the leading American or European strategic journals to realize the broader Middle East was now the top foreign policy challenge. The ESS signaled a clear shift in Europe's strategic attention beyond its current borders. In the view of Javier Solana (2003), a key element was the need to stabilize what he called the European neighborhood: 'the Middle East is a challenge and must lie at the heart of our neighborhood strategy,' he argued. 'Our task is to promote an arc of well-governed states in our neighborhood with whom we enjoy close and cooperative relations, creating a circle of good governance on the perimeter of the Mediterranean to the Caucasus.'

To be sure, there were and are key differences of view between Washington and Brussels, especially when it comes to the means that should be employed to address these threats and the need to build internal order and further develop international law as a tool to help manage a potentially dangerous world. The American emphasis on a 'balance of power that favors freedom' finds no rhetorical equivalent in the ESS. While one can argue that the European Union is the world's most interesting experiment in the application of neo-Wilsonian principles, one does not find the same transformational hue in the ESS that exists in its American counterpart.[5] The real difference in the two documents lies in the European Union's eschewing of any discussion of military preemption and its repeated reaffirmation of the need to build on international order and strengthen international law. One could continue the list of such real and at times important nuances.

Yet it was the commonality of threat analysis and analytical thrust in terms of the need for early intervention to defuse threats and crises before they become acute that caught Washington's attention and generated a positive reaction. While the ESS was the subject of few (if any) headlines in the United States, in both public and private administration officials went out of their way to commend it as an important step forward for the European Union as such, as well as a step towards bridging transatlantic differences. In the American strategic community, it was generally seen as a positive step and was greeted with almost universal applause. At a time when beleaguered Atlanticists in and outside of the government were confronted with claims that Europe had become strategically marginal and the alliance was dead, this document was received as a kind of tonic, which suggested that Europe was capable of a strategic rethink akin in important ways to the one under-way in the United States. As one senior administration official put it to the author at the time, the ESS was certainly not written with the same 'ruthless clarity' as the NSS. Still, it demonstrated that Europe was taking a key step in a similar direction and reaching many of the same conclusions as strategic thinkers in Washington.

The ESS also became an important data and reference point in a burgeon-ing internal debate in Washington over Europe's future importance and role in American foreign policy. That debate had started much earlier in the 1990s – catalyzed by war in the Balkans and NATO enlargement – and centered on how important the Europe and the US–European relationship was or should be in a post-Cold War world where Europe was no longer the locus of global conflict and was increasingly democratic and secure. It was accelerated by 9/11, which graphically underscored that the major threats to America came from very different parts of the world – and no longer from Europe.

From an American perspective, the central issue was whether Europe could evolve from what had been, in historical terms, a strategic problem into a new global partner. In other words, could a part of the world that for nearly a century had bedeviled American statespersons during two world wars and the Cold War, now that it was unified and secure, step forward on an increasingly global stage as a partner of the United States in projecting Western influence to address new challenges to common interests? In the aftermath of 9/11, what had been a somewhat theoretical debate among insiders in the strategic community became a much more explicit political and partisan dispute, as two very different views and policy alternatives emerged. One group of commentators, largely but not exclusively consisting of conservatives, asserted that US–European strategic cooperation during the Cold War had been driven by a specific strategic need and that it was an illusion to think that the same kind of close strategic cooperation with Europe could be extended to other issues and areas given our diverging stra-tegic cultures and interests (see Kagan 2002, 2003).[6] To replicate it, they argued, would potentially hamstring America from pursuing its own national interest and asserting its unique power at a crucial juncture in history. Some commentators even went a step further and argued that the United States should seek to prevent the emergence of a strong and unified Europe lest it become a hindrance to or competitor with the United States.

It was this logic that, in part, contributed to the Bush administration's decision to downplay NATO's Article V offer of assistance in the wake of 9/11, and to embrace Donald Rumsfeld's vision of 'coalitions of the willing' instead of the alliance as a collective set of allies; and which led to loose talk about an American policy of seeking to disaggregate the European Union. While the Bush administration would subsequently move to correct some of these early mistakes and repair transatlantic ties, such policies, along with widespread doubts about the war in Iraq, contributed to a wave of public estrangement vis-à-vis the United States in Europe. While President Bush distanced himself from such views, these voices and views remain a potent force in American conservative circles. Paradoxically, they find their counterparts in an unholy alliance with Europe's own unilateralists – often found on the left on the continent – who argued that Europe must emancipate itself from American influence and go its own way.

The opposing view was and is that the transformation of the US–European partnership to meet these new threats is the logical and natural extension of the original Atlanticist vision that motivated American and European leaders first to come together in the late 1940s and establish NATO and the European project. Proponents of this view argue that such a strategic leap is politically doable and indeed a prerequisite if either side of the Atlantic hopes successfully to face the new strategic challenges likely to dominate the twenty-first century. They also argue that the focus of this new transatlantic agenda must be the broader Middle East and that it will require a new set of policies designed to prevent and preempt crises politically, economically and, if need be, militarily. While it is true that the United States and Europe do not have the tradition or track record of working together in the wider Middle East, East Asia or other more distant parts of the globe, the same was true when it came to dealing with Russia in the late 1940s. What made the founding fathers of the alliance successful was precisely their ability to generate the will to create the structures that led to those common efforts. The same, they argue, could and must be done today – provided there is commitment, at the highest political levels, to a rethink of both the role of NATO and American policy towards the European Union (see Asmus and Pollack 2002; Asmus 2005). For obvious reasons, the ESS became an important reference point. Both sides of the debate pointed to the similarities and differences between it and the NSS to justify their viewpoints as to whether the glass was half empty or half full, and whether the Atlantic Alliance, at the end of the day, still had a future.

Rethinking the rethink

In August 2004, at the height of the American presidential election campaign – and paradoxically at a time when the Republican Party criticism of Senator John Kerry and the Democratic Party for being too eager to cooperate and compromise with European allies was also at its height – President Bush and National Security Adviser Condoleezza Rice called in a small group of trusted aides to the White House and tasked them to prepare a strategy to repair transatlantic relations in the president's second term if he was re-elected.[7] To the surprise of many, almost immediately following his electoral victory in November 2004, President Bush moved quickly to restore US–European relations. National Security Adviser Rice was promoted to Secretary of State and quickly traveled to Europe to underscore this new message. In February 2005, the president made the first of a series of trips to the continent to mend ties, visiting the European Union's institutions for the first time and delivering a major speech underscoring the need for a new transatlantic agenda and partnership to tackle the challenges of a new era.[8]

The challenges the president spoke about in his Brussels speech were in many ways the same issues and concerns that he and his team had highlighted in the NSS. Despite all the controversy that President Bush's tenure in office and initiatives such as the NSS had produced at home and abroad, perhaps the one area where there was and still is common ground in the United States across the political aisle was the recognition that 9/11 was the dawn of a new strategic era, that the threat of the use of a weapon of mass destruction against the United States was very real and growing, and that the American national security strategy needed to be overhauled for a new era. Similarly, the contention that US policy must focus more on the internal nature of regimes, and elevate the importance of democratic development in regions such as the Middle East as part of a strategy to battle terrorism, was an insight likely to outlast this president. While one can criticize the Bush administration for how it packaged and launched the NSS, as well as certain elements of this document, it remains true that the NSS captured some basic truths about a new strategic age that would serve as a point of departure for any future president, be he or she Republican or Democrat.

At the same time, it was hard not to conclude that the warnings of critics of the administration about the potential costs of this strategy had been proven correct. At the time of writing (early 2006), the administration's course looked increasingly unsustainable at home. The broad bipartisan consensus that existed after 9/11 had fractured and led to one of the most partisan and polarizing foreign policy debates in Washington in decades. The risk of the rise of a new wave of neo-isolationism was growing. By early 2006, the United States was becoming isolated around the world with its global standing at an all-time low. The administration was unable to generate the kind of broad international support needed successfully to prevail in postwar Iraq and on other critical issues. Washington had opened the Pandora's box of preemption but without a serious effort to build international norms that would guide and legitimate its use or deal with the risks of the unintended consequences.

In other words, the NSS analysis of the threats facing the United States in the twenty-first century, and the push for a more expansive set of policy objectives to combat terrorism, including a greater emphasis on democracy promotion, were likely to prove enduring features of future American foreign policy even if the packaging and formulations would change, perhaps significantly, with future administrations. This would be especially true in the case of a future Democratic administration which would bend over backwards to look different from the Bush team. But the real debate will be over the 'how'. And here it seemed obvious that the Bush administration's failures and setbacks in Iraq and elsewhere would only heighten and reinforce the sense that different and more effective approaches would be needed.

Conclusion

What does all this mean for the transatlantic relationship? Is Europe likely to become more or less important in the future for American policymakers? If Washington turns back to viewing Europe as a major partner, is it more likely to focus on the European Union, NATO or some new combination of the two in forging a new agenda? Already the key to future transatlantic cooperation seems increasingly to lie beyond Europe and in the ability of the United States and EU to cooperate on the challenges of the future and not the past. To be sure, there remains an important agenda requiring attention in Europe – consolidating Balkan peace, anchoring a democratic Ukraine to the West, addressing Russia's drift toward autocracy, reaching out to the Black Sea region, and so on. As critical as this agenda is, the central strategic issues remain combating terrorism and working for positive change in the broader Middle East, as well as dealing with Asia and China's rise down the road. If one could measure the amount of time and energy devoted by the United States and the European Union to issues on the continent versus this broader global agenda, the balance has already shifted toward the latter.

Second, if the United States and Europe were to succeed in developing a strategy to address such challenges, it would need to be based much more on a US–EU dialogue than in the past – for both European and American reasons. From an American perspective, these new challenges and America's changing strategic needs are making the United States more rather than less dependent on the European Union and its success. If we simply take the Bush administration's top goals – defending the US homeland, winning the war on terror and promoting liberty and freedom around the world – all these are areas where the European Union has considerable say and resources. Achieving them would require a strong, politically cohesive and outward-looking European Union in addition to NATO. Thus US policy needs to rethink its approach to the European Union while continuing to maintain its traditional support for NATO as the political-military security arm of a new community of Western democracies (see Asmus 2005).

Third, if the neo-imperial moment in American foreign policy is over, it is not yet clear whether a new multilateral moment has yet arrived. The challenge for critics and opponents of the Bush administration is to develop a credible alternative that could address the same threats and pursue the same goals while being more effective, multilateral and contributing to international order. Although the Democrats in opposition in the United States are starting to sketch out alternative national security strategies, it is fair to say that they were still closer to the beginning rather than the end of the process in early 2006.

Was there, for example, a more legitimate and internationally acceptable form of preemption that American and Europeans could embrace? One that recognizes that preventive wars of regime change should indeed be a matter of absolutely last resort but that there will be circumstances in which future policymakers will want to use force preventively? Can the UN be reformed in a manner that brings it into this new strategic era, which modernizes foundational principles and norms that are no longer tenable, and which makes it an asset as opposed to the hindrance that conservative critics claim it is (see Daalder and Steinberg 2005)? Today we still live in what might accurately be called a Trumanesque moment. The question is whether policies worthy of Truman's name and legacy are within reach.

Notes

1   In this author's view, the best analysis of the intellectual origins of the NSS from someone sympathetic to the administration and the NSS is by Philip Zelikow. In addition to being a well-known scholar of US foreign policy in his own right, Zelikow was a confidant of then National Security Adviser Condoleezza Rice, and was brought in as a consultant to assist in the conceptualization of this document. See his thoughts on the NSS in Zelikow (2003), and interesting clues to his and Rice's thinking on Europe in Zelikow and Rice (1997). For excellent critical views of the NSS, see Ikenberry (2002b) and Daalder and Lindsay (2003).
2   An excellent overview of US strategic thinking on the eve of the 9/11 attacks as well as in the immediate aftermath of those attacks can be found by reading the reports of the National Commission on Terrorist Attacks (2003). This report and the testimony the Commission organized captures a sense of how the American strategic community had suffered a fundamental failure of imagination and its determination never to let it happen again.
3   Private conversations with senior EU officials.
4   This is one conclusion that can be clearly drawn from the data gathered in a series of annual polls conducted by the German Marshall Fund of the United States since 2002. That evidence can be found at www.transatlantictrends.org. See also Asmus *et al.* (2004).
5   At the same time, it is interesting to note that the same German Marshall Fund polls mentioned above also found European publics as supportive as Americans when it came to democracy promotion.
6   To be fair, Kagan lamented what he saw as an inevitable transatlantic drift driven by the asymmetry in power across the Atlantic. Other conservative commentators were far less regretful.
7   Private conversations between the author and senior administration officials.
8   Bush's February 2005 Brussels speech is available online at http://www.useu.be/TransAtlantic/Feb2105BushSpeechConcertNoble.html (accessed 7 January 2006).

3   The US National Security Strategy

European reactions

Jolyon Howorth

The National Security Strategy (NSS) was published by the White House almost a year to the day of the terrorist attacks on New York and Washington of 11 September 2001. It acquired instant notoriety, not only in Europe but around the world, both because of its apparent function as a response to 9/11, and its ominous implications for Iraq and other 'rogue regimes'. The combination (or rather the conflation) of these two distinct issues was one of Europe's primary concerns about the NSS. The document appeared in September 2002, as the entire world began to debate the case for war against Saddam Hussein. Unsurprisingly, much of the public comment was coloured by the passion of the moment. Beyond the drama generated in the European press,[1] informed comment on the document was more readily forthcoming from Americans than from Europeans – even in 'European' international relations journals.[2] Two of the most sophisticated 'European' responses (Freedman 2003; Heisbourg 2003) were published in an American journal. Perhaps the most substantial and significant 'European' response to the NSS was eventually expressed in the ESS itself.

At the most general level, there was a European distaste for the triumphalism of the NSS. Stanley Hoffmann (2003), in his guise as a Frenchman, was merciless in his denunciation of the document's 'triumphant unilateralism'. Pierre Hassner (2002: 46) deplored

> the absolute right that the US currently claims to make sovereign judgments on what is right and what is wrong, particularly in respect of the use of force, and to exempt itself with an absolutely clear conscience from all the rules that it proclaims and applies to others.

But the tone and tenor of the document were minor irritants. There were really few surprises in European reactions. In general, and predictably, multilateralism was preferred to unilateralism, pragmatism to ideology, root causes prioritised over symptoms, diplomacy over military force, the long-term over the short-term, the known over the unknown, caution preferred to risk.

European reactions can be differentiated thematically and chronologically. Given the immediate context of a looming – ostensibly pre-emptive –

'war of choice', it was hardly surprising that the main focus of the immediate European reaction was on the controversial issue of pre-emption. Somewhat later, after the Iraq war had started, there were various European reactions both to the impact on alliance relations of the notion of 'coalitions of the willing', and to the strictures within the NSS about fighting the 'war on terror'. Perhaps paradoxically, it was even later still – long after the Bush administration had declared an end to 'major combat' and embarked on the process of 'nation-building' – that Europeans really began to pay appropriate attention to the issue which is arguably the single most important new departure in the NSS: the export of democracy.

Who says pre-emption and who says prevention?

The initial reactions of informed Europeans to the NSS were actually quite restrained. A number of key papers all suggested that the new questions being asked in the NSS were legitimate – though ambiguous – and that what was required was more transatlantic discussion. François Heisbourg (2003: 75) offered reflections on the NSS as a 'work in progress'. He focused tightly on 'the semantics at play – notably the wide use of the words "pre-emption" and "prevention" interchangeably to summarise this new strategy', and situated this shift within the context of a discursive leitmotif which had become a constant in all US strategic pronouncements after 9/11: the need to take the fight to the enemy before they struck again. For Heisbourg, the fundamental significance of the document lay in Chapter V ('Prevent Our Enemies from Threatening Us, Our Allies, and Our Friends with Weapons of Mass Destruction'), and its several worrying features. The first was that the NSS tended explicitly to downplay the novelty[3] of the notion of pre-emption:

> We must adapt the concept of imminent threat to the capabilities and objectives of today's adversaries … The United States has long maintained the option of pre-emptive actions to counter a sufficient threat to our national security … The United States will not use force in all cases to pre-empt threats nor should nations use pre-emption as a pretext for aggression.

Such a 'classical approach', commented Heisbourg, was difficult to reconcile with the revolution in strategic thinking implicit in Paul Wolfowitz's December 2002 comment: 'Anyone who believes that we can wait until we have certain knowledge that attacks are imminent has failed to connect the dots that led to September 11' (Wolfowitz 2002). The doctrine of pre-emption, for Heisbourg, had broken important new ground in relation to previous precepts of international law, sloughing off any juridical framework and becoming a dangerous new doctrine of war-fighting.[4] Heisbourg noted that the terms 'pre-emption', 'prevention' and 'anticipatory action' were used almost interchangeably in the NSS and in public discussion of it – whereas they had always been, and needed still to be, kept rigorously distinct at both semantic and juridical levels. Even the word 'prevention', he noted, had itself acquired contradictory connotations, having been traditionally used (especially in European discourse) to imply *crisis prevention* or *preventive deployment*, as for instance in the case of the deployment of United Nations (UN) peace-keepers in Macedonia in the 1990s. The NSS usage, on the other hand, clearly implied *war-fighting*. The semantic conflation of the concepts of pre-emption and prevention could, Heisbourg (2003) argued, lead to a revolution in the 'legitimization of the use of force'. Three further problems arose.

The first, according to Heisbourg, was the danger that the 'loose language' evident in the NSS, coupled with the explicit threat of unilateral military action, could in fact *prevent* the general adoption, by the international community, of a new legal definition of pre-emption – something which the drama of 9/11 suggested was urgently required in international law. Second, by shifting, with no allied consultation, from the tried and trusted strategies of deterrence and containment, to the vague and inchoate notions of pre-emption and prevention, the United States risked plunging the Atlantic Alliance into paralysis. This would be all the more regrettable in that certain allies, notably France, had no theoretical, cognitive or strategic problem with notions of prevention and pre-emption, provided there was proper discussion about the new parameters. Third, the new strategy of pre-emption, linked as it was to the fight against the proliferation of WMD, would almost certainly lead to the acceleration of WMD programmes in what were at that time euphemistically called 'states of concern'. Since some of these were close to Europe's strategic space, this could render the European allies increasingly vulnerable. By the same logic, conscious of the price to be paid for being on the US 'blacklist', other states, currently allied to the United States (though more out of convenience than conviction, Saudi Arabia and Pakistan being obvious examples), might be tempted covertly to accelerate their own WMD programmes against the day when alliance preferences in Washington might shift to their disadvantage. Heisbourg concluded by making a plea to the United States. In the post-9/11 context, he argued, new legal definitions for both pre-emption and prevention were necessary and justified. The Europeans needed such definitional and doctrinal clarity just as much as the United States. But while agreement on the definition and scope of pre-emption was vital, this had to be a multilateral process involving intensive alliance discussions in order to ensure resumed transatlantic convergence rather than further divergence.

An important corollary to Heisbourg's thoughts on pre-emption was provided by Lawrence Freedman (2003), who stressed that much of the semantic discussion was misplaced. The NSS, he implied, was simply incorrect in its use of words. Pre-emption, he insisted, was a response to a situation which had already got out of hand. It was a last-minute act of desperation, a quest to reverse a developing imbalance of power. As such, it was likely to be sub-optimal strategically and counterproductive militarily. It had been in vogue at times during the Cold War with discussions around first-strike capacity, but ultimately ruled out as too risky. Nothing on this score, argued Freedman, had changed with the end of the Cold War. Neither in the case of humanitarian intervention, nor in that of action against rogue states developing WMD, nor even in that of action against terrorists was there any logical case to be made for pre-emption. On the other hand, *prevention*, hitherto the outcast of international law, could now, he suggested, come into its own: 'prevention provides a means of confronting factors that are likely to contribute to the development of a threat before it has had the chance to become imminent' (Freedman 2003: 106). When used in conjunction with classical elements of deterrence, he concluded, 'an ounce of prevention is better than a pound of cure'. Freedman (2003: 114) called for a vigorous transatlantic debate around 'an updated notion of prevention' which 'might encourage recognition that the world in which we live is one in which the best results are likely to come from a readiness to engage difficult problems over an extended period of time'.

These two immediate European responses, formulated by two of Europe's foremost strategic thinkers, both reflected concerns that US strategy had embarked on a form of knee-jerk, ill-thought-out, strategic revisionism that would put Europeans in a bind and almost certainly exacerbate EU–US tensions at precisely the moment when a shifting security dilemma and unprecedented new threats called for a lucid, legitimate and collective re-assessment of the overall rules of the game. Both analysts suggested that, with enough good will and determination to confront bold new questions, the Europeans and the Americans could probably reach agreement. However, both papers were written before the outbreak of conflict in Iraq.

A similarly confident 'European' reaction was produced by the London-based International Institute for Strategic Studies (IISS 2002). Reassuring its readers that the NSS was 'not proposing to abandon deterrence or to make pre-emption the focus of US defence policy', the IISS paper identified a major strategic shift in the designation of 'terrorists of global reach' and of 'rogue states' as the main threat. While granting some validity to the pre-emptive option in the former case, the IISS insisted that pre-emption was inappropriate in almost all other cases and concluded, perhaps presciently, that 'pre-emption will not become the defining feature of US military strategy'.[5] The paper regretted the extent to which the language of the NSS was driven by ideology, and warned against the dangers of other states hijacking some of the US arguments in favour of pre-emption. The task facing both the United States and the international community, according to the IISS, was to 'define the line separating justifiable pre-emption from unlawful aggression in ways that will gain widespread adherence abroad'. Once again, the basic message was: here are some interesting and valid ideas – let's discuss them. Overall, the initial response of most Europeans was to suggest that the NSS was guilty of departing from traditional realism and verging too radically towards idealism. Robert Kagan was being turned on his head.

British and French commentators might have been expected to embrace the logic of military intervention more readily than other Europeans. Yet, interestingly, even German commentators were similarly unperturbed. Thomas Risse (2003: 22), in a sober re-appraisal of the 'transatlantic security community' in light of the NSS, argued that nothing fundamental yet threatened the traditional ways of doing business across the Atlantic:

> The transatlantic security community is still intact, resting on a combination of collective identity based on common values, (economic) interdependence based on common material interests, and common institutions based on norms regulating the relationship.

While recognising the dangers of some of the 'imperial tendencies' in contemporary US foreign policy discourse, and while accepting that there were elements in the NSS which were 'partly at odds with some principles of the world order that have been part of the western consensus in the post World War II era' (which must count as a rare Germanic instance of litotes), Risse (2004: 230) nevertheless noted that there were countervailing messages within the document itself (where due obeisance is indeed made to the importance of alliances and multilateralism), and concluded: 'In sum, the much-criticized National Security Strategy document actually represents a policy compromise between the neoconservative unilateralists and the traditional conservatives in the Bush administration.'

Karl-Heinz Kamp (2003: 18), from the other side of the German politico-intellectual spectrum, went even further:

> Given the dangers of terrorism, allies should have no problem in principle with the new American National Security Strategy endorsement of preventive as well as pre-emptive war. The UN Charter must be reinterpreted in light of threats from non-state actors in failed states.

One seasoned Berlin-based observer noted that there was a major difference between the emotional reactions of the European press and the much more measured response of the policy community and even of governments, most of which in these initial months between September 2002 and the outbreak of the Iraq war considered that 'the principle of pre-emption' gave no real cause for alarm (Pond 2004: 36). The senior EU official Robert Cooper is even quoted in this same study as having argued that prevention had been the principle on which, throughout the nineteenth century, the United Kingdom had decided whether or not to intervene in continental Europe (see Pond 2004: 60).

So far, almost all comments on the NSS implied that multilateral discussions could – with good will on all sides – generate consensual answers to the tough questions the document posed. Part of the explanation for this measured initial response was the timing. The document appeared one day after the anniversary of 9/11 and the very day of George W. Bush's speech to the United Nations General Assembly calling on the unity of the international community to solve the Iraq problem. After a summer of alarmist and bellicose rumours, during which many members of the commentariat confidently predicted an ideologically driven unilateral US invasion of Iraq, early September appeared to have consecrated an administration shift back to multilateralism and reason. Transatlantic harmony seemed, once again, to be within reach and the initial reactions to the NSS reflected that perspective.

Less sanguine, however, with respect to the prospects for transatlantic harmony emerging out of NSS, was an instant analysis provided by Jean-Yves Haine and Gustav Lindstrom of the EU Institute for Security Studies (Haine and Lindstrom 2002). They considered that the key innovation of the document was the identification of the new threats to the United States: 'the combination of terrorism, tyranny and technology'. The 9/11 attacks, they noted, had put an end to 1990s-era American self-doubt about the desirability of US hegemony and had generated, in part – and paradoxically – as a reaction to a new sense of vulnerability, a new US assertiveness. Coupled with the messianic language of 'good and evil', 'with us or against us', the document, Haine and Lindstrom (2002) argued, clearly presaged an entirely new version of US 'grand strategy' – one to which Europeans needed to pay close attention because of four disturbing features: the willingness to use military force; a less risk-averse approach to 'exit strategy' (go in rapidly and worry later about getting out); the preference for 'coalitions of the willing' over fixed alliances; and a new crusading mission around 'nation building'. All of these new features, it was noted, contradicted the previous cautious realism of the Bush team in foreign affairs. The authors concluded that the NSS posed for European policy-makers two significant sets of questions. First, how to *read* US policy ambiguity through all the loose talk of pre-emption (US attitudes towards Iraq and North Korea were quite different). Second, how to avoid being forced simply to react to US strategic decisions – the latter likely to be taken with no consultation. The authors suggested that the European Union should 'set up its own criteria and operating procedures for the use of force and preventive measures' (Haine and Lindstrom 2002) – a proposal somewhat at odds with the general European optimism with respect to EU–US policy convergence arising out of open discussion. The ESS was, at one level, a follow-up to this suggestion.

As the war in Iraq became protracted, European criticism of the doctrine of pre-emption was massively stepped up. It was castigated as a 'recipe for turning the world into a jungle' (Hoffmann 2003: 103). The London-based *Guardian*, in a leader on 26 November 2003, predicted that it 'will make nuclear warfare both more doable and more likely'. To the extent that the war in Iraq came to be widely perceived in Europe as a 'mistake', one major consequence was the growing European perception that the primary result had been an increase in terrorist recruitment rather than a decline, the creation of a less stable rather than a more stable Middle East and the exacerbation rather than the improvement of relations between the 'West' and Islam (Royal Institute of International Affairs 2004). Chris Patten (2004b) voiced this concern in September 2004 in a withering rhetorical statement about pre-emption to the European Parliament:

> Is the world today safer than before the overthrow of the appalling Saddam? Is global terrorism in retreat? Are we closer to building bridges between Islam and the West? Is the world's only super-power more widely respected? Have the citizens in our democracies been treated in a way that will encourage them to give governments the benefit of the doubt next time they are told that force needs to be used pre-emptively to deal with an imminent threat? I simply pose the questions. Honourable Members will have their own answers.

It is important to remember that Islam is a growing presence in the European Union as a whole. It is thus unsurprising that Europe gradually became appalled at the extent to which the first application of the NSS – the military occupation of Iraq – was widely perceived as a war against Islam, thus fuelling jihadist tendencies,[6] especially among youth and other groups (Errera 2005). More generally, especially once the European Security Strategy document was made public, analysts began stressing the growing divergence between the underlying values which informed the two approaches (Bailes 2004; Spears 2003).

'The mission determines the coalition'

Another major European objection to the NSS concerned the Bush administration's increasingly overt policy of forging 'coalitions of the willing' instead of relying on the formal structures and resources of the Atlantic Alliance. Although the NSS insisted that 'The United States is committed to lasting institutions like ... NATO', the document foresaw no military role for the European Union per se and went on to stress the value of coalitions of the willing. 'Coalitions' effectively replaced permanent alliances as the US instrument of choice for the implementation of the NSS. This was true in Afghanistan, even before the drafting of the NSS, where the military campaign which famously cold-shouldered NATO was only made possible by the diplomatic construction of an unprecedented ad hoc coalition embracing countries as diverse as Russia, Uzbekistan, Tajikistan, Kyrgyzstan, Kazakhstan, Azerbaijan, Pakistan, China and India. And it was true again in Iraq. Of the 45 official members of the 'coalition' which fought its way to Baghdad in spring 2003, only one (the UK) fielded substantial numbers of troops (45,000) and only one other (Australia) supplied more than token forces (2000). Only three other countries, Albania (70), Poland (200) and Romania (278), fielded any combat troops at all. The remaining 40 'coalition partners' provided essentially political support, with varying levels of credibility and enthusiasm. As was pointed out in a number of sceptical studies (see Anderson *et al.* 2003), 17 of the countries in the coalition could not claim to have 'free' or even 'partially free' democracies, while 24 (more than half) had high levels of corruption. The US State Department's own human rights survey reported that torture and/or extra-judicial killings were carried out by security forces in 11 coalition members.[7]

The slogan 'the mission determines the coalition', with its unilateralist connotations, has been profoundly disruptive of NATO. Opinions on this issue have been sharply divided across the Atlantic. A major research project conducted in 2004 revealed that, while US analysts and actors considered it normal that coalitions had become the default US preference, their European counterparts still hankered for the relative comfort of alliances in general and of NATO in particular (Howorth *et al.* 2004). A 2004 Council on Foreign Relations report on *Renewing the Atlantic Partnership* stated unequivocally that 'reliance on coalitions of the willing ... has become the policy of the United States' (CFR 2004: 1). There are several reasons for this change: the absence of any existential threat; the near impossibility of achieving unanimity at a political level; the growing problems of military interoperability; the restructuring of the US military away from massive overseas forward basing (especially in Europe); and the growing US need for flexibility in response to crisis management. The NATO alliance is increasingly seen in the United States as being in a state of decline (see Rupp 2006). While Europeans interviewed about the implications of 'coalitions' in summer 2004 understood much of the US logic in their favour, for the most part, they deeply regretted the new reality. This was especially true of senior military officers who (even in France) remained deeply nostalgic for NATO. Moreover, there was a general sense in most European countries that the relative demise of the alliance reflected a growing EU–US gap not only in values but also in interests. Even more significantly, there was general agreement that the new US 'imperialism' was problematic for Europe, in part (paradoxically) because the United States did not have the mindset or reflexes of a 'true' imperial power.

Despite considerable pro-NATO official rhetoric in Paris, few believed that there was much future in trying to reinvigorate the alliance. The American switch to reliance on coalitions was widely seen as having blown apart the internal dynamics which previously held NATO together: on the one hand, a workable balance between political credit, acceptable risk and financial viability; on the other, a balance between values, interests and responsibilities. A political-military strategy based on ad hoc coalitions dispenses altogether with such delicate considerations.

Most Europeans agree that the 'tool-box' function of NATO remains its key asset. The alliance, over long years, has developed its own structures, processes, functional commonality, standards, ways of sticking together and inter-operability. It is, of course, precisely these features which allow for the construction, from within the alliance, of effective coalitions of the willing.

Perhaps the most lasting impact on European militaries of the coalitions doctrine will come from the choice that has to be made by all EU member states: whether to continue even trying to be able to fight alongside the US military in high intensity warfare. The UK and (to a somewhat lesser extent) France still aim to achieve inter-operability. Most other EU member states have implicitly accepted a military role confined to 'peace support' (Venusberg Group 2004: 68). Behind the almost innocuous reference to coalitions of the willing in the NSS, there lies the entire question of the future functionality of the Atlantic Alliance. It is in part that uncertainty that has been driving the European Security and Defence Policy (ESDP). But that is another story.

Debating the 'global war on terror'

Europeans generally refused to follow the United States in declaring a 'global war on terror' (GWOT) (Andréani 2004–5). The NSS proclaimed that 'The United States is fighting a war against terrorism of global reach' and warned that other nations could not sit on the fence: 'History will judge harshly those who saw this coming danger but failed to act.' This black-and-white approach to the world was widely regarded across Europe not merely as simplistic, but, in the words of the eminently establishment UK historian Sir Michael Howard, as a 'terrible and irrevocable error'. For Howard (2002: 8–9), 'to declare war on terror, or even more illiterately, on terrorism, is at once to accord terrorists a status and dignity that they seek and that they do not deserve'. Worse still, he argued, the 'war' cannot be 'won' militarily, but the public will expect precisely such an outcome. Across Europe, diplomats and soldiers alike inwardly cringed at the hubristic words with which Bush chose to introduce the chapter devoted to defeating global terrorism: 'The conflict was begun on the timing and terms of others. It will end in a way, and at an hour, of our choosing.'[8] Despite official Bush administration disclaimers to the effect that this was not a war like any other, it did eventually, in the words of Andréani (2004–5: 31), go 'far beyond metaphor to acquire a strategic reality'. Furthermore, contrary to what almost all European commentators on pre-emption counselled, the vital distinction between state actors and non-state actors is absent from the NSS. Indeed the conflation between terrorism and Iraq, between Bin Laden and Saddam Hussein – implicit throughout and explicit from time to time – eventually became an item of administration faith.[9] The 'war' was thus extended beyond terrorism to 'rogue states' along the 'axis of evil' (Bush) but also, potentially, to a longer list of states now categorised as 'outposts of tyranny' (Rice). This war psychosis was aptly exemplified by the glib remark attributed to Radek Sikorski of the American Enterprise Institute: 'Baghdad is for wimps. Real men go to Tehran' (Everts 2004a: 35). Furthermore, this extended war – particularly the one fought in Iraq – succeeded in attracting and in creating terrorists in numbers unseen in the past, and in fuelling a 'war' between terrorists and the United States which did not previously exist, a development now officially recognised by US intelligence sources (National Intelligence Council 2005: 93–5; Stephens 2005). All this has been widely perceived in Europe not only as regrettable but also as highly counter-productive. It has, in effect, according to many Europeans (and also to many Americans[10]), amounted to a massive distraction from the 'real' fight against terrorism in general and against Al Qaeda in particular (Muller 2003; Gordon and Shapiro 2004).

With the occasional exception (Delpech 2002), Europeans collectively winced at most aspects of the treatment of 'terror' in the NSS (Muller 2003; Keohane 2005). They deplored the simplistic depiction of terrorists as 'evil' and 'immoral', the equation of terrorism with 'slavery, piracy, or genocide', and the lack of any serious attempt to address root causes. The main explanation for terrorism produced by the Bush administration at the time was that 'terror grows in the absence of progress and development ... terror lives when freedom dies' (Rice 2003). Moreover, despite repeated assertions from leading European statespersons that there is no structural connection between terrorism and Islam, the NSS, despite its own denial, appears to fall squarely into a 'clash of civilizations' trap in declaring the need for:

a different and more comprehensive approach to public information efforts that can help people around the world learn about and understand America. The war on terrorism is not a clash of civilizations. It does, however, reveal the clash inside a civilization, a battle for the future of the Muslim world. This is a struggle of ideas and this is an area where America must excel.

Even more deplorable, from a European perspective, was the ironic fact that, in waging this struggle of ideas, the United States preferred to use the sword rather than the word (Berenskoetter 2005: 83). Although the European Union has regularly insisted that a military component will be a necessary part of its counter-terrorist activities,[11] it has never explained in any detail what specific role it foresees for military instruments. This remains an unanswered question in the European Union's approach to counter-terrorism. It is yet another significant contrast to the approach adopted by the United States.

A further target of European criticism of the GWOT was the perceived US disregard for the norms of international law both with respect to the Geneva Convention and with respect to human rights (Greenwood 2002; Roberts 2003; Ignatieff 2005). There was considerable disquiet across Europe about the Patriot Act and its restrictions on human rights and basic freedoms – all of which are explicitly protected in the European Union's Charter of Fundamental Rights. This is a theme which is regularly – albeit diplomatically – raised by visiting EU counter-terrorism officials in the United States. Gjis de Vries on his first visit to Washington in May 2004 insisted that 'we must be careful to preserve and protect the rights and liberties, the principles and values terrorists are seeking to destroy' (Center for Strategic and International Studies 2004: 2–3). It has also constituted the main concern among European analysts of the impact of the GWOT on basic freedoms and human rights (den Boer 2003; Centre for Defence Studies 2005: 17–20).

The July 2005 reports that the Bush administration had decided to *re-brand* its 'war' under the new acronym SAVE (struggle against violent extremism)[12] merely underlined the continuing gulf between the two sides. The fact that it took the administration over four years to begin publicly to emphasise that the 'struggle' should be 'more diplomatic, more economic, more political than it is military'[13] cut little ice with most Europeans. UK officials attempted, at a 8 June 2005 Special Operations seminar in Tampa, Florida, to demonstrate that British experience of heavy-handedness in Northern Ireland had led to the conclusion: 'Kill five, recruit ... how many?' But they suspected their US audience of being deaf to such wisdom and doubted that US officials genuinely believe that military instruments should take a back seat. They saw few signs of the United States accepting anything but a leading role in the ongoing struggle (Fox 2005). A major challenge for the Europeans is to convince their US allies that a holistic new approach to the 'new' terrorism is essential. Unfortunately, the Europeans, though convinced of the virtues of such a holistic approach, are still struggling to assess how the different parts of the whole fit together.

'Extending the peace' or compounding the problem?

Connected to this criticism has been widespread concern across Europe about US approaches to 'winning the peace' in Iraq. The United States has been perceived, even by senior former officials of the Bush administration, as having badly misjudged the challenge of democratisation in Iraq (Diamond 2005; Phillips 2005). In Europe, the Bush administration was (perhaps unfairly) widely accused of wishing to move too quickly towards an 'exit strategy' (Chesterman 2005; Dodge 2004).

Arguably, the most important component in the NSS, on which analysts were slow to pick up, was the notion of 'extending the peace' by exporting 'the hope of democracy, free markets and free trade to every corner of the world'. The Bush administration's 'Greater Middle East Initiative' (GMEI), which translated this chapter of the NSS into a form of 'grand strategy', thereby producing yet another causal justification for the war in Iraq, was only formally presented to the world in early 2004 (Cheney 2004). Cynics might suggest that this was not unconnected with the fact that the two earlier reasons for going to war in Iraq (WMD and the linkage between Saddam Hussein's regime and Al Qaeda) had proved to be dead ends.[14] As it turned out, the GMEI was to prove a nine days' wonder, partly – but only partly – because of European scepticism and resistance (Achcar 2004). Europeans, as Robert Cooper (2005b) insists, have nothing against the export of demo-cracy. At one level, the democratisation (and stabilisation) of the European continent, East and West, has been the European Union's single biggest historical achievement. But Europeans tend to apprehend democratisation rather differently from the missionary approach favoured by those in the United States – from Woodrow Wilson to Paul Wolfowitz – who see the messianic spread of the 'American dream' as the only viable alternative to circling the wagons against an evil external world. European objections to the US proposals assumed three basic forms: the insistence on socio-economics rather than idealism (or ideology – the so-called 'forward strategy for freedom') as the basis of any plan; the insistence that the Israel–Palestine issue should be seen as central and primary; and the insistence on Arab ownership of the democratisation process itself.

The underlying American logic behind the GMEI was originally a security logic: extending democracy would promote stability and security. If neces-sary, it should be done by the application of military force (Cheney 2004). Such a proposal was rendered somewhat more palatable to European sensi-tivities by suggestions (Hagel 2004; Lugar 2004) that the appropriate body to drive the process forward should be NATO. The first European reaction to these proposals came from Joschka Fischer in February 2004 (Fischer 2004). The German foreign minister offered 'a completely new perspective to the countries of the Middle East: enhanced co-operation and closer partnership in the fields of security, politics, the economy, law, culture and civil society'. In outlining this new initiative, Fischer emphasised that it should be based on sustainability and a long-term perspective. Already, the European Union approach based on a variant of the Barcelona Process – emphasising a strong socio-economic basis to reform – is clear. Instant European reactions to the GMEI came thick and fast in the early months of 2004 (Peel 2004; Gnesotto 2004b; Patten 2004a; *Oxford Analytica* 2004). Taken together with Arab objections to the initial crusading enterprise, these responses succeeded, by mid-year, in shifting the entire ethos and focus of the project.

By the time of the G-8 summit in June 2004, the title, phrasing and content of the project had been substantially modified. The very notion of an initia-tive (US-driven), with all that that implied about control and agenda-setting from Washington, was dropped in favour of the title 'Broader Middle East and North Africa *Partnership*' (emphasis added; G-8 summit 2004). The original space involved (basically from Mauritania to Afghanistan), which had caused generalised eye-rolling across Europe, was reduced to that of the Arab world. One cardinal point argued by all European governments – that resolution of the Israel–Palestine conflict should be seen as an indispensable top priority – also found its way into the G-8 statement. Against US officials who argued that Arab governments simply used the pretext of the Israeli–Palestinian conflict as a way of avoiding reform, Europeans successfully made the point that the permanency of that conflict seriously compromised all efforts to promote broader reform across the Arab world. Against Bush and Cheney who called for democratisation of the Palestinian Authority as the primary route to change, European analysts insisted that, without some measure of socio-economic hope for the Palestinian people, democracy was little more than an abstraction. Virtually all European commentators had rejected the all-inclusive nature of the GMEI as a disingenuous attempt to dilute the Israeli–Palestinian problem in a much wider framework. Chris Patten (2004a), citing a Zogby International survey of attitudes in the Arab world, noted that the situation of the Palestinians, 'after more than three generations of conflicts ... appears to have become a defining one of general Arab concern'. It had, he noted, become personalised within the Arab psyche. Patten deplored the fact that 'this apparently incontestable point is, for a particular school of American thought,[15] a deliberate and alarming blind-spot'.

One final area of robust European reaction to the NSS policy of exporting democracy came over the issue of ownership of the reform process. The original GMEI proposals were to some extent based on the UN Development Programme's 2002 *Arab Human Development* report, which stressed three main challenges: governance, gender and education. The success of that report across the Arab world, where it engendered intense discussion, derived from the fact that its authors were Arab scholars and policy-makers, not UN bureaucrats or US ideologues. The NSS serves up, by contrast, a stark series of technocratic fixes designed to maintain control of the reform process in Washington and in institutions such as the World Bank. Indeed, the very fact that the NSS and the GMEI were drafted with no outside consultation speaks volumes about US notions of agenda-setting. European commentators all insisted that 'it is imperative that the agenda of modernisation ... should be owned by the Arab countries themselves' (Patten 2004a). This principle found its way into the eventual statements on the project both through the notion of 'partnership' and through recognition that 'ownership' was structurally linked to success. Grand ideals, however, are no substitute for results and it has subsequently become clear that the ownership principle is undermined by at least three factors: lack of democratic enthusiasm among regional (Arab) governments; the weakness of independent civil society actors; and raw class conflict within most Arab nations. The US ambition, most dramatically being implemented in Iraq, to export democracy to the Middle East, was first formulated publicly in the National Security Strategy. To say that Europeans remained sceptical would be an understatement.

Conclusions: 'half full' or 'half empty'?

It is hazardous to draw any general conclusions about European responses to the NSS. Analyses, like public opinion, varied considerably from country to country, especially among elites. The basic divide between old and new Europe, which Donald Rumsfeld mischievously detected, certainly existed at one level (Levy *et al.* 2005). But even while many Central and Eastern

European elites expressed support for the NSS, their publics did not. Even as the Iraq war was shifting from combat phase to post-conflict reconstruction phase, many of those former members of the Warsaw Pact were already beginning to move away from an almost intuitive pro-Americanism to a greater understanding for and identification with the security objectives of the European Union (Valásek 2005). Moreover, the intensity of the passions generated in 2002 to 2003 led to exaggerated predictions about the seriousness of the clash which proved, with time, to be unfounded (Lindberg 2005). European analysts differed widely in their assessment of the elements of divergence and convergence between the NSS and the ESS. Most insisted that the two documents reveal important – and by now structurally conditioned – differences between their respective approaches to the task of 'doing' international relations (Bailes 2004; Spears 2003). For his part, Robert Cooper (2005b) puts the emphasis on similarities between the two documents, arguing that the European Union and the United States share a basic foreign policy agenda centred on the need to defend themselves proactively and to promote democratisation. While noting the parallel existence of basic differences, Cooper chooses to see the glass as half full. Felix Berenskoetter (2005: 71–92), on the other hand, sees the glass as seriously half empty. By subjecting the two documents to a comparative analysis in terms of their respective visions of 'responsibility, threats and means', he argues that 'what on the surface appears to be a common set of means and ends turns out to be quite different once the semantic shells are removed'. While both documents, argues Berenskoetter, seek to formulate a response to the new world disorder, they are above all guided by very different readings of history. For the United States, history is a linear process moving inexorably towards universalisation of the American dream. For Europe, history is a hopelessly messy process which tells us, above all, that we have to learn to live with diversity. This fundamental difference structured by historical experience is likely to prove the most difficult hurdle facing any attempts to bridge the gap.

Notes

1 See, for example, David E. Sanger, 'Bush to Outline Doctrine of Striking Foes First', *International Herald Tribune*, 20 September 2002; Gaidz Minassian, 'Les Fondations de la Doctrine Bush sont jetées', *Le Monde*, 20 September 2002; 'La Nouvelle Doctrine américaine de défense embarrasse les alliés européens', *EurActiv*, 24 September 2002.

2 See, for example, Blinken (2003–4); Brzezinski (2003); Calleo (2004a); Hunter (2004); Litwak (2002–3); Mazaar (2002–3); Slocombe (2003).

3 John Gaddis (2004: 16–22) argues that *pre-emption* was the cardinal feature of US grand strategy in its very first (John Quincy Adams) guise throughout the nineteenth century.

4 The French president, Jacques Chirac, in his major interview in the *New York Times* on 8 September 2002 (that is, *prior to* the publication of the NSS), had

already castigated the doctrine of pre-emption: 'I think this is an extraordinarily dangerous doctrine that could have tragic consequences.'

5 This prediction was also made by Martin Woolacott in 'Now Bush's Doctrine of War Will Be Put to the Test', *The Guardian*, 21 March 2003: 'this may prove to be a one-war doctrine, even if that war goes very well, a doctrine tailored for Iraq and only distantly relevant to other situations'.

6 A typical comment was that 'bin Laden ... has been able to capitalize on the growing resentment of the Muslim diaspora, especially in Europe' (Center for Strategic and International Studies 2004: 6).

7 The list included Albania, Azerbaijan, Colombia, Eritrea, Ethiopia, Georgia, Macedonia, Nicaragua, the Philippines, Turkey and Uzbekistan.

8 George W. Bush, in his 30 August 2005 speech in California, repeatedly promised 'victory', a word he used no fewer than nine times: 'President commemorates 60th anniversary of VJ Day'. Online. Available: http://www.whitehouse.gov/news/releases/2005/08/20050830-1.html (accessed 8 January 2006).

9 The conflation was even formalized with the US Pentagon-organised 'Freedom March' in Washington DC on 11 September 2005 to honour both victims of 9/11 and the US soldiers who died in Iraq.

10 This was a point John Kerry made repeatedly towards the end of his presidential election campaign in 2004. See also Jervis (2005: 353).

11 This was first made explicit in the Declaration on the Contribution of the CFSP, including the ESDP, to the Fight Against Terrorism issued as Annex V to the Presidency Conclusions of the 22 June 2002 Seville European Council.

12 Or, in some versions, G-SAVE (G being for global, rather than for God!) (Schmitt and Shanker 2005; Kaplan 2005). In fact, the 're-branding' exercise was soon dropped as too blatant a form of PR.

13 General Richard Myers quoted in Matthew Davis, 'New Name for "War on Terror"', BBC News, 27 July 2005. Online. Available: http://news.bbc.co.uk/1/hi/world/americas/4719169.stm (accessed 8 January 2006). In fact, this message was made clear in the February 2003 paper, *National Strategy for Combating Terrorism* (Online. Available: http://www.whitehouse.gov/news/releases/2003/02/20030214-7.html (accessed 8 January 2006)) as early as page 1: 'The struggle against international terrorism is different from any other war in our history. We will not triumph solely or even primarily through military might.'

14 In fact, when Condoleezza Rice testified before Congress on 19 October 2005, she defined the administration's objectives as being:

> Break the back of the insurgency so that Iraqis can finish it off without large-scale military help from the United States. Keep Iraq from becoming a safe haven from which Islamic extremists can terrorize the region or the world. Demonstrate positive potential for democratic change and free expression in the Arab and Muslim worlds, even under the most difficult conditions.

Before the war, there was of course no 'insurgency', no prospect of 'safe haven' for terrorists, and little talk of 'democratic change'. See 'Iraq and US Policy'. Online. Available: http://www.state.gov/secretary/rm/2005/55303.htm (accessed 8 January 2006).

15 Patten fingers Richard Perle and David Frum as prime culprits (see Frum and Perle 2003).

4 Security strategy

What roles for institutions?

Fraser Cameron

The transatlantic political crisis of 2002–3 was arguably the most traumatic in post-war history. It centred on how to respond to international security threats and pitted Washington, London, Warsaw (and for a time Madrid) against Berlin and Paris (and Moscow). German Chancellor Gerhard Schroeder won re-election on an anti-American war ticket in October 2002. Some of the largest anti-war demonstrations in European history took place in February 2003. The crisis shook NATO and the European Union to their very foundations.

The crisis occurred less because of transatlantic differences on security perceptions than over how to respond to the new threats, and in particular the threat posed by Saddam Hussein and his alleged possession of weapons of mass destruction (WMD) and links to international terrorism. How did these different security perceptions and responses arise? What are the prospects for future agreement on security threats and the appropriate response to them, in particular if it involves the use of force? To what extent has the second Bush administration learned lessons from the Iraq war?

These questions lead us inevitably to other questions that are central about the future role of institutions, both transatlantic and international. These institutional questions, with the US and European security strategies used as reference documents, form the central focus for this chapter. Can the European Union and the United States work together in the United Nations and other international organisations? What are the implications for the future of the European Union and NATO? How will the European Union emerge from its political crisis of 2005 after failing to ratify the Constitutional Treaty?

The changing nature of security

With the end of the Cold War, it was inevitable that the United States and the European Union would reassess their strategic interests (Buzan and Waever 2003). The fall of the Berlin Wall in November 1989 became the defining moment for Europe as much as the terrorist attacks of September 2001 became the defining moment for the United States. With the collapse of communism, the European Union embarked on a process of integrating the two halves of a continent that had been divided for half a century. With the attack on the Twin Towers, the United States embarked on a global mission to eradicate terrorism. The US front line was no longer in Europe but in every country or region that engaged in terrorism or sheltered terrorists or was alleged to be developing WMD. There was little overlap between the two agendas. The United States was pleased that the European Union was finally taking greater responsibility for its own continent, but expected Europe to do more in the global war on terrorism. Most Europeans were concerned about the American approach to tackling terrorism, with which Europe had lengthy experience. Even after the Madrid and London bombings of 2004–5, many in the European Union doubted whether the use of military power was a very effective instrument in combating terrorism (Dittrich 2005).

The terminology used to describe the response to the terrorist threat highlights differences in approach between the European Union and the United States. While Americans speak of a 'war on terror', Europeans talk about the 'fight against terrorism'. The European attitude was perhaps best articulated by Professor Michael Howard (2002: 3–4) shortly after 9/11 when he wrote:

> By conceiving of the struggle against international terrorism as a war, loudly proclaiming it as such, and waging it as one, we have given our enemies the battle they aimed to provoke but could not get unless the United States gave it to them. To declare that one is at war also tends to create a war psychosis that may be totally counterproductive for the objective being sought. It arouses an immediate expectation, and demand, for spectacular military action against some easily identifiable adversary, preferably a hostile state. It also helps create the perception that terrorism is an evil that can be eradicated rather than a more complex phenomenon with different aspects to be considered.

According to President Bush, nations were either 'with us or against us', and would need to show what side they were on. The main tool in the war on terrorism was to be the US military machine, the most daunting fighting force in history. In a swift one-sided military encounter, the Taliban were defeated in Afghanistan. The ease with which the US military imposed regime change in Afghanistan brought a frenzy of calls for further military action to oust Iraqi President Saddam Hussein. There was broad support for the Iraqi adventure as hubris reigned in Washington. From leaked reports of meetings of the National Security Council and also of meetings between President Bush and Tony Blair, it would appear that the United States took the decision to topple Saddam Hussein in the summer of 2002. It was later claimed, especially by US Democrats as well as by some Bush administration insiders (see Hersch 2003; Clarke 2004), that American and British intelligence reports were manipulated to seek to demonstrate that Iraq possessed

WMD. Despite failing to secure UN Security Council (UNSC) authorisation, the United States together with the United Kingdom and a handful of other smaller allies invaded Iraq in spring 2003 and by the summer had again imposed regime change in a Muslim country.

The decision to go to war led to a major crisis in transatlantic relations. Both Bush and Blair tried to pin the blame on French President Jacques Chirac for threatening to use France's veto to block a UNSC resolution in support of military action. The French retorted that Hans Blix, the UN chief weapons inspector, should be given more time to complete his work. At the height of the conflict, National Security Adviser, Condoleezza Rice, was quoted as saying that the United States 'should punish the French, ignore Germany and forgive Russia'. For several months the White House refused to take any calls from the German Chancellor's office.

The initial euphoria over the swift military victory in Iraq soon gave way to misgivings as the United States encountered increasing guerrilla resistance which was to increase and continue into 2006. There was widespread criticism of the failure to plan for the post-conflict reconstruction of Iraq, and American and civilian casualties continued to rise in the two years following the invasion. Yet, despite these problems, President Bush fought and won the November 2004 election as a war president.[1]

The neo-conservatives that dominated the first Bush administration were soon to learn that the power to act did not equate to power to persuade. Many American strategists derided Europe's military weakness and argued that the United States could and should 'go it alone'. Many Europeans wailed at the growing asymmetry in military power but argued that the European Union was an important proponent of 'soft power' (see Nye 2003). Few stopped to consider the possibility of complementarities in what the European Union and the United States brought to the table. The first Bush administration seemed more willing to divide and rule in Europe than to argue the virtues of a strong, united European Union.

An additional problem was that a new generation was taking power on both sides of the Atlantic. Gerhard Schröder, for example, did not have the same wartime experience as his predecessor, Helmut Kohl, and few of the closest advisers around Bush had experience of the European Union. For most young Americans, Europe did not figure on the radar screen. For most young Europeans (and Canadians), the United States was a danger to world peace. The elder statespersons on both sides of the Atlantic issued various statements condemning the situation but with no evidence that they were being heeded.

The early months of the second Bush administration seemed to indicate a willingness to change tack and to reach out to erstwhile allies in Europe that had been scorned during the first Bush term. In February 2005 President Bush chose to visit Brussels, including the EU headquarters as well as NATO, and Germany. He spoke of the enduring importance of the Atlantic Alliance but also emphasised the US wish to see a strong, united Europe. He repeated this message at the EU–US summit in Washington in June, just a few weeks after the European Union was plunged into crisis as a result of the two failed referendums on the Constitutional Treaty in France and the Netherlands. He also went out of his way to receive European Commission President Barroso at the White House in October 2005, a further indication of his changed views on the importance of the European Union.

Coming so soon after his re-election, Bush's February 2005 visit to Brussels was especially warmly welcomed by European leaders keen to heal the transatlantic rift. Yet European public opinion remained hostile to Bush and US foreign policy. According to several polls taken after the US elections, a staggering 75 per cent of Europeans had no confidence in Bush's foreign policy. Polls in Canada, the Middle East and elsewhere in the world showed similar popular misgivings about the style and direction of American policy. In many countries China was more trusted in international relations than the United States.[2] What upset many Europeans was the style and rhetoric of the Bush administration, which were both so different from Clinton's. Bush also propagated a different theory of leadership. The United States should articulate clear goals and others would follow. Allies would be punished or ignored if they did not follow. Dissent was equated with disloyalty. This grated with European governments as well as public opinion.

America – the special nation

US security perceptions are coloured by the fact that America has always seen itself as a special nation with a special mission to save civilisation (see Mead 2002). Moral and religious fervour have always been present in presidential speeches, but reached new heights during the Bush presidency, suggesting a heightened sense of crisis and a shift in the very categories of thinking about international relations. The argument for an American special mission was put with force by Robert Kagan (2003) who asserted that 'Americans are from Mars and Europeans from Venus'. A high priest of the neo-conservatives, Kagan (2003: 1) argued that 'it is time to stop pretending that Europeans and Americans share a common view of the world, or even that they occupy the same world. They agree on little and understand each other less and less.' Nor was this a superficial or transitory phenomenon: 'when it comes to setting national priorities, determining threats, defining challenges, and fashioning and implementing foreign and defence policies, the United States and Europe have parted ways' (Kagan 2003: 1–2).

Kagan's thesis struck a raw nerve in Europe and led to a plethora of counter-arguments. But Bush (2005) himself was constantly promoting the idea of America as a special nation with a special mission and special responsibilities – and after 9/11 facing a unique sense of vulnerability. Prior to 1989 the principal mission was the containment of communism. Now Bush was arguing, rather like John Kennedy, that the United States would pay any price, bear any burden, to eradicate terrorism (see Bush 2005). As leader of the 'civilised' world the United States was expected to assume certain responsibilities. Its wide range of economic and strategic interests had increasingly extended the net of its commitments. Some traditional constraints still existed on American activism but the context had changed radically since 1989 and especially after 9/11. The United States was the undisputed world leader: it had no rival globally, whether measured by overall size of national economies, defence budgets, sophistication of weapons systems, global military reach, global economic influence and so on. Despite many social and economic problems, the basic ingredients of American power remained intact. With the Cold War over, America was apparently freer to act on the global stage than at any time since the Second World War. The suggestions that America was engaged in a special mission and was 'bound to lead' were made plausible by a powerful sense that America had been violated on 9/11 as well as by the geopolitics of what was often viewed as a unipolar world.

On the other hand, the end of the Cold War complicated matters as far as American global leadership is concerned. It is not the often remarked absence of a clearly defined enemy so much as the absence of a ready set of rules and justifications for overseas interventions. Rather than the blanket justification of containment of communism, each intervention has to be justified on its own terms or in relation to some as yet not clearly formulated programme – Bush Senior's 'New World Order' or Clinton's 'democratic enlargement' (Haas 1999). If Cold War realism had supplied the necessary basis for policy choices in the period of East–West confrontation, in the more fluid world that followed the collapse of communism various elements of idealism came to the fore, including a renewed interest in promoting the spread of democracy. The idealist and realist visions came together in the Middle East, where the United States jettisoned six decades of support for 'stability' in favour of democracy and human rights.[3] Crucially, a world in which terrorism was the chief threat simply did not accord with the familiar patterns of conflict and policy choices, to the extent that it was necessary to reinterpret that threat to accord more clearly with realist precepts; hence the 'war' on terrorism and the war on Saddam Hussein's Iraq, and policy choices that acted to split the transatlantic allies.

The ESS and NSS

The European Security Strategy (ESS) and the US National Security Strategy (NSS) are the two most important reference documents for any analysis of transatlantic security differences. Detailed comparison of them is difficult because of their different lengths, structures and ambitions. The US paper is twice as long, providing a fairly detailed and concrete programme statement on behalf of a single sovereign entity. The ESS reads more like a declaration of intent and a platform for continuing debate. It avoids descending into detail, not just because of the number of nations it was designed to please and the multiplicity of European and national instruments needed to give it effect, but also because it was published in the wake of a major internal disagreement on Iraq and amidst a sensitive debate on the future of the European Union's security and defence policy (ESDP) (Cameron and Quille 2004).

Each paper was designed for domestic audiences. The NSS sought to demonstrate that Bush had a clear vision of the threats facing the United States and understood what was required to counter such threats. The ESS sought partly to overcome the painful rift over Iraq and partly to demonstrate that the European Union also had a global view of security threats and was determined to meet them. The NSS was peppered with phrases about promoting freedom and what it called the 'non-negotiable demand of human dignity'. Claims were made on behalf of America's own history and values, on behalf of American leadership and on behalf of the civilised world, whose values are taken to be at one with those of the United States. In his introductory statement to the NSS, Bush noted that 'the allies of terror are the enemies of civilization'.

The introduction to the ESS states that Europe has never been so prosperous, so secure and so free. It adds that this Union of 25 states with over 450 million people producing a quarter of the world's GNP, and with a wide range of instruments at its disposal, is inevitably a global player. It should be ready, therefore, to share in the responsibility for global security and building a better world. The ESS is then organised into three chapters: on the security environment, strategic objectives, and the policy implications for the European Union.

In its opening section on the current security environment, the ESS begins by listing the negative aspects of globalisation, arguing that poverty, disease, competition for scarce resources and global warming degrade the security of EU member countries. Anticipating that 'large scale aggression against any member state is now improbable', the ESS identifies five key threats that are interconnected, namely: terrorism, proliferation of WMD, regional conflicts, state failure and organised crime. The ESS then identifies three strategic objectives. The first is 'Addressing the Threats', and here the document notes progress in adopting an EU arrest warrant, in tackling proliferation and dealing with regional conflicts. The second is 'Building Security in our Neighbourhood'. Here, the ESS touches on the importance of enlargement and the EU's neighbourhood policy. The third objective is an international order based on *effective multilateralism*. Finally, in considering the policy implications for Europe, the ESS suggests that Europe should be more active, more capable and more coherent in responding to the new security threats.

Threats are dominant throughout the NSS, which considers all policy areas in the light of the fight against WMD proliferation, rogue states, and particularly the 'war against terrorism'. The ESS speaks cautiously of failed states, whereas the US language towards these regimes is much stronger and far more explicit. However, the ESS recognises the nightmare scenario of a nexus between terrorism, WMD and failed states. Both the NSS and the ESS refer to the underlying sources of terrorism. The NSS, for instance, states 'that the US will support moderate and modern governing to ensure that conditions ... that promote terrorism do not find fertile ground in any nation, and that it will try to diminish the underlying conditions that spawn terrorism'.

It should be noted that the ESS's first draft had a much stronger emphasis on threats, especially on terrorism and WMD, and was thus closer to the NSS. In comparison to an earlier June 2003 draft (considered at the Thessaloniki EU summit), the final adopted version of the ESS was broadened and toned down (see Chapter 10). The final version paid more attention to the effects of globalisation, while state failure and organised crime became separate entries in the list of key threats. The ESS also added regional conflicts as a key security threat. Moreover, while the first draft considered WMD proliferation 'the single most important threat', the adopted ESS considered it as 'potentially the greatest threat to our security'.

Although the NSS was written a year earlier and with an overall tougher approach than the ESS, there are a number of similarities in the papers. Both are optimistic about the progress made since the end of the Cold War, take a comprehensive view of threats, and recognise the complexity of new challenges. Both also touch on values and emphasise the need for a proactive approach. The ESS does not, however, embrace the doctrine of pre-emption. This difference was without doubt widely noted when the ESS was published, not least because it resonated so directly with US–European differences over Iraq and as pre-emption became mixed up with preventive war.[4] The European Union recognises the importance of the United States, but there is not a single mention of the European Union in the NSS and only one of NATO (briefly towards its end). As for multilateralism, the ESS states that 'no single country is able to tackle today's complex problems entirely on its own'. The NSS accepts that 'no nation can build a safer, better world alone', but the emphasis is very much on US dominance and determination, with the United States leading the war on terrorism alone or at the head of a coalition. International institutions are presented as playing a mere supporting role. In contrast, the ESS gives far greater prominence to the importance of the UN as a legitimising authority.

The ESS's comprehensive approach towards security also contrasts with NATO's Allied Strategic Concept, whose current version was agreed at the 1999 Washington summit, and revised at the 2002 Prague summit. While NATO's approach to security was broadened after the end of the Cold War, the Strategic Concept is comparatively narrower in focus, reflecting its role as an alliance of collective defence. The 1999 Washington declaration identified the alliance's core functions: providing the basis for a stable Euro-Atlantic security environment; a forum for transatlantic consultation; deterrence and defence; and strengthening the security and stability of the Euro-Atlantic area through conflict prevention, partnership, cooperation and dialogue. In 2002 at Prague, NATO recognised terrorism, WMD, and failed states as the defining security challenges of the twenty-first century. Heads of state and government adopted a package of measures designed to strengthen NATO's readiness and ability to take on the full spectrum of security challenges, including sending forces to wherever they were needed to meet these challenges.

Changes since the NSS and ESS appeared

After the NSS and ESS were published, the United States underwent a very difficult learning process as a result of events on the ground in Iraq. Talk of further pre-emptive strikes against Iran and North Korea almost disappeared. The United States changed its approach towards both states and swung behind diplomatic efforts to curb their nuclear ambitions. In particular, the United States changed tack on Iran and supported the European Union's diplomatic efforts. On North Korea, the United States recognised that the six-party talks – involving the United States, China, Japan, both Koreas and Russia – were the only way forward.

There has also been a noticeable change within the US foreign and security policy elite about the limitations of military power to achieve political goals (see Gaddis 2005). The creation of a Peacebuilding Unit within the State Department signalled recognition that the United States would have to become more involved in nation-building, something the first George W. Bush administration publicly eschewed. The decision in late 2005 by the White House formally to give authority to Condoleezza Rice to take the lead in planning and reconstruction efforts in conflict areas such as Iraq was a sign of the rising confidence of the State Department under her leadership.[5] The United States could not simply withdraw from Iraq and, if it wanted outside assistance, let alone legitimacy for its aims, it would have to accept difficult compromises.

The widely propagated neo-conservative view that regime change in Iraq would deal a body blow to terrorism was proved quite wrong. President Bush himself admitted that Iraq was a magnet for terrorists in a speech to the nation in June 2005. By midsummer 2005 there were also attacks on President Bush from within his own party as well as from Democrats. Republican Senator Chuck Hagel worried about Iraq becoming 'another Vietnam' while launching his 2008 presidential bid. Senator Joseph Biden spoke for many Democrats in lambasting Bush for his 'staggering series of failures on Iraq'.[6]

For its part, the European Union sought to bury its differences over Iraq and agreed not only the ESS but also a series of treaty changes (that were stalled in 2005) and a new relationship with NATO. The European Union also continued with its enlargement process, albeit with notably more caution and reservations since the French and Dutch referendums on the Constitutional Treaty, agreeing to open accession negotiations with Turkey and Croatia in October 2005. For his part, EU foreign policy chief Javier

Solana tried to stress the importance of 'human security' – giving more attention to individual security as opposed to traditional state security – within EU circles (see Centre for the Study of Global Governance 2004; see also Chapter 10).

Popular views on security

Numerous surveys of popular opinion during and after the 2002–3 transatlantic crisis revealed considerable similarities in the United States and European Union, albeit with some marked differences.[7] Neither Europeans nor Americans any longer fear any kind of direct Soviet-style attack. Americans give more priority to terrorism and weapons of mass destruction, while crime looms larger for Europeans. The United States tends to place more emphasis on external threats, the European Union on internal threats.

In contrast to elite views, there is considerable convergence in popular views about how both Americans and Europeans consider threats should be tackled. Both sides of the Atlantic would appear to wish for a non-unilateralist United States, an active European Union (perhaps even a European superpower), cooperative modes of action using non-military as well as military instruments, and respect for the United Nations. Americans, however, are more willing to bypass the UN when vital national interests are at stake, and more willing to accept the use of military power. The Iraq war seems to have been a major factor in reducing levels of European trust in and approval for the Bush administration's policies (most sharply of all in Germany) more than it has affected American attitudes towards Europe. European leaders, especially in France and Germany, no longer find it a vote-winner to be seen photographed with George W. Bush.[8] Popular opposition to the war in Iraq brought millions on to the streets throughout Europe and was probably the most important demonstration of European public opinion on a major foreign policy issue for decades.

The European Union as a security actor

The European Union has made enormous strides in the past decade as a security actor (see Gnesotto 2004b; Howorth 2005). It is now the principal stabilising regime for the entire continent. The enlargement process has been a powerful element in this effort to attempt peaceful regime change in central and eastern Europe, the Balkans and now Turkey. As the European Union has enlarged it has also deepened and attempted (at least) to adopt a new Constitutional Treaty that promised further to enhance its ability to act on the world stage. The Constitutional Treaty provided for structured cooperation, jargon for allowing those member states ready, willing and able to act in the name of the European Union to do so even if others choose not to join them. Perhaps most significant were steps to enhance Europe's military capability. New specialised, rapidly deployable 'battle groups' were formed to combine national resources at the hard end of European military capability.

As neo-conservative influence in Washington has declined, there has been a renewed interest in what Europe can deliver on security matters. At the time of writing (early 2006), it remained to be seen, after the French and Dutch referendums, whether anything could be salvaged from the Constitutional Treaty. There appeared to be a broad consensus that the proposals to improve the European Union's foreign and security policy should somehow be salvaged. At the same time there was concern that attempts to 'cherry-pick' parts of the treaty could provoke a popular backlash. What were most likely, therefore, were incremental improvements to Common Foreign and Security Policy (CFSP) and no institutional 'big bang'.

Leaving the Treaty aside, the past decade has witnessed significant progress on the ESDP. It now has a permanent bureaucracy in the form of the EU Military Committee and military staff, a framework for conducting operations and securing force goals from the member states, the beginnings of a European Defence Agency for armaments cooperation, and a security strategy that specifies, at least in broad terms, the political mechanisms and conceptual reasons for how and when this force would be used. In short, within a decade ESDP has gone from vague idea to developing institution, one that is conducting small but significant operations in the Balkans, Africa and Asia. Although there are many commentators who confidently predict that ESDP will never lead to a truly integrated EU military organisation, it is worth noting that there were those who confidently predicted in the 1980s that a single currency would never exist.

There are differing conceptions of what ESDP should become in the future. At one end of the spectrum, some see it as a major step forward in the European integration project (Gnesotto 2004a). The creation of a European force capable of acting autonomously would give the European Union some 'hard' power to back up the CFSP. Eventually, ESDP would lead to a more common military force. The force would not necessarily be a European army, but certainly a military force capable of conducting a range of missions without resorting to assistance from NATO or the United States when the member states of the European Union agree that military force is needed. The need for such a force is not purely theoretical. It has its roots in the inability of Europe to act in the face of successive crises in the Balkans in the 1990s without American assistance.

Also on this end of the spectrum is the view that the European Union may eventually be responsible for the collective defence of Europe. As General Gustav Hägglund, the then (in 2005) chairman of the EU Military Committee, asked rhetorically, 'If 280 million Americans can take care of their homeland security without European involvement, isn't it fair to expect the 450 million Europeans to arrange the defence of their area without the Americans?'[9]

At the other end of the spectrum, however, this conception of the European Union as an institution encompassing a mutual security guarantee is opposed by many Europeans. In this view, ESDP is a more limited and pragmatic development. ESDP is a means to building better capabilities because it may be easier to convince European publics that they should support the development of military capabilities within an EU context than it is to do so within a NATO context (Larrabee 2004). The same ships, aircraft and troops would be used for either NATO or EU missions. So, for those on this end of the spectrum, ESDP is less of a radical concept and more of an adjustment to political realities after the end of the Cold War and the existential threat to Europe posed by the Warsaw Pact. In this view, ESDP can only be seen as a means of improving European capabilities to take on certain activities in which NATO declines to participate.

Whatever the case, it is important to keep ESDP in perspective. There is no possibility of the European Union fielding a military capability that is remotely comparable in size or firepower to that of the United States (see Chapter 9). Even at its full strength, and assuming a massive increase in European power projection capabilities, the planned European Rapid Reaction Force (RRF) would be about the same size as one of the three US Marine Corps expeditionary forces. The European Union is also not attempting to build a force for high-intensity operations and is concentrating on stability operations, humanitarian relief and similar operations. Thus, while at one end of the continuum some see ESDP as an important part of the overall process of European integration, at the other end some are more focused on the pragmatic aspects of military cooperation to make Europe more capable of playing a larger role within or outside of the NATO alliance.

Where does this leave the European Union and NATO?

For 40 years NATO provided a secure shield for West Europeans to engage in rebuilding their half of the continent and develop the process of European integration (Sloan 2005). When the Berlin Wall fell in November 1989 there were many who predicted the end of NATO. But rather than contract or atrophy, NATO expanded from 16 to 19 to 26. It also conducted its first operations out of area. Yet the Kosovo experience in 1999 led many in the Pentagon to doubt whether the United States could or should ever fight a war by committee. When NATO proposed invoking its article V guarantee in the wake of 9/11 the United States declined the offer. According to the US Secretary of Defense, Donald Rumsfeld, the mission defined the coalition, not the other way round. During 2002 and until the summer of 2003 hubris ruled. The greatest fighting machine in the world could do it all alone. But then reality set in and Washington pushed for an expanded NATO role in Afghanistan in order to relieve US forces, and subsequently urged a NATO role in Iraq.

In terms of mission the NATO summits at Prague (2002) and Istanbul (2004) camouflaged deep differences between member governments. NATO had its hands full in Afghanistan as it attempted to set up its own rapid reaction force. The alliance had expanded its dialogues with just about every region of the world. It had tried to develop a role for itself in fighting terrorism. It agreed (in 2005) to build a new headquarters. But it still could not shake off the impression, as one US Senator said, of being 'a bureaucracy in search of a pension'.[10]

In February 2005, the German Chancellor Gerhard Schröder raised a number of sensitive institutional issues in a speech at the annual transatlantic security conference in Munich. He stated that the American presence in Europe was no longer the security priority that it used to be. He also said that the new threats did not require a military response, echoing a widespread European fear of being dragged into American wars. Schröder went on to note that one of the major problems in transatlantic relations was the absence of any forum to discuss strategic issues.

Certainly Schröder was right to state that the EU–US dialogue in its current form – let alone NATO – did not do justice to the Union's growing importance or meet demands for increased transatlantic cooperation. The current structures were based on the 1995 New Transatlantic Agenda (NTA) that provided for regular consultations at political and official levels. Originally there were two NTA summits a year but there was only one after 2001. Ministerial meetings were held twice a year and so were senior official meetings. But these meetings were often rushed and had to cope with an overloaded agenda of issues that had not been resolved at lower levels. The main body holding the NTA together was a Task Force comprised of mid-level officials. On the US side the head of the European Bureau in the State Department would normally lead, while on the European side there would be a double chair from the Presidency and the Commission. Few argued for abandoning the NTA outright (see European Commission 2005) but, equally, few could deny Schröder's contention that it was inadequate as a framework for strategic dialogue.

However, Schröder failed to prepare the diplomatic ground for his remarks and there was little instant support for his speech, apart from France's President Jacques Chirac. The French press certainly welcomed the passage in the speech that stated 'NATO was no longer the primary venue where transatlantic partners discuss and coordinate strategies'. German and French public opinion were aligned insofar as both were unlikely to accept the primacy of NATO for political matters. But President Bush reacted by stating that 'the relationship between the United States and Europe is a vital relationship, a necessary relationship, and our relationship within NATO is the cornerstone of that relationship' (Dempsey 2005a). Donald Rumsfeld confirmed that the United States would continue to favour coalitions of the willing. NATO Secretary General De Hoop Scheffer said that NATO was in full transformation and not terminally ill (Dempsey 2005b; Dombey 2005).

The United States has fluctuated between regarding NATO as an opportunity to gain European support for its foreign policy and as a useful toolbox for its operations elsewhere (Hamilton 2004). The United States continues to give more attention to NATO than most European partners. The short annual EU–US summits and the usually rushed and overloaded ministerial meetings have been unable to find time for these matters. Consequently, in 2002–3 the two sides largely talked past each other. While there was a general common analysis of the threats, there were significant differences about how to tackle them. For the Bush administration the military was the first instrument. For Europeans (and Canadians), the military was but one of several instruments and any military action should have UN approval. The European approach emphasised a comprehensive approach involving a mix of political, economic, financial, technical and development instruments, highlighting the importance of 'effective multilateralism' and working through a rules-based international system. A significant part of the US foreign and security policy establishment viewed all such international bodies, including the UN, with great suspicion. The differences in EU and US approaches also extended to political issues such as the Israel–Palestine conflict, the wider Middle East including how to deal with Iran and autocratic regimes, so-called rogue states, climate change, the international criminal court (ICC) and a host of arms control treaties.

One area where the European Union and NATO *were* working together was Afghanistan. Yet this theatre was a difficult and highly sensitive one, with the United States providing over 90 per cent of all forces deployed in 'hard' tasks under 'Operation Enduring Freedom' and Europeans responsible under NATO's International Security Assistance Force (ISAF) for 'soft' (mostly reconstruction) tasks, to which it contributed 70 per cent of all troops (Lindstrom 2005: 51). There was considerable acrimony between the two sides concerning this division of responsibility.

Another point of sensitivity concerned the idea of a reverse Berlin Plus. Some argued that if NATO stood ready to provide assets for EU operations then NATO should be able to benefit from EU assets when it was leading crisis management operations. This proposal was not met with great enthusiasm by EU member states. Similarly the idea of joint NATO/EU headquarters for crisis management did not gain general approval.

For the next few years the United States will most likely try and work through both institutions, normally showing a preference for NATO but recognising that it brings little to the table in tackling terrorism or other new threats. Indeed the Department of Homeland Security has been to the fore in promoting the European Union as a main partner in the fight against terrorism. By early 2006, there was little sign that Washington would wish to change the status quo. But if and when the European Union developed more coherence in foreign policy and brought greater military capabilities to the table, then there was always the prospect, at least, of a change of heart in the United States that would lead to a de facto EU–US strategic relationship.

Prospects for wider cooperation

After the unilateralist approach of the first Bush administration, what are
the prospects for the European Union and the United States working
together in the multilateral system, especially via international institutions?
There is some evidence that there has been a change of approach in Washington with the influence of pragmatists, led by Rice, rising (see Fukuyama
2005). The Mitchell/Gingrich report on the UN argued for a stronger US
engagement with the UN, and called on the United States to support some
key proposals in the High-Level Panel report such as the Peacebuilding
Commission and the proposed Human Rights Council, and agreeing an
internationally recognised definition of terrorism (United Nations 2004).
But John Bolton's arrival in New York as US Ambassador to the UN,
the result of a controversial recess appointment, raised renewed concerns
about America's commitment to a strong and effective UN. Bolton tried to
water down the recommendations in the draft document prepared for
the UN summit and refused to commit the United States to any binding
mechanisms.

This was particularly regrettable because there was little doubt that the
United States, as much as the European Union, would need to turn to the
UN for support as it tackled the problem of failed states in future. Both the
European Union and the United States had an interest in securing early
action, as well as a coordinated international response, to tackle situations
like the Congo, Somalia, Aceh and Kosovo. The creation of a Stabilisation
and Peacebuilding Unit in the State Department was an indication of a
change in official American attitudes, but it remained to be seen whether the
State Department would be able to win the inevitable battle over resources
for the UN. An interesting statistic was that the Pentagon spent the entire
budget of the UN in less than 48 hours by the mid 2000s.

The establishment of the UN Peacebuilding Commission, although a
weaker body than the European Union would have wished to see, may also
offer new possibilities for cooperation between the European Union and the
United States. The prospects for EU–US cooperation in other international
bodies are mixed, given continuing, and at times visceral, American opposition to international treaties that may limit the ability of the United States to
act. The vociferous attacks of the religious right on international organisations that promote birth control are another area of dispute between the
European Union and the United States. There are also disagreements over
human rights (Guantanamo, the death penalty), development policy (with
the United States preferring to reward those states with a proven track
record in good governance), and the priority given to working through
multilateral institutions. At the same time there is agreement on many other
issues, including the Balkans, Ukraine and tackling HIV/Aids. The transatlantic relationship is also based on very strong economic and trade ties
that seem both (mostly) immune to political friction and to have the effect

of ensuring that political disputes are kept within limits (see European Commission 2005). However, even here, as on issues of high politics, transatlantic cooperation is only tenuously, at best, institutionalised.

Conclusion

This chapter has examined the transatlantic rift on security, focusing on the respective security strategies and prospects for cooperation within transatlantic and international institutions. While the gap has narrowed as a result of the Iraq experience, there remain substantial differences in approach, which will inevitably colour future transatlantic institutional relations. The European Union and the United States have moved closer as a result of the lessons learned in Iraq and the recognition that they are far better equipped to tackle new security threats by working together than by going their separate ways. Pragmatists have regained lost ground and there now seems to be an opportunity for the United States and the European Union to strengthen the UN by agreeing to support the Peacebuilding Commission. Both the United States and the European Union clearly need further to develop their non-military capabilities for nation-building. The European Union needs to strengthen its military capabilities. To maximise their ability to realise joint goals, and to identify them in the first place, both sides need to engage in a regular strategic dialogue and seek better to understand each other's motives and interests.

There was growing interest by the mid 2000s in the idea of working within existing structures but with additional provision for informal contact group arrangements. Partly, such ideas reflected frustration with the EU–US New Transatlantic Agenda framework, which was accentuated by the difficulties the European Union had in negotiating as 25 with the United States. Even before the 2004 EU enlargement, the NTA agendas were packed with issues of high and low politics. Discussions might cover Iran and Iraq as well as steel tariffs and genetically modified organisms. Rarely was there time at any level for what might be termed strategic dialogue. The American side was usually better prepared to discuss political-security issues and often distributed speaking notes in advance, hoping that this would impress the Europeans. Given the complicated institutional arrangements on the European side, the European Union tended to be more reactive than active in discussions. Even when the European Union did take a position, American officials often complained about the rigidity of EU views, which especially and necessarily reflected the common view of 25 member states after 2004.

Given the limitations of the NTA, it was not surprising that there were ad hoc additions to the dialogue process, such as when President Bush invited Jose Manuel Barroso, the President of the Commission, to a lengthy one-on-one meeting in October 2005. Another suggestion was to revive discreetly the informal *directoire* that existed to discuss Berlin issues during the Cold War, involving the United States, the United Kingdom, France and

Germany. Given the reality of international relations, this 'quad' had a powerful leadership role to play – assuming they could agree – as shown (with decidedly mixed results) on nuclear diplomacy with Iran.

For the foreseeable future, however, there is unlikely to be any radical change in the institutional structures of transatlantic relations. If and when the European Union moves forward in agreeing a new treaty that enshrines most of the provisions in the Constitutional Treaty on external affairs, then it might be time to revisit the idea of an EU–US treaty. Until then the European Union and NATO are likely to continue to be the two main structures of a changing transatlantic relationship, with the European Union gradually gaining more and more importance in the eyes of Washington. With both the United States and the European Union weakened, the former due to Iraq and the latter due to its constitutional failure, the second half of the 2000s might be a good time to try and establish a transatlantic strategic dialogue in a calm manner, on the basis of what each side identifies as a shared agenda, perhaps in very turbulent times but on the basis of the security strategies of the early part of the decade.

Notes

1 For coverage of the foreign policy of the first Bush administration, see Daalder and Lindsay (2003); Hersch (2003); Clarke (2004); Woodward (2004); Cameron (2005).
2 Pew Institute polling results, January–June 2005 and GMF Transatlantic Trends, September 2005. Online. Available: http://people-press.org/ and http://www.tran satlantictrends.org (accessed 8 January 2006).
3 See Condoleezza Rice, 'Remarks at the American University in Cairo', 20 June 2005. Online. Available: http://www.state.gov/secretary/rm/2005/48328.htm (accessed 8 January 2006).
4 It is worth noting that the United Kingdom and France have been no strangers to pre-emptive strikes, especially in Africa.
5 See Caroline Daniel, 'Bush Hands Rice Lead Role in War Zones', *Financial Times* (UK edition), 15 December, p. 12.
6 Quoted in *Washington Post*, 14 May 2005, p. 1.
7 The Transatlantic Trends and Eurobarometer polls on which this discussion and the tables are mainly based can be found at http://www.transatlantictrends.org and http://www.eu.int/comm/public_opinion/standard_en.htm respectively.
8 In Germany, 68 per cent of respondents thought strong US leadership in the world desirable in 2002, and only 45 per cent in 2003. The number of German respondents who accepted the United States as the world's sole superpower fell from 22 per cent to 8 per cent, and the number wishing the European Union to become a superpower rose from 48 per cent to 70 per cent over the same year (see Transatlantic Trends polls at web link in note 7).
9 Speech at the Konrad Adenauer Stiftung, Brussels, 14 February 2005. Online. Available: http://www.kas.de/proj/home/home/9/2/index.html (accessed 8 January 2006).
10 Private conversation.

5   Security strategy and the 'war on terror'

Seán Molloy

In an age of global terrorism, the question of how to deal with an entirely new security dilemma becomes ever more important. 9/11 demonstrated that the new primary threat to most states' national security emanates not from a rival state or bloc of states, but rather from networks, groups of individuals and organisations that exist as viruses within traditional international society. The viral nature of transnational terrorism is difficult to counter effectively. To date the American response has not been to concentrate on the viruses, but rather to attack those who have played host to the viruses by seeking to quarantine the states that harbour or sponsor terrorism. To this effect, the United States has launched two major wars against Afghanistan and Iraq as theatres in a wider 'war on terror'.

The European Union has also suffered the effects of Islamist terrorism, most evidently in the attacks on Madrid in 2004 and on London in 2005. It has also developed its own security strategy in the face of the threat presented by Al Qaeda and its allies. The aim of this chapter is to examine the effects of the EU and US security strategies on the transatlantic relationship, to determine if the American and European approaches are complementary in that they pursue parallel goals by different means, or if they are in fact incompatible in both means and ends, destined to drive a wedge between an increasingly Martian America and Venusian Europe (Kagan 2003).

The chapter begins with a brief overview of the development of post-Cold War American security strategy in both Bush presidencies and the Clinton presidency. The primary purpose of this section is to determine whether or not the National Security Strategy (NSS) of George W. Bush's presidency is qualitatively different from that of his predecessors. In other words, to what extent was the 2002 NSS a revolution in strategic affairs, as opposed to a continuation of longstanding trends? This question is not only of interest to academics. If there has been a genuine revolution in the strategic outlook of the United States, and the means by which it seeks to obtain policy ends, this has profound ramifications, not just in terms of the transatlantic relationship, but also for global politics more generally.

Caught between Atlanticist and European factions, the European Union's room for manoeuvre is slight, but progress in the development of a European security strategy has increased apace from the time of the Kosovo crisis in

1999 through a phase of accelerated development in the aftermath of the 9/11 and Madrid attacks. The underlying principles of the European Security Strategy are the primary focus of the second part of the chapter.

The third section of the chapter will identify where and when the Americans and the European Union have acted in unison, and when they have parted ways on the question of how best to wage a war on terror. In the context of an international society that is dominated politically, culturally and economically by these two powers, the question of whether the United States and the European Union are capable of collective strategic action will be one of the most important factors in determining the near-term evolution of the war on terror.

American security strategy in the 1990s and beyond

With the demise of the Soviet Union in 1991, American strategy emerged vindicated from the Cold War. Through periods of conflict, deterrence and détente, the Americans had successfully (if narrowly) averted open warfare with the only other superpower, while at the same time exerting sufficient pressure on the USSR, which, coupled with the internal stresses and tensions within the Soviet Union itself, ultimately forced the Soviets to conclude the Cold War on terms favourable to America and its allies. After the Cold War ended, however, a new strategic vision was necessary. After tarrying with a straight like-for-like swap of the Evil Empire of the USSR for a shifting Islamic enemy (generally Iran, but after 1990, Saddam Hussein's Iraq also featured prominently), the first Gulf War in 1991 provided an opportunity for a redefinition of America's security strategy and place in the world. The most significant statement of intent regarding the future conduct of America in global affairs was provided by President George H. W. Bush (1991a) in his State of the Union address of January 1991, when he described the action against Saddam Hussein's Iraq as the dawn of a new age:

> For two centuries, we've done the hard work of freedom. And tonight, we lead the world in facing down a threat to decency and humanity. What is at stake is more than one small country; it is a big idea: a new world order, where diverse nations are drawn together in common cause to achieve the universal aspirations of mankind – peace and security, freedom, and the rule of law. Such is a world worthy of our struggle and worthy of our children's future.

This 'big idea' of New World Order was a radical break with the Cold War notion of implacable opposition to an encroaching and deadly enemy. In its place was a vision of the world under American leadership in which cooperation under its benign hegemony would result in a more democratic and stable international order.

The National Security Strategy (NSS) that emerged from the first Bush presidency is a remarkable attempt to reorient both American strategy and global politics in the aftermath of the Cold War. It is characterised by an almost managerial mentality according to which the allocation of resources and the processes of world politics should be determined in a layered, multi-lateral manner with the United States, destined by its size and influence to play a leading role, as *primus inter pares*, complemented by other powers such as the Europeans (particularly the Germans) and the Japanese, directing through international organisations the economic, diplomatic and military affairs of global politics (see Bush 1991b).

The Bush Senior NSS was not so much a military security strategy as a project for global stability. Where the military featured it was largely in the context of maintaining security in an era of cutting defence expenditure and the standing down of American forces in Europe. Armies were to become smaller and stealthier, maximising return on a smaller investment. The army required for the massive stand-off of the Cold War was to be replaced by an army more suited to the new circumstances: in particular, an army designed to respond to regional crises and emergencies that threaten global stability.

Stability and security are assumed to be one and the same thing throughout the document, with economic, diplomatic and military measures to be taken to preserve balance and avoid turbulence. In essence this was a conservative policy of preserving the status quo. It would be achieved through international institutions, in particular the 'new' United Nations (UN), which during the Gulf war had played 'the role dreamed of by its founders, with the world's leading nations orchestrating and sanctioning collective action against aggression' (Bush 1991b: xiii).

In both the scale and scope of its ambition, the NSS of Bush 1 is clear and coherent. Very specific actions are directed towards specific goals, with a clear multilateral logic and modus operandi underlying these goals. The strategic environment was to be transformed by addressing the logistics of American military endeavour, which in turn would limit and define the nature of American intervention in the 1990s. The New World Order was to be a technocratic realm, with force deployed only when necessary and then in a strictly delimited, rational manner. Legitimacy and logistics would be the lodestones of this New World Order.

The immediate bête noire of the project for a New World Order, as he was to prove for successive presidencies, was Saddam Hussein of Iraq. Dealing with Saddam was to provide the template for the New World Order of American hegemony. This template, while recognising 'American leadership', insisted on following the protocols of international law (especially the offices of the United Nations) and engaging the support of allies under the rubric of collective resistance against aggression (Bush 1991a).

The actual operation of the New World Order lasted approximately six months, until June 1991 when the secession of Croatia and Slovenia sparked the Yugoslavian civil war. The vaunted American leadership that was supposed to underpin the New World Order was shared with (or foisted upon) what was then still the European Community, which itself was either unwilling or unable to formulate a coherent response to the implosion and disintegration of Yugoslavia. From a position of leadership, America was now content to act merely as an endorser of European Community diplomatic efforts (Fitzwater 1991; Bush 1991c).

Africa, long seen in merely instrumental terms as a theatre of the Cold War, began to assume a different character in the era of the New World Order. US National Security Directive 75 argued: '[b]ecause of its conflicts and poverty there is a long-term humanitarian imperative to help alleviate acute suffering as much as possible'.[1] Operation Restore Hope, designed to assist the UN in Somalia, was the most visible manifestation of this commitment to humanitarian imperatives and democratisation in National Security Directive 75 (Bush 1992).

Operation Restore Hope also passed the baton of national security to President Clinton's administration. This administration, at first largely oblivious to questions of security strategy as it pursued domestic economic reform, did not rush to endorse a New World Order, but nor did it seek to differentiate itself from the previous regime. Instead, we saw the Clinton regime largely reproduce the rhetoric of the Bush regime, but replacing the all-encompassing sense of an international society that under American leadership would establish a rule of law in international politics. Clinton advocated an alternative perspective:

> Emphatically, the international community cannot seek to heal every domestic dispute or resolve every ethnic conflict. But within practical bounds, and with a sense of strategic priorities, we must do what we can to promote the democratic spirit and economic reforms that can tip the balance for progress in the next century.
>
> (Clinton 1993)

This was a more realistic assessment of the capabilities of international society (even under American leadership). Equally, it represented a continued American commitment to engage with international conflicts on a case-by-case basis, with the US response to be determined by pragmatism and strategic analysis. However, in the aftermath of Operation Restore Hope, American interventions could only be undertaken if there was a threat to American security and there was no serious threat to US forces. Hence Rwanda was left to its own devices, while American ground troops were not deployed in Bosnia or Kosovo. If an aspiration towards a New World Order was the hallmark of the first President Bush administration, then pragmatism would be the defining characteristic of the Clinton administration.

Somalia demonstrated the tendency of the Clinton administration to run the full gamut from idealism through pragmatism to cynicism. American interventions in global hot spots were undertaken during the Clinton administration not according to lofty principles, but largely because to allow them to escalate would have posed a massive threat to regional and global order, or because they required relatively little investment of political capital for considerable foreign policy returns. Thus the Clinton administration remained largely uninvolved in the Balkan wars until it became clear that the European Union did not have the ability to solve the problem, and the UN could not provide a platform either for conflict resolution or effective peace-keeping. Elsewhere, acting as an honest broker, the Clinton administration cajoled the various parties in Northern Ireland and the Middle East peace processes to a position where peace was in sight.

This is not to say that the Clinton administration was not, in its way, as revolutionary as that of the first Bush administration. The Clinton adminis-tration may have lacked an ideological vision on the scale of the New World Order. But perhaps because of its more 'problem-solving' approach it was willing to engage in more drastic actions in order to achieve its aims. The Kosovo crisis, and the American-led response to it, effectively rewrote the book on what states can and cannot do to each other politically, militarily and legally. It established a set of radical innovations that continue to impact on the conduct of international relations.

The Clinton administration, chary of allowing an escalation of the Kosovo crisis to the level of the Bosnian crisis of the early 1990s, resolved to take measures against the Federal Republic of Yugoslavia. The dense and intricate strands of diplomatic, institutional and finally military power that the United States employed in order to secure its objectives provided ample evidence of the Clinton administration's mastery of both soft and hard power strategy and tactics. Circumventing the issue of Kosovo's status as a province within a sovereign state, and hence an internal matter for the Federal Republic of Yugoslavia (FRY), the American-led NATO operation launched in 1999 was predicated in terms of humanitarian intervention, not the right of Kosovo to declare independence or otherwise secede from the FRY. Humanitarian intervention is, however, a slippery norm, and a dangerous precedent. As Chomsky (1999) has asked, how and when does one determine it is just, or appropriate to intervene on humanitarian grounds? Why not intervene in Turkey's war with the Kurds, or in Palestine's war with Israel?

The most important effect of the Kosovo crisis was the retooling of the transatlantic security sphere and a reorientation of its primary institution, NATO. During the Kosovo crisis NATO morphed into more than simply a Cold War relic looking for a purpose. It became instead the vehicle through which the Americans could act in a multilateral fashion without having to worry about the Russian Federation or China's veto in the Security Council of the United Nations. In more general terms, the concept of sovereignty underwent a serious challenge. A precedent for intervention by self-appointed guardians of right behaviour, an international posse so to speak, had been established. Established principles and procedures of international law had been challenged by practices that could be described as deriving from an almost frontier-style concept of international justice.

From neo-isolationism to war on terror

Initially, the first George W. Bush administration was characterised by an almost pathological desire for insulation against the rest of the world, as demonstrated by the missile defence shield that was presented as the showpiece of its security strategy pre-9/11. Also symptomatic of the disengagement of the United States was the renunciation of the American commitment to the International Criminal Court and outright refusal to participate in the Kyoto Protocol on Climate Control. The sabre-rattling and sniping with China over the shooting down of an American spy plane over Chinese airspace provided the tone for American involvement in global politics in the pre-9/11 Bush administration.

The terrorist attacks of 2001, however, changed the tenor and scope of US security strategy. The action taken against Afghanistan was, in the main, conducted according to established practice, and given the failure of the Taliban regime to cooperate with America's request to hand over Osama Bin Laden, not all that controversial. The United States assembled a coalition of the willing – refusing to conduct the campaign via NATO – and duly led it to victory in association with the anti-Taliban forces of the Northern Alliance.

The truly radical phase of the Bush administration began after the Afghan war and the promulgation of the Bush Doctrine and the further articulation of post-9/11 strategy in the 2002 NSS. The first reorientation was against the former insulationist approach of the pre-9/11 Bush administration. Although the missile defence shield remained on the agenda, the overall sentiment towards the Other beyond America's border had changed from one of diffident disinterest to one of hyper-security consciousness.

At first sight, the NSS is disappointing as a blueprint for dealing with the problem of transnational terrorism. There is very little about terrorism in the document, and what little there is relates to the relationship between states and terrorist organisations. This lack of focus in what is ostensibly a security strategy for dealing with terrorism is puzzling. Clearly, the terrorist organisations themselves are not attributed much significance in the NSS.

Viewed from an alternative perspective, the perspective of the practice of power in international politics, an altogether different picture emerges. It is in this context that the definitive breaks with previous American administrations are most manifest. For the Bush administration, multilateral international organisations are dismissed from centre stage. The United Nations, one of the mainstays of the New World Order of 1991, is conspicuous by its absence. The step away from multilateralism is accompanied by a stated preference for bilateral, state-to-state relations as a more effective means of securing international order. The rule of law as determined within international organisations is shunned as part of a turn towards a more direct exercise of power in global politics, a shift from hegemonic to relational power. Those international organisations that are promoted in the NSS are those that America either dominates or can influence to its will, such as NATO.

International law as a principle is also undermined throughout the NSS. The so-called Bush Doctrine of pre-emptive strikes against perceived threats allows for American intervention anywhere and at any time that US security or even its interests are threatened. This is justified under the principle of imminent threat: specifically, that the United States cannot afford to prove or demonstrate a threat in an era of weapons of mass destruction. While an understandable reaction to the shock of 9/11, the effect of the Bush Doctrine is to reinstitute a global regime of insecurity, ceaseless scrutiny and the possibility of lightning strikes against prospective threats.

The strategic environment of the NSS

The Bush 2 presidency offers a very different take on national security to the managerial aspirations of the New World Order and the pragmatically limited idealism of the Clinton administration. The strategic environment is one in which terrorists and tyrants offer a new and radically different threat to the United States from the one in which regional instability threatened the peaceful operation of global politics in the Bush 1 and Clinton presidencies. Instead of states, the NSS identifies 'shadowy networks of individuals' employing technology and weapons of mass destruction as the primary threat to the United States:

> The United States of America is fighting a war against terrorists of global reach. The enemy is not a single political regime or person or religion or ideology. The enemy is terrorism – premeditated, politically motivated violence perpetrated against innocents.

In terms of international security, the question has to be asked: is terrorism an enemy to be fought, or a tactic employed by an enemy who has chosen to use this tactic? Does the use of the word terrorism as 'enemy' deflect from the fact that it is committed by 'terrorists'; that is, specific agents with a particular agenda? Identifying these agents as terrorists would limit the range and scope of actions available to the United States and call into question the wisdom of attacking regimes that had little or nothing to do with 9/11. By calling the enemy 'terrorism' the NSS provides the United States with much more latitude in terms of fighting a war on terror as opposed to a war on terrorists. In any case (as mentioned earlier), dealing with terrorists, and by extension terrorism, occupies surprisingly little space in the NSS, and in fairly vague terms: 'The struggle against global terrorism is different from any other war in our history. It will be fought on many fronts against a particularly elusive enemy over an extended period of time.' The war will be fought by efforts 'to disrupt and destroy terrorist organizations of global reach and attack their leadership; command, control, and communications; material support; and finances. This will have a disabling effect upon the terrorists' ability to plan and operate.' One is left with the impression that the war will be infinite in both space and time. Simultaneously, the NSS stresses that American resources are limited: 'We have finite political, economic, and military resources to meet our global priorities.' Here we see one contradiction between means and ends out of several that are found throughout the document.

Despite an awareness that shadowy networks are the problem, the NSS's formulation of a response to the problem of terrorism is couched mostly in terms of states and alliances. The NSS claims that 'Our immediate focus will be those terrorist organizations of global reach.' Yet in its military campaigns to date the United States has focused not on terrorists, allowing (for example) the Al Qaeda leadership to escape from Tora Bora, but rather on securing the territory of Afghanistan and Iraq. The United States, with its military oriented towards fighting wars with states, cannot cope with the swarming effect of individuals. Rather, it must seek to discipline these individuals by proxy: that is, by 'hold[ing] to account nations that are compromised by terror'. Attacking state sponsors of terrorism is justified according to the NSS in terms of complicity: 'We make no distinction between terrorists and those who knowingly harbor or provide aid to them.' The effect of attacking these state sponsors of terrorism is to deprive terrorists of safe havens from which to threaten America. Afghanistan is the NSS's segue from terrorism (and it was terrorists based in Afghanistan who launched the 9/11 attacks) to what becomes clear is its primary focus: rogue states. This focus on states rather than terrorists is evident even in the National Strategy for Combating Terrorism, a later document published in early 2003 which again stressed the need for a territorial understanding of the problem of terrorism, and a territorial solution to the problem (White House 2003).

Back to the future: states, alliances and rogue states

The strategic policies of the NSS are expressed in a series of totems: positive totems such as freedom and liberty, and negative totems such as terrorism and weapons of mass destruction. Of these, the oddest is the concept of a 'balance of power that favours freedom', a phrase which appears five times in the NSS. This notion betrays a peculiar understanding of the primary function of the balance of power, namely the preservation of order, not liberty or freedom. Power itself may be used to promote liberty and freedom, but the exercise of this power in a world unwilling to accept the legitimacy of the actor employing that power cannot be termed a balance of power. It is at best an extension or an imposition of power. In any case, for there to be a balance there would have to be someone to balance against. The NSS clearly lays out that those who oppose America are merely an 'embittered few': rogue states and terrorists. The very meaninglessness of the phrase provides evidence of the nostalgia that permeates both the NSS and the practice of American power under the Bush administration. The balance of power and the balance of terror served as effective strategic concepts during the Cold War, while the occupation of Japan and Germany served as models for the occupation of Iraq. The grafting of concepts and practices suited to the Second World War, Cold War and the classical age of European diplomacy onto an era characterised by the conflict of terrorists and states speaks of a pathological relationship with the past that is not historical, but rather ideological: a dehistoricised nostalgia for a victorious age that also provides evidence of an inability to determine a strategy suited to the demands of a new age.

At the systemic level, it is states and alliances, not multilateral organisations, that are to form the basis for the war against terror and their focus shall be on rogue states, not terrorists. Where the United Nations is mentioned it is merely as one among many actors charged with the responsibility to rebuild Afghanistan. The war on terror must be fought, according to the NSS, by coalitions of states, in a manner similar to that pioneered by President Clinton:

> America will implement its strategies by organizing coalitions – as broad as practicable – of states able and willing to promote a balance of power that favors freedom. Effective coalition leadership requires clear priorities, an appreciation of others' interests, and consistent consultations among partners with a spirit of humility.

In practice, the failures of the United States in the war on terror lie in an inability to make rhetoric correspond with military and political choices, with 'appreciation of others' interests' and 'consistent consultations among partners' being particularly conspicuous by their absence: this despite the fact that the NSS recognises that there 'is little of lasting consequence that the United States can accomplish in the world without the sustained cooperation of its allies and friends in Canada and Europe'. Yet this failure in practice to recognise the shortcomings of a security policy that neglects its allies is consistent with one of the first principles of the NSS:

> While the United States will constantly strive to enlist the support of the international community, we will not hesitate to act alone, if necessary, to exercise our right of self-defense by acting preemptively against such terrorists, to prevent them from doing harm against our people and our country.

It is the very exercise of this right to pre-emption in Iraq that cost America support in Europe and Canada. Arguing that Iraq had both the means and intention to make an attack on American allies, the Bush administration insisted that Iraqi non-compliance with various UN resolutions, and especially the activities of the UN Weapons Inspection Committee, justified a pre-emptive military attack. The invasion went ahead despite Hans Blix's protestations that there was no real evidence of weapons of mass destruction in Iraq. The Bush administration then shifted its primary casus bellum from actual possession of WMD to non-compliance with UN resolutions.

The 2002 National Security Strategy is a revolutionary document. It combines the grand vision of the NSS of George H. W. Bush's New World Order with a codification of American disdain for both the rule of law and multilateralism that underpinned that document. It is essentially an exercise in *Machtpolitik*, asserting that America's identity and power are legitimate in and of themselves, requiring no justification and recognising no legitimate brake on the exercise of its power in its interests, expressed through the notion of security. In this it represents an evolution of elements of the Clinton presidency's impatience with the structures of international governance. In common with the New World Order era of George Bush Senior, and the Clinton administration's 'full spectrum dominance', the NSS posits a world recast in the image of America, but insists on this transformation rather than arguing for it. Instead of persuading the world, the NSS condemns it to freedom.

From a European point of view, the Bush administration has on one hand offered the European Union a place at the centre of the war on terror, while at the same time insisting on America's right to act unilaterally and preemptively. The European Union thus has been caught between its advocacy of the rule of law in global politics and its support for America in the fight against terrorism. In any event, the European Security Strategy announced in December 2003 was the culmination of a series of enormous strides in the self-definition of what in former times was called a European Security and Defence Identity, particularly after the Kosovo crisis and as seen in the development of a European Security and Defence Policy (ESDP) within the broader context of the Union's Common Foreign and Security Policy (CFSP). The extent to which the NSS of President Bush and the ESS of 2003 are compatible will go some way to determining the efficacy of the transatlantic alliance in dealing with the problem of Islamist terrorism in the coming decades.

A unity of vision?

On a number of levels the NSS and the ESS share similar concerns. Both documents stress the importance of globalisation and the interdependence of security and economic development. There is likewise a commitment to democracy and the rule of law. The ESS has a little remarked upon tendency to stress the necessity of 'robust' responses to emergent threats. Like the NSS, the ESS identifies terrorism and the proliferation of weapons of mass destruction as the foremost threats facing the European Union, with failing states and regional conflicts also identified as issues of concern. In terms of hyperbole, the ESS goes beyond even the NSS as it stresses 'We live in a world that holds brighter prospects but also greater threats than we have known.' Echoing the NSS, the European Union's security strategy states: 'There are few if any problems we can deal with on our own ... International cooperation is a necessity.'

Differences emerge, however, in both the strategic objectives and the nature of responses to the terrorist threat. In keeping with its bureaucratic bent, the European Union stresses an institutional response as the framework of its strategy towards terrorism and effective counter-terrorism. The introduction of a European Arrest Warrant, the targeting of terrorist funding and the agreement of legal assistance with the United States, strengthening the International Atomic Energy Agency, measures against illegal shipping and procurement of WMD are identified as key components of the European Union's response to terror. In addition to these specific actions, the European Union reaffirms its commitment to 'achieving universal adherence to multilateral treaty regimes, as well as to strengthening the treaties and their verification provisions'.

The ESS attaches much more significance to the revolutionary nature of the threat posed by terrorism. It recognises that the nature of the battlefield has changed:

> Terrorists and criminals are now able to operate world-wide: their activities in central or south-east Asia may be a threat to European countries or their citizens ... Our traditional concept of self-defence – up to and including the Cold War – was based on the threat of invasion. With the new threats, the first line of defence will often be abroad. The new threats are dynamic. The risks of proliferation grow over time: left alone, terrorist networks will become ever more dangerous ... we should be ready to act before a crisis occurs. Conflict prevention and threat prevention cannot start too early.

Interestingly, the means by which the terrorist and proliferation threats should be confronted are presented as multi-layered, involving

> a mixture of instruments. Proliferation may be controlled through export controls and attacked through political, economic and other pressures while the underlying causes are also tackled. Dealing with terrorism may require a mixture of intelligence, police, judicial, military and other means.

Unless one files pre-emptive strikes under the ominously broad category of 'other means' the ESS is far removed from the Bush Doctrine of pre-emptive warfare. Only restoring order in failed states may require 'military instruments'.

The section of the ESS headed 'An International Order Based on Effective Multilateralism' provides the most detailed vision of world order in the ESS and the means by which it should be achieved. As the first paragraph makes clear, 'The development of a stronger international society, well functioning international institutions and a rule-based international order is our objective.' Crucial to this rule-based international order is the place of international law and the United Nations charter. The UN Security Council is presented as having 'the primary responsibility for the maintenance of international peace and security', and strengthening the UN is a clear European priority. Other organisations are presented as playing important roles in multi-level global governance – the World Trade Organisation (WTO) and other international financial institutions among them – while the transatlantic relationship is singled out as a core element of the international system, of which NATO is an important expression. Regional organisations such as the Organisation for Security and Cooperation in Europe (OSCE), the Council of Europe, ASEAN (the Association of Southeast Asian Nations), MERCOSUR and the African Union also play a role in the managerial aspects of contributing to 'a more orderly world'.

This commitment to multi-layered global governance by the European Union obviously impacts on the type of security policy to be pursued. Typically, this policy is couched in terms of coherence (foreign policy) and efficiency (crisis management). According to the ESS, it is necessary 'to develop a strategic culture that fosters early, rapid, and when necessary, robust intervention'. With a defence expenditure (combined) of €160 billion, the European Union should be able to 'sustain several operations simultaneously'. In contrast to the American insistence on unilateralism and bilateralism, the ESS makes no commitment to support any ally other than the UN: 'the EU should support the United Nations as it responds to threats to international peace and security'. Yet at the same time the European Union is committed to 'preventive engagement' with deteriorating countries.

The issue of coherence has more potential for disagreement within the European Union than that of developing an effective response to terrorism, proliferation and failed states. The ESS stresses that the use of assets must be 'systematic' while EU diplomacy should combine 'the resources of Member States with those of EU institutions'. The closer coordination of the European Union's external action and Justice Home Affairs is also 'crucial in the fight both against terrorism and organised crime'.

The incompatibility of the security strategies

In both the ESS and the NSS the authors take great pains to stress the importance of the transatlantic alliance and the closeness of the relationship between Europe and America. Although they share the same vision of a perfectly ordered international system composed of democratic states and based on the operation of free markets and the rule of law, the American and European security strategies are not fundamentally compatible with each other. Ultimately, differing conceptual bases for how to bring this vision of the international system into being is what separates the European Union and the United States. Although there is some convergence in terms of the ends to be achieved – democracy, free trade, and so on – there are fundamental differences in terms of both how these aims should be achieved and the basis and nature of the international system that would result from the institution of these respective visions of world order.

Policy has been extensively coordinated on matters of homeland security as well as on the extradition of suspects under a Mutual Legal Assistance deal brokered in 2003. Yet these remain the most impressive of a rather piecemeal effort at coordination that has become the norm in transatlantic efforts at targeting terrorism. Even as officials on both sides do what they can to coordinate their efforts, they are always likely to run up against the hard limits that arise from a fundamental incompatibility of strategy. The European Union's commitment to a regime based on multilateralism and international law as the bases for international governance cannot be squared with an American philosophy based on ad hoc alliances and the right to act according to unilateral interests (albeit within a certain form of multilateralism akin to an international posse with America at the head) in the last instance. The European Union's strategy for global order is based on going beyond the concept of alliances and interests upon which the American strategy for the preservation of its interests is based.

There was no contradiction between the two bodies in the first year of the operation of the NSS. The Afghan war was broadly consistent with the NSS and the future ESS in that the terrorist haven of Afghanistan under the Taliban had been destroyed, the Al Qaeda leadership was on the run, and the beginning of a process of democratisation and nation building had begun. The lead-up to the Iraq war, however, revealed the very real problems within the 'indispensable' transatlantic alliance.

We now know that the targeting of Iraq began almost immediately after 9/11, when it was unclear who was behind the attack. Those elements of the Bush Doctrine that were expressed in his June 2002 speech at West Point, pre-emptive war and the deadly immediacy of the WMD threat, became central justifications for removing Saddam Hussein from power.[2] Speech after speech by members of the Bush administration stressed the possibility of collusion between Saddam Hussein and Al Qaeda or other terrorist organisations. The alleged attempts by Saddam Hussein to secure materials necessary for a nuclear bomb from Niger were adequate (if fictitious) grounds to launch an all-out attack on Iraq according to the logic of the NSS.

The Iraq war's justifications were remarkably consistent with the NSS, and almost a textbook demonstration of its core principles: that is, that America would act according to its interests, in a 'coalition of the willing' in which it was the leading figure (it is unlikely that Micronesia or Costa Rica had much say in planning the elements of shock and awe that were to characterise Operation Iraqi Freedom). A further justification for this war was the threat of the use of weapons of mass destruction. What did not factor into this equation as significant considerations were the European Union, the

UN or any other international organisation or body of global governance. The lip-service paid to these in the NSS was revealed as mere window-dressing. By its actions the Bush administration demonstrated that it is coalitions of willing American partners, not the agencies of global governance, that are the primary actors of international security. The use of UN Security Council resolutions as a justification for American actions was somewhat offset by the refusal of the UN to sanction American actions against Iraq. The Americans acted as the NSS prescribed: specifically, by ignoring the objections and suggestions of the UN and doing what it thought necessary, or desirable, regardless.

The European Union, which in December 2003 (several months after the outbreak of the Iraq war) insisted that one of the central aims of European integration should be to establish 'an effective and balanced partnership with the US', reacted in a much divided manner to the war. The internal cohesion of EU foreign policy was lost when the United Kingdom, Spain, Italy, Denmark and several of the accession countries, notably Poland, signed up, at least in principle, as participants in the Iraq war. As a result, EU coherence and capability, two of the lodestones of the ESS, were among the greatest diplomatic casualties of the war in Iraq.

The choice before the European Union

The Iraq war's most important consequence for the European Union was, however, that it revealed that the United States was not interested in a partnership of equals, but was in fact determined to act in a manner that could not but alienate an EU committed to 'effective multilateralism'. The need of European states to calibrate their response to American unilateralism has and will continue to dictate the agenda between the two Western power centres. In the face of seeming US intransigence, the incompatibility of security epistemes forces the European Union into a limited number of strategic options. In practice, it can accept and support America's actions (choosing to bandwagon), oppose US actions (seeking to balance American power) or accept an uneasy co-existence with American initiatives in the war on terror.

Conflict

Although open warfare with the United States is not an option in even the most severe of circumstances, the possibility of EU–American security relations becoming increasingly less amicable is not unthinkable. With no Soviet threat, there is no strategic necessity for EU–US unanimity. Certainly US actions that would result in a massive increase in the price of oil, or affect the oil supply, or on the other hand violate human rights (as already seen in Guantanamo Bay or in allegations of secret prisons run by the US Central Intelligence Agency (CIA) in Central and Eastern Europe), could provoke the European Union to openly and forcefully condemn American actions. The extent to which the European Union could oppose the United States is, however, very limited. There is no provision in the ESS for any such policy. The most the European Union could do would be to make life difficult for the United States at the level of international organisations and if its members revoked their NATO commitments. While this would not be ideal from an American perspective, it would not be a disastrous blow to its military capabilities and could precipitate a major split in the European Union between Atlanticists (and certainly the United Kingdom) and the Europeanist factions that would effectively torpedo a coordinated CFSP – a case of the game (opposing America) not being worth the candle.

Cooperation

In certain circumstances, the European Union and the United States may be able to cooperate. The ESS and the NSS are not incompatible in all instances and at all times. In particular, even the Bush administration recognised both the significance and potential of transatlantic relations in addressing issues of homeland security. Cooperation on customs issues post-9/11, including container security and information-sharing on airline passenger records, became a growth area in the US–EU dialogue, with the European Union surprising many in Washington as well as European capitals with its capacity for collective action (see Aldrich 2004; Monar 2004; Nielsen and Hamilton 2005). In particular, as it struggled to find its institutional feet and identity, the new US Department of Homeland Security found the European Union to be a 'steadfast ally' on matters of border and transport security.[3]

Yet a reorientation of European strategic identity to the extent that the European Union would begin actively to support all of America's actions in the war on terror is unlikely. Given the stated opposition of many of the leading states of the European Union against the war in Iraq, it is unlikely that such a position would gain support outside the United Kingdom and certain members of Donald Rumsfeld's 'New Europe'. Diplomatically, the European Union would gain little except confirmation of its secondary status and almost certainly alienate existing allies and/or jeopardise existing security relationships.

Co-existence

Perhaps the most realistic option for the European Union is to continue as it is doing: neither actively supporting, nor actively opposing American actions. Certain member states may oppose or support American actions but these postures could be kept outside the growing remit of the European Union's foreign and security policy. The European Union as an institution is steering a middle course that both diplomatically and in terms of its internal politics secures the most gains for the least input of efforts or resources. The strategic position seems to be to allow America its head. This has two possible outcomes: first, that the Americans destroy Al Qaeda and other terrorist groups, spread democracy and create free market economies on a global basis or, second, that America fails in its mission and the war on terror spirals out of control, after having been fought on too many fronts simultaneously. In either case the United States is likely to be massively indebted to the states of the European Union and other creditor nations, giving these actors considerable leverage over American foreign policy and giving the European Union a stronger position from which to negotiate the shape of the global order in the aftermath of either a pyrrhic American victory or a Vietnam-like failure in the war on terror.

Conclusion

At present the European Union and the United States are pursuing parallel security strategies. One is based on unilateralism and the right to pre-emptively attack perceived threats to national security. The other is based on a multilateral approach to collective security predicated upon international law and institutions. Although they share a concern with rogue states and terrorist organisations, arguably the most important similarity is that neither the ESS nor the NSS focus on effective strategies for dealing with these problems. The war on terror is an ideological conflict, waged against states by private, stateless individuals. Neither the United States nor the European Union seems willing to grapple with the element of information and intelligence-led warfare. Targeting individuals, using effective intelligence, and engaging with the Islamist propagandists by using Islam against them in a prolonged media campaign, would be more effective than either the shock-and-awe approach of the Americans, which has been shown to be largely counter-productive, or the schizoid nature of the European response.

If the Americans and the European Union are serious about developing a joint approach to new security threats, they will have to develop one that goes beyond such competing shibboleths as 'balance of power that favours freedom' or repeated mantras about the need for 'global governance' – both of which are meaningless in the context of a war on terror. An effective security strategy for a war on terror cannot be fought on the basis of ideas, rules and resources carried over from previous eras. As a war of intelligence it is essential that the European Union and the United States coordinate with reliable allies in the Middle East, such as Jordan, with a vested interest in halting the spread and effectiveness of Islamist extremism, and coerce or cajole others into sharing information. There is some evidence that the Americans have at least grasped this particular aspect of the war on terror. Rather than blowing up half of Baghdad, targeting Al Qaeda man for man would spread much more fear within Islamist ranks than the rather indiscriminate tactics currently employed by the coalition of the willing. The establishment of counter-terrorist cells would go some way to establishing both the effective intelligence and the means to target the relevant individuals. The focus has to shift from the punishing of deviant states to the excision of terrorist clans, networks and individuals from an international society that has moved into a new, more erratic 'neo-medieval' form.

Recent attempts to tighten container security and to keep a more coordinated record of passenger information on air travel testify to the efforts of the American and European authorities to coordinate their intelligence activities. There is no doubt growing awareness of the need to coordinate and effectively control international space, in keeping with the particular nature of the current security threat of transnational terrorism. This coordination is, however, in its infancy (despite a long gestation whose beginnings many locate in the 1970s), and far more needs to be done in the intelligence field to break down the territoriality of the intelligence and security agencies of both Europe and America (Aldrich 2004: 731–2). The compartmentalised 'integrity' and separation of national intelligence agencies may have been necessary in the age of competing and antagonistic nation states. But it cannot serve as the template for dealing with transnational terrorism.

Notes

1 See 'National Security Directive 75: American Policy Towards Sub-Saharan Africa', 23 December 1992. Online. Available: http://bushlibrary.tamu.edu/ research/nsd/NSD/NSD%2075/0001.pdf (accessed 12 December 2005).
2 'President Bush delivers graduation speech at West Point', 1 June 2002. Online. Available: http://www.whitehouse.gov/news/releases/2002/06/20020601-3.html (accessed 8 January 2006).
3 See transcript of remarks by Secretary of Homeland Security Tom Ridge at 'Transatlantic Homeland Security Conference', Washington, DC: Johns Hopkins University Center for Transatlantic Relations, 13 September 2004. Online. Available: http://www.dhs.gov/dhspublic/display?content=3994 (accessed 12 December 2005).

6 The Middle East and security strategy

Anoushiravan Ehteshami

Introduction

The Middle East and North Africa (MENA) region has been the source of key security dilemmas for the West for over a generation. It was here that the American military machine launched its biggest military campaign after Vietnam (in Iraq in 1990–1), and where the NATO alliance developed its largest network of regional partners – from Morocco in the west to Oman in the east – on the strategic chessboard of the Cold War. It was here that the Western and Eastern power blocs manoeuvred for strategic space, often subverting unfriendly governments, and more often supporting authoritarian regimes for the sake of NATO or Warsaw Pact security (Halliday 1997). Moreover, in so far as Turkey straddles the northern edge of the region (neighbouring Iran, Iraq and Syria), the region also has been home to NATO's only Muslim country and its only Eurasian Cold War 'front-line' state. This added to the importance of the Middle East to the East–West confrontation of the time.

Since the 1960s the Middle East has had to endure the consequences of the modern world's longest running regional conflict within its boundaries (namely, the Arab–Israeli conflict), one of the last century's longest wars (the eight-year-long Iran–Iraq War which resulted in over 500,000 casualties), rampant civil war (in Lebanon and Sudan, in particular), insurgencies (Algeria, Yemen, Western Sahara), and intermittent low-level conflict between members of the regional system. To cap it all, MENA is also home to one undeclared nuclear power, Israel, and at least one other nuclear aspirant, Iran.

If one throws into the equation running territorial disputes, ideological confrontations, and inter-communal strife, then it becomes clear that regime security is very tightly tied up with regime legitimacy, foreign relations and the international political economy in this region. This complex and dynamic region has equally complex relationships with the international system. In strategic terms, its geopolitical value, sitting at the crossroads of three important continents, is further underlined by the vast hydrocarbon resources of the Persian Gulf and North African sub-regions. Together, they provide over 75 per cent of the world's known hydrocarbon reserves, on which the West as well as the Far East is becoming increasingly more dependent for economic survival. But rapid population growth of over 3.5 per cent a year in some parts of the region, compounded by unresponsive governments and substantial discrepancies in income and wealth within and between MENA countries, means that the regimes which sit atop these reserves are not fully secure either.

Interest in the region has heightened even further in the twenty-first century with the dramatic rise of Islamic terrorist networks, most importantly Al Qaeda, and their ability to hit at high-value Western military and civilian targets at home and abroad. In many ways, 9/11 was the key catalyst, shifting the international focus on the MENA region. Not only did the terror attacks on the United States resonate in the Bush administration's 2002 National Security Strategy (NSS), but also accelerated the development of European thinking on its neighbourhood policy. 9/11 also raised a wide range of questions about the societies of the Middle East themselves, in terms of the health of the region's cultural and political conditions, its regime structures and future prospects.

Very rapidly after 9/11, as is self-evident in both the NSS and the European Security Strategy (ESS), increased security concerns and geopolitical cross-fires became intertwined with MENA regime politics. This unfortunate mix, in terms of the NSS, culminated in the 2003 forceful removal by an United States-led military coalition of arguably the Arab world's most notorious (but largely ineffectual in regional terms) dictatorial regime – the Baath regime in Iraq. It will be argued here that in strategic terms the application of the NSS in this region, leading to the overthrow of the Sunni-dominated Baath regime in Iraq, has had significant and unforeseen regional implications, generating extraordinary challenges for the Sunni and Arab-dominated regional order which slowly emerged from the ashes of the Ottoman Empire over a century ago. Indeed, this change has left the European Union (and its ESS) with a series of dilemmas in practical policy terms, and has had a further impact on its other major policy areas, such as Iran's nuclear programme, the Israel–Palestine peace process, approaches to democratisation and, of course, terrorism. The pretext for regime change in Iraq, coming less than two years after the forced removal of the Taliban from Afghanistan, was the presence of weapons of mass destruction (WMD) – a terror threat that the Baath regime allegedly posed to American security and its wider interests abroad. Since then, fears of nuclear proliferation by Iran and the persistence of terrorism in Iraq and elsewhere have continued to define much of the transatlantic approach to the region.

It was fear of the linkage between WMD proliferation and terrorism, therefore, and the core recommendation of the NSS for the United States to prevent the rise of regional challengers to its hegemony, which should form the basis of our understanding of the transatlantic policy options towards this region. Moreover, the distinctiveness of the respective European and

American security strategies vis-à-vis the Middle East should also be understood in the same context, in which the European Union (which has a unitary foreign policy only in form) has had to try and behave more like a single actor when devising security policy. To allow a fresh look, it is useful to frame the analysis of the Middle East and security strategy into three distinct periods: first, the era of the Cold War; second, the immediate post-Cold War period; and, third, the post-9/11 period which provides the main backdrop for an examination of the current nature of the international politics of the Middle East region.

The Cold War era

During the Cold War, the United States and Europe tended to speak through NATO with one voice over security matters pertaining to the Middle East region. The key concerns were preventing Soviet military encroachments southwards and limiting communism's influence in the region, even by nurturing political Islam as an effective anti-Soviet weapon. To forestall Communist infiltration, the West, albeit unsystematically, took steps to prevent the rise or establishment of apparently anti-Western nationalist regimes in the region. Western action included military intervention. France and the United Kingdom, Western Europe's military and political power-houses of the day, launched a military attack on Gamal Abdel Nasser's Arab nationalist administration in Egypt in 1956. An Anglo-American destabilisation campaign saw off the nationalist government of Iran under Premier Mossadeq in 1953 and brought back to power the much more compliant young Pahlavi monarch (the 'Shah of Iran'). But the Soviets did not surrender the Middle East to the West. Moscow soon developed a proactive strategy of befriending many of the new political, largely military-led, elites of the region that were sweeping into power. The Warsaw Pact countries thus developed substantial military and political links in Egypt, Syria, Iraq, Libya, Algeria, Yemen and Sudan.

Both the United States and the Soviet Union worked hard to limit each other's zones of influence, but the Middle Eastern regimes themselves often struggled to distance themselves from both superpowers, and in so doing sought collaborative ties with countries of Asia and Europe instead. In Western Europe's case, historic links with the region have meant that their voice in shaping NATO's strategy towards the Middle East resonated more forcefully than in many other 'out of area' concerns. Thus, in the Persian Gulf sub-region, an Anglo-American security partnership developed, with the United States emerging as the dominant partner after 1971, enduring the fall of the monarchy in Iran in 1979 and providing the bedrock of two major military campaigns against Iraq in 1990–1 and 2003. The United States and the United Kingdom continue to maintain a high-level presence in the sub-region, with the United States providing first-line security for a number of the small Arab states. Bahrain, Qatar, Kuwait, the United Arab Emirates,

Oman and even Saudi Arabia (whose relations with the United States have been somewhat strained since 9/11) all have intimate military and broader security ties with the United States. Some also have similar links with the United Kingdom, and to a lesser extent France. One could go further and argue that the NSS and ESS owe much of their evolution to the security dilemmas posed by this strategically vital sub-region of the Middle East. In Iran (revolution, Islamic radicalism and proliferation), Iraq (military aggression, development and use of WMD, severe political repression), and Saudi Arabia (Salafi militancy, support for radical Sunni groups in Afghanistan and elsewhere) the transatlantic alliance has faced a series of unparalleled challenges.

In the Levant, the heart of the Arab–Israeli conflict, American power has prevailed since the 1956 Suez debacle, providing the main security guarantee for the state of Israel. But it is also true that European powers such as France have played a big part in shaping the European Union's strategy of engagement in this arena, and in landmark European policy positions such as the 1979 Venice declaration, which adopted a two-state solution for Palestine more than 20 years before the United States followed suit. In North Africa, furthermore, France has been the prime actor since the end of its rule in Algeria, Morocco and Tunisia. This background is important for, over time, Paris has used these ties to advance the European Union's post-Cold War strategy of deeper engagement with the Maghreb, as exemplified in the Euro-Mediterranean Partnership 'Barcelona process' which was formally launched in 1995.

The 1990s: the New World Order

To recap, the West's key strategic concerns during the Cold War era were security of the oil states and the flow of oil out of the Persian Gulf, Israel's security, and the survival of the moderate pro-Western regimes in the region. These general goals were shared by the alliance as a whole, despite subtle differences in the foreign relations of its members with the Middle East, or indeed their own competing interests in this region. While some of these objectives did not endure beyond the Cold War, Gulf security and the Arab–Israeli conflict did, leading to the pursuit of a new post-Cold War order in the Middle East. President George H. W. Bush's 'New World Order' was built on the swift success of the 1991 Operation Desert Storm to liberate Kuwait from Iraq's clutches and had, at its heart, a new American security strategy for the MENA region.

With the Cold War and the Soviet threat gone, the West could now look beyond containment and purely strategic gain and try to change conditions on the ground so as to minimise the threat of warfare in this region. Security of oil and the state of Israel continued to top the American agenda. Yet in the absence of a Soviet challenge the West could envisage adopting more creative policies for dealing with the region's many trouble spots. The threatening regimes of Iraq and Iran would be marginalised and the resolution of the Arab–Israeli conflict could finally become the international community's highest priority. The October 1991 Madrid 'peace' conference was the zenith of collective action on that front.[1]

By the early 1990s, therefore, the United States was more of a local 'pervasive' power than an 'intrusive' one, with commensurate military might and political presence in virtually every theatre in the Middle East. There were more countries dependent on US security patronage and support by the end of the 1990s than there had been at any time during the Cold War. US security strategy in the Middle East had, as a consequence, become increasingly pervasive and local by the end of the century.

Europe too had increased the 'local content' of its security strategy towards the region, as exemplified in the Euro-Mediterranean partnership. A relatively more nuanced security strategy, however, was to be found in Europe's partnership framework for the region. With regard to the Persian Gulf sub-region, while the European Union accepted the full containment and shackling of Iraq, it chose a policy of engagement and dialogue with the Gulf's other key power, Iran. From its 'critical dialogue' with Iran, which was launched in the early 1990s, it had by the end of the decade moved the agenda to one of 'constructive engagement' with the Islamic regime. In the absence of diplomatic relations between Tehran and Washington, the open-ended and wide-ranging engagement policy raised Europe's economic and diplomatic profile considerably in Iran, paving the way for a much deeper relationship between the two sides. The fact that the United Kingdom, Germany and France became the key Western interlocutors in Iran's nuclear stand-off with the West bears testimony to the Europeans' patient building of relations with Tehran and preparedness to treat it as a worthy negotiating partner. At the same time, the European Union also initiated (beginning in 1998) an EU–Gulf Cooperation Council (GCC) dialogue in order to broaden its ties with other important players of this vital sub-region.[2]

In the Mediterranean the European policy was even more daring, in that the European Union's Barcelona process had three main aims: first, to create 'a zone of peace and stability, based on the principles of human rights and democracy'; second, to construct 'a zone of shared prosperity' by the gradual setting up of an area of free trade between the European Union and its Mediterranean partners and between these same partners, accompanied by extensive financial support from the Community 'to facilitate economic transition and help partners deal with the socio-economic challenges caused by this transition'; and, third, to improve 'mutual understanding between the peoples of the region and the promotion of free and flourishing civil society' (Patten 2001). The three-pronged European security strategy of the time focused on the socio-economic roots of conflict in the southern Mediterranean, encouraging political reform while also trying to ease the burden of the necessary economic reforms with assistance, and 'incentivising' the southern partners to initiate and stick with the agreed programme of action.[3]

The Euro-Med partnership soon evolved into a multilateral forum for dialogue between the European Union and its southern partners, engaging them within a complex web of associations, conferences, workshops, and links with civil, military, political, diplomatic, legal, educational, industrial and non-governmental actors from across the partnership countries. Cynics might suggest that these MENA societies were locked into the European sphere through an enforced process of dialogue, which essentially shadowed the European agenda, itself being part of the European Union's strategic response to globalisation and the perceived need to strengthen the Union's position internationally. EU encroachment through the Barcelona process, over and above the Association Agreements being reached with the southern Mediterranean countries, might go some way to explaining the drive of a number of southern Mediterranean countries, including Algeria, Morocco, Tunisia and even Libya since 2004, to court American support.

But the fact remains that the Euro-Med partnership provided the perfect staging post for broader dialogue between Levant protagonists after the 1991 Madrid conference. Over time it also helped in easing the reform process in a number of North African countries. In the absence of a heavy stick in its repertoire, however, the European Union's powers of persuasion did not always yield fruit: the European Union failed to moderate Israel's settlement building, or stop its destruction of the Palestinian security and socioeconomic infrastructure largely financed by European taxpayers, or prevent the spiralling of the al-Aqsa Palestinian intifada. More generally, it failed to bridge the gap between Israel and Libya in the Barcelona process, or to advance its primary goal of democratisation. EU offers of funds for various initiatives also encouraged a culture of clientelism, which generated tensions not only between the Arab states and the European Union, but also within the southern Mediterranean countries themselves.

On the bright side, the Arab–Israeli conflict today would have been in an even more dangerous state had the European Union not launched the 'roadmap' to peace between Israel and Palestine in 2002, and therefore persuaded the United States, Russia and the UN to agree to the principle of land for peace as the basis of a final and negotiated settlement. A 'Quartet' of interested parties was born, bringing to bear the influence of arguably the most important global actors. With the creation of the Quartet the European Union had managed to internationalise its own collective approach to problem-solving. Thus, today the road-map to peace between Israel and Palestine (as a condition of the resolution of the wider Arab–Israeli dispute) has become one of the cornerstones of the security strategies of both the United States and the European Union. The fact that the United States has failed to force the parties to follow it in full is of course a measure of the limitations of American brokering influence, but is also a feature of the diplomatic weaknesses of the European Union and its other Quartet partners to help push forward the agenda in the absence of support from Washington.[4] The European Union may have created the international vehicle for enforcement and may even have drawn the road-map to a lasting peace. But it has not been able to persuade the parties to progress along it.

The post-9/11 disorder

As already noted, 9/11 brought into even sharper focus the security dilemmas being faced in the MENA region. At the same time, it also altered some inter-state norms by including the war on terror as a mandatory part of the West's relations with the Muslim world in general and the United States' contacts with the Middle East in particular. The war on terror demanded the adoption of a new grand American strategy which would seek to eradicate the three key sources of threat to America and its interests worldwide – terrorism, the proliferation of weapons of mass destruction in the hands of rogue actors (states or groups), and regional states pursuing policies deemed hostile to the United States. For the neo-conservatives in the US administration, the terror attacks provided the logic for pre-emption, or 'anticipatory self-defence', as the country's first line of defence. As Michael Hudson (2005: 299) notes:

> The greater Middle East became the testing ground for the new America project, and within it the Arab world was 'ground zero' – the source of what the US administration insisted was the new danger, a danger even worse than the old Soviet threat. The new task of American foreign policy was not just to use force proactively but also to reshape the domestic environment of several 'failed states' in the Middle East whose educational systems, religious organisations, incompetent governments and stagnant economies nurtured anti-American terrorism.

On another front, the role of intervention as part of a grand strategy was further reinforced by the democratisation component of the Bush Doctrine. President Bush brought this issue to the forefront of US security strategy in November 2003 in the course of two major speeches, delivered in Washington and London. In speaking of a 'forward strategy of freedom in the Middle East', he spoke of the need to change America's relations with the region. In Washington, the president put the emphasis on the need for reform:

> the freedom deficit has terrible consequences for the people of the Middle East and for the world. In many Middle Eastern countries poverty is deep and it is spreading, women lack rights and are denied schooling, whole societies remain stagnant while the world moves ahead.[5]

In London, however, Bush was more critical of the inter-state bargain between the West and the Middle East's authoritarian elites. He said that:

> we must shake off decades of failed policy in the Middle East ... in the past

[we] have been willing to make a bargain, to tolerate oppression for the sake of stability. Longstanding ties often led us to overlook the faults of local elites. Yet this bargain did not bring stability or make us safe. It merely bought time, while problems festered and ideologies of violence took hold.[6]

Thus, the United States launched a 'root and branch' reform strategy, finally ditching one of the main planks of the West's Cold War policies in the Middle East, namely extending full support for all those rulers deemed to be friendly to the West and its interests.

Interestingly, the new US strategy mirrors in places the older Euro-Med initiative of the European Union. For the European Union itself, 9/11 also shifted the agenda, with the perceived need to find the means of matching its soft security approach with hard security tools. The 2003 European Security Strategy is a testimony to this rapid evolution. Indeed the June 2003 EU Action Plan on preventing WMD proliferation could be regarded as an even more concrete response to the changing security environment. Still, it was the European Union's new European Neighbourhood Policy (ENP) which most comprehensively encompassed an enlarged Europe's post-9/11 security strategy. The ENP aimed to strengthen the European Union's security with respect to the new neighbours it acquired after its 2004 expansion. It is noteworthy that nine of the 17 ENP-linked countries were MENA ones, thus revealing the relevance of the ENP to the European Union's Middle East strategy.[7] Overall, these various initiatives gave substance to the tri-pillar architecture of the ESS: a developed security zone around the expanded European Union; building a consensus on effective multilateralism as the fundamental framework of international action (prevention and not pre-emption); and recognition that, in the post-9/11 disorder, the first line of defence is not at home but abroad.

Despite its recognition of the changed international security environment after 9/11, the European Union did not abandon its strategy of dialogue. It did not endorse regime change in Iraq, nor did it boycott Yasser Arafat after President Bush's snub of him from 2002 until his death in November 2004. Over Iraq, though, European policy was in complete disarray. On one side stood France and Germany (usually with Belgium and Luxembourg), and on the other a pro-United States, pro-war camp including the United Kingdom, Spain and Italy. The open division in European ranks robbed the European Union of a strong hand in the debates about Iraq, rendering the organisation impotent when the invasion finally took place in March 2003.

Despite the European Union not being a unitary actor in foreign and security terms, Rosemary Hollis (2005: 308) rightly observes that in the MENA region the European Union has 'a totally different orientation to that of the United States and the difference is between advocacy of an international system based on international law and institutions versus one defined by US hegemony'. This analysis has been accepted by American strategic planners themselves, who see the United States as being largely responsible for shaping Middle Eastern events between now and 2020. For them, the United States is

> the dominant military power in the region and it is the forger of a new political and economic system in Iraq. It is the principal security guarantor of several Middle Eastern states and the principal bête noire of several others. And it is the main source of an alien culture that is admired by many Middle Easterners but disdained by others ... the Middle East now plays, and is likely to continue to play, at least as large a part in US foreign policy discourse as ever before.[8]

In the context of this strategic reality, transatlantic concerns over Iran's nuclear programme acquire crucial importance. While Washington had argued since 2002 that Iran's programme was for weaponisation and should therefore be referred to the Security Council as a matter of priority, the European Union opted to engage Iran through an Anglo-Franco-German partnership in a debate about its nuclear programme. Between 2003 and summer 2005 the so-called EU3 pushed Iran to accept certain limitations on its nuclear research and even fully to suspend its uranium enrichment and reprocessing activities. At their height, the intense negotiations produced the Paris agreement of November 2004, in which both parties espoused their commitment to a negotiated deal and the need for finding an inclusive security dialogue across the Persian Gulf. For the European Union, the Paris agreement marked a significant departure from its traditional role. In these negotiations the EU3 laid down the basis for joint action on de-escalation, and went as far as supporting the case for collective security with a non-European regional actor. The European Union's position was in sharp contrast to that of the United States, and signified a clear divergence in approach to global security issues. The protracted negotiations also showed that the European Union was able to take what amounted, in transatlantic terms, to unilateral action on major international security matters.

Nonetheless, so long as Tehran viewed the EU3 discussions as a vehicle for dealing with the United States (either to buy time against military action or to exchange bargaining chips with Washington), the EU3's ability to extract a final binding agreement from Tehran on its enrichment activities was likely to fail. The failure, leading to the British request to refer Iran to the Security Council in September 2005, was itself a measure of the European Union's structural weaknesses and ability, though certainly not of its larger political ambitions. From Tehran's perspective, its active nuclear programme could be seen in a similar light: a tool for reinforcing its regional weight in the new order and as a strong card in strengthening its hand in the geopolitical struggle with the United States and its closest regional ally, Israel.

The political front

Having considered the evolution of the American and EU security strategies with regard to the Middle East, the question now arises: can such schemes as the 2004 Greater Middle East Initiative (GMEI) help to advance US and transatlantic security strategy and encourage reform in the MENA region? Or will it hinder both? The initiative, first brought to light by the US Vice-President Dick Cheney at the World Economic Forum meeting in Davos in January 2004, was called 'the most ambitious U.S. democracy effort since the end of the Cold War'.[9] Its existence was made public a year after the Arab world's own 'Arab Charter', which Saudi Arabia tabled in January 2003. The Charter, which was seen as a revolution of sorts in its own right, called for 'internal reform and enhanced political participation in the Arab states'.[10] The later American GMEI plan, by contrast, encompassed a wide range of diplomatic, cultural and economic measures. The GMEI deliberately advanced the agenda by calling for the United States and its European allies and partners (in the G-8 Group, NATO, and the European Union) to press for and assist the holding of free elections in the Middle East (through support for civic education, the creation of independent election commissions in MENA countries and comprehensive voter registers); foster the growth of new independent media; press for judicial reforms; create a 'literate generation' by helping to cut regional illiteracy rates in half by 2010, and train 'literacy corps' of around 100,000 female teachers by 2008; finance the translation of Western classical texts into Arabic to foster better understanding of the West amongst Muslims; and establish a European-style Greater Middle East Development Bank, a type of International Finance Corporation (IFC),[11] to assist the development of larger enterprises, and give $500 million in micro-loans to small entrepreneurs, especially women, in order to spur 1.2 million small entrepreneurs out of poverty.

As reform of the region has become a high US post-9/11 priority, the launch of the GMEI should be seen in the context of the perceived American need 'to drain the swamp' which breeds Islamic terrorists in this region. The concern from the region, however, has been that the 2004 US initiative, as with the NSS in 2002, explained its logic in purely Western security terms. Its early 2004 draft states that 'so long as the region's pool of politically and economically disenfranchised individuals grows, we will witness an increase in extremism, terrorism, international crime and illegal migration'.[12] Furthermore, the initiative perceived the region in largely Cold War terms. The GMEI, for example, spoke of creating MENA security structures based on the 1975-launched Helsinki process and NATO's Partnership for Peace programme. It anticipated that a complex set of security structures could bring six Middle East countries, including Egypt, Morocco, Tunisia, Qatar and Israel, into partnership with NATO. But leaving such prominent regional players as Iran, Syria and Saudi Arabia out of such regional security arrangements was always likely to fuel discontent, creating new divisions, and breeding further instability across national boundaries. In MENA's dynamic setting, drawing parallels with the East–West Helsinki process did nothing to assuage fears; indeed it accomplished the opposite. On more than one occasion regional policymakers stated that the Helsinki process first ended the alternative power bloc to the West and then caused an internal collapse of the Soviet Union. 'Is that what's in store for the Muslim world as well with this initiative?' is what several leading Arab (and Iranian) policymakers asked.[13]

Other important concerns were the extent to which the initiative would take notice of the situation on the ground in the Middle East, and how much attention it would pay to the legitimate concerns of the region's ruling regimes.[14] It was precisely because of the ambiguities attached to the original proposal that President Husni Mubarak of Egypt 'denounced with force the ready-for-use prescriptions proposed abroad under cover of what are called reforms'. As he headed home from a meeting with King Fahd and Crown Prince Abdullah of Saudi Arabia, Mubarak told Egyptian journalists:

> we hear about these initiatives as if the region and its states do not exist, as if they had no sovereignty over their land … these kinds of initiatives do not deserve a comment, [but] need to be confronted by scientific and convincing answers from thinkers, so as not to leave people to fall prey to misleading impressions and misconceptions disseminated by such initiatives.[15]

In Riyadh, an official Egyptian–Saudi statement noted that:

> imposing a certain model of reform on Arab and Islamic states from the outside is unacceptable … [Arab countries are] progressing on the road to development, modernisation and reform, but in a way that is compatible with the needs, interests, values and identities of their peoples.[16]

The voices of some other Arab leaders, including those from Jordan, Morocco and Syria, similarly rejected the plan as an external imposition as news of it began to filter out in February 2004:

> No matter how well-intended the Americans and Europeans say their initiatives are, it will take more than words to comfort sceptical Arab rulers and a worried Arab public. The regimes see many signs suggesting that the United States is determined to enforce change or 'reforms,' while the public – initially desperate for real reforms – suspect that the foreign calls for democracy are only an excuse to interfere in the region and redraw it in accordance with the West's own interests. The occupation of Iraq and the disinterest in Palestinian suffering have reinforced those fears.[17]

Former US National Security Adviser, Zbigniew Brzezinski, added that:

> There is no question that the administration has its work cut out for it. For starters, the democracy initiative was unveiled by the president in a patronising way: before an enthusiastic audience at the American Enterprise Institute, a Washington policy institution enamoured of the war in Iraq and not particularly sympathetic toward the Arab world. The notion that America, with Europe's support and Israel's endorsement, will teach the Arab world how to become modern and democratic elicits, at the very least, ambivalent reactions. (This, after all, is a region where memory of French and British control is still fresh).[18]

Yet, as the initiative provided the first indication of a concerted drive to reform the region, many civil society groups and liberal voices in the region came (albeit quietly at first) to welcome the GMEI, with the proviso that it must enjoy 'high local content'. According to the *Al-Ahram*, at least one opposition leader welcomed the initiative, noting that:

> sadly enough, it was only this kind of pressure that forced [Egypt's ruling party] to finally relinquish its 22 years of stubborn refusal to embrace any kind of political reform, establish a human rights council and allow a remarkable amount of press freedom.[19]

The German 'partner' of the GMEI, its Foreign Minister Joshka Fischer, had this factor in mind when he presented its content to the Egyptians in terms of the two highly critical Arab Human Development Reports, in which Arab economists had identified key political as well as socio-economic obstacles to development.[20] It was said that 'by 12 February [2004], the ambassador to Cairo Martin Cobler had given Osama El-Baz, President Mubarak's chief political adviser, a copy of the new US–EU transatlantic initiative'. Clearly, Europeans were trying to promote the American GMEI plan as they were already associating themselves with it. While it is clear that the Germans were engaged in some fence-mending of their own with Washington over their strong opposition to the Iraq war, the ambassador had told Egyptian officials that the initiative aimed at securing a full partnership between the transatlantic coalition and the greater Middle East, 'in the light of US and European consensus that reforming the Middle East must be a top priority'.[21]

The geopolitical context

The geopolitical context of the MENA region today provides another backdrop for the pace and nature of change. Broadly speaking, there are five countries in the 'greater Middle East' region that have the ability actively to shape the geopolitical setting of the area. The first two are Iraq and its non-Arab Shia neighbour, Iran; the third is Israel, an economically powerful nuclear-weapon state which holds the key to the Arab–Israeli conflict; the fourth is Libya, an oil-rich Maghreb state with geopolitical presence and influence in the Middle East, Europe and Africa; and the fifth is Pakistan, a nuclear weapon state and former supporter of the Taliban in Afghanistan and today a US ally in the war on terrorism.

Of these, Iraq is perhaps the most important and uncertain, and Iran the most challenging, both further clouding the security conditions of the Persian Gulf. Here, as Nasr (2004) notes, the geopolitical context is being shaped by a dangerous conflict between Iraq's Shia majority and militant Sunnis, including Al Qaeda. The primary focus of the guerrilla operations in Iraq began to shift in the second half of 2003 towards the Shia community. It has been noted by Sunnis in general, and Al Qaeda and the Wahhabis in particular, that large sections of Iraq's Shia community not only did not rise against the US occupation but also have worked with the United States to facilitate a transfer of power that will make them the dominant political and socio-economic force in Iraq. Al Qaeda and Sunni militants believe that the Shia, with the connivance of the United States, are busy implementing their plan for the domination of the important Arab state of Iraq as a base for targeting their Sunni-dominated hinterland, most notably Islam's heartland in Saudi Arabia. The terror campaign in Iraq, therefore, has acquired a dangerous geocultural slant to it, perilously threatening the stability of Shia–Sunni relations, non-Arab Iran's ties with its Sunni neighbours in the Arab world, as well as Iran's and Iraq's relations with Sunni-dominated Pakistan, Turkey and Afghanistan.

The militant Sunnis' perception of the growing political role of the Shia in Iraq has therefore increased the frequency and intensity of terror attacks on the Shia communities there. These attacks reached a highpoint on Ashura (Shia Islam's major religious occasion) during the Islamic month of Muharram in early March 2004, with the deadly synchronised attacks on the main Shia shrines in Baghdad and Karbala which killed at least 170 people and injured hundreds more.[22] If not contained, the anti-Shia terror campaign in Iraq will sooner, rather than later, resonate in Iraq's Sunni hinterland as well, and will stir greater hostilities between the Shia minorities of the Arabian Peninsula states and their governments, as well as between the Shia-dominated states of Iran and Iraq and their neighbours. As a direct consequence of these developments, a clash of religious factions, if not 'civilisations', could eventually ensue to engulf the entire region. The Muslim world could again be set on a course of self-inflicted pain and inter-factional collisions over ideology and identity.

The United States will probably not be an innocent bystander in this situation. Having occupied Iraq and 'liberated' its Shia community, voices in Washington have begun to speak of the need to 'free the eastern province of Saudi Arabia' where the majority of Saudi Shia reside. Max Singer, the co-founder of the Hudson Institute, is amongst those who have suggested that Saudi Arabia's strategic oil region, its eastern al-Hasa province, should be separated from the rest of the country in an effort to curb Wahhabi extremism.[23] Other Washington insiders, such as Richard Perle, David Frum (President George W. Bush's former speech writer) and Senator Sam Brownback, have also recommended that the fight against terror be taken to Saudi Arabia. They argue that the Saudis need to be told to follow the United States' lead in its anti-terror campaign or watch the United States encourage separatist tendencies of the Saudi Shia in al-Hasa (Fahim 2004). By denying access to its oil, the argument goes, Riyadh can be 'tamed' and Saudi fundamentalists deprived of the funds to support Al Qaeda.

It is into this grave situation that neighbouring Iran treads. As the world's only Shia and expressly Islamist state, Iran in its post-revolutionary mode has been careful not to stray too far from the wider Arab region in its policy pronouncements. It has remained loyal to the Palestinian cause, has developed cooperative relations with virtually every Arab state, and has ensured that it keeps in close touch with its Gulf Arab neighbours. Yet the tempo of its domestic politics is hopelessly out of sync with them. One commentator has speculated that:

> In 20 years, perhaps less, Iran will be a powerful democracy and a solid US ally. Having rejected its own Western stooge and endured an indigenous, orthodox replacement, the Iranians realise there is no alternative to liberal democracy. If the Arab world is entering a pre-revolutionary phase, Iran is in a post-revolutionary one. The Iranian polity is already more dynamic than many of its Arab counterparts. Its demographics – a growing population of young, secular reformers and a dwindling pool of ageing clerics – are working in favour of stability.
>
> (Glain 2003: 20)

On the basis of this scenario Iran will have as much to fear from the tide of Sunni-Arab Islamism as its Western counterparts. Yet, Islamist Iran finds itself in a geopolitical struggle with the United States and its main regional ally, Israel, and as such cannot act as a natural ally of the West in the war on Al Qaeda. Although both Tehran and Washington fear Al Qaeda, they have been unable to form a Western–Islamic front against Al Qaeda and Salafi Islam. Irrespective of bilateral problems, Iran is destined to play a critical role in the unfolding drama of the region. Susser (2003: 6) notes that in the Persian Gulf, 'Iran is the only regional power of consequence. Iraq is out for the count, and the Saudis are a broken reed'. Such an assessment would have seemed hardly credible a decade ago. Thus the combination of Iran's internal political dynamism, its relations with the Arab Shias in Iraq, Kuwait, Bahrain, Saudi Arabia, Lebanon, Afghanistan, Pakistan, India and Azerbaijan, and its geopolitical advantages, will continue to give the leaders of this country a powerful voice in the region.

It is therefore the apparently sudden shift of focus in US policy to the geocultural link between Persian Gulf oil and the Shia communities in the region that alarms the (largely Sunni-dominated) Arab regional actors, particularly Saudi Arabia and the Gulf states. The West, suggests Yamani, has 'woken up to the accident of geography that has placed the world's major oil supplies in areas where the Shi'ites form the majority' (quoted in Fahim 2004: 30). It is the awareness of this geocultural cross-section in US policy terms that petrifies the Arab leaders and fuels their suspicions of the US end-game in the region. In the tense post-Saddam environment of the Persian Gulf sub-region, even faint suspicion of US-backed sectarian power struggles between the Sunni and the Shia can ignite a much bigger fire to engulf the entire Arab world.[24] Gulf Arab leaders, therefore, may be forgiven for not fully buying into the American-led Iraq mission nor its grand democratisation drive. If both of these initiatives are to result in the empowerment of the Shia communities of the Arab world, it is hardly likely that Sunni leaders will embrace them with any warmth. Where Arab regime survival is at stake, the United States could be fanning flames of antagonism that could sustain many decades of trench warfare between militant and jihadist Islamists and the West. As we have seen in Iraq, the Shia of course do not also uniformly welcome the American intervention on their behalf. US backing, short of delivering a defensible Shia protectorate, could threaten their efforts at co-existence with their Sunni brethren. As a minority in a sea of Sunnis in the Muslim world, the Shia are very careful not to fan the sectarian flames that could lead to their further marginalisation or, even worse, annihilation.

US grand designs, therefore, for regime change, reform, counter-terrorism and counter-proliferation are creating new, unpredictable and uncontrollable instabilities in the Middle East, which are not being helped by the impasse in the Arab–Israeli peace talks. With Israel's unilateral with-drawal from the Gaza Strip in August 2005, the prospects of reaching a permanent settlement in the Palestinian–Israeli dispute according to the road-map seems also to have disappeared. The White House's unconditional support for Israel, exemplified in President Bush's letter to Prime Minister Sharon in 2004 that questioned the continuing validity of the UN resolutions 242 and 338,[25] has given Israel the green light to draw its borders unilaterally and without regard for the needs and aspirations of the Palestinian party. This in itself is highly destabilising and will further radicalise the Palestinian population. But American unwillingness to force the issue has also prevented the European Union from pursuing its own unilateral strategy of finding the way to the two-state solution advocated in the road-map. The result will be further radicalisation of Europe's 'near aboard'. American security strategy, pursued without reference to the ongoing conflict between Israel and some of its neighbours, is likely to lead to a weakening of prag-matic forces in the region, further insecurity for Israel and its neighbours, and the bolstering of radical forces in Palestine and elsewhere. Further radi-calisation of the region in response to the crisis in Palestine will also prevent a slow pro-Western realignment from taking place, deepening suspicions in the region of the West's hegemonic ambitions.

Conclusion

The geopolitical map of the MENA region has changed dramatically over recent years, and at every juncture the United States and the European Union have had to respond creatively to the regional security challenges. Both now have security strategies in place with the Middle East very much in mind, and both increasingly tend to mirror each other. The European Security Strategy of 2003 affirms the link between the democratic deficit and security in the Middle East: for example, in ways suggestive of the Bush administration's 'forward strategy for freedom'. The GMEI, endorsed by the G-8 summit in 2004, neatly distils the linkages which have been drawn between violence, stability and politics of the Middle East. Moreover, NATO has been brought in as a partner to provide support for security governance in what it calls the 'broader Middle East' (which for the first time in NATO's structural commitments includes the Persian Gulf) through its 'Istanbul Cooperation Initiative' (ICI).[26] So, while differences of emphasis continue to separate the EU and US security strategies in the Middle East, and although the European Union remains very much opposed to regime change as a practical solution to complex problems of the region, in reality both sides of the Atlantic accept the critical linkages between politico-cultural and socio-economic problems in the region and insecurity (including terrorism). Also, although both sides continue to implement their own policies in regard to countering Middle East-generated insecurity, through NATO, the GMEI, and other fora, they also work together.

For its part, the European Union continues to suffer from an image problem in the Middle East, in that it is not seen as a powerful single actor; nor is it regarded as a powerful force for dealing with the region's multiple security challenges. 'Yet,' note two prominent commentators,

> the EU does need to better mobilize its own security assets in terms of confidence-building measures and proliferation initiatives. With the United States not being able to eradicate regional differences, prevent conflicts from breaking out, or promote a more stable security environment, the Europeans have a qualitatively different role to play in the region.
>
> (Koch and Neugart 2004: 13)

The security picture in the Middle East is likely to get even more complicated in the next 15 years. First, both the European Union and the United States will need to absorb the geopolitical implications of NATO member Turkey joining the European Union as a full member. Second, the nuclear stand-off with Iran will more than likely not be resolved to the satisfaction of Washington, leaving a huge uncertainty in Iran's future relations with its neighbours, as well as with its main nuclear negotiating partners in the European Union. Third, it will be at least another five years before the final shape of post-Baathist Iraq can emerge. In the meanwhile, Iraq will continue to act as the security black hole of the region, with all the mysteries and uncertainties associated with a black hole. Fourth, the Arab–Israeli conflict must be resolved, and to the satisfaction of all the parties, if the region is to pull away from the cycle of militarisation. And, finally, both the European Union and the United States must be careful with the implementation of their reform strategies. It is vital to bear in mind that democracies, as we have seen in Germany, Spain and Italy in the inter-war period, can turn erstwhile allies into distant relatives. Were democracy to take hold in the Middle East – in Iraq, Egypt, Morocco, Algeria, Lebanon, Jordan, Palestine, Yemen – it is by no means certain that the popular governments of these countries would pursue the West's agenda. Indeed, the popular election of an anti-Western neo-conservative, such as Iran's new president in June 2005, shows the dangers to the West of the MENA masses being empowered to articulate their political aspirations through the ballot-box. In looking for an effective security strategy based on the establishment of democracy in the Middle East, therefore, both Europe and the United States will have to be very careful about exactly what they wish for! The same democratically elected forces can tomorrow expect from the West what Nasser, Mossadegh and their followers were demanding at the height of the Cold War. But this time the nationalist garb will have been replaced with an Islamist cloak.

Notes

1 During the 1990s, this process led to an embryonic dialogue between Israel and Syria, the Palestinian–Israeli Oslo Accords of 1993 and 1996, the establishment of formal diplomatic relations between Jordan and Israel in 1994, and Israeli withdrawal from southern Lebanon in 2001.
2 The GCC was created in 1981 and includes Bahrain, Kuwait, Oman, Qatar, Saudi Arabia and the United Arab Emirates.
3 The three baskets of the Euro-Med partnership are political and security, economic and financial, and social and cultural.
4 The Palestinian–Israeli Rafah border crossing agreement of November 2005 again shows the European Union's political weakness. Despite the fact that it is as a body responsible for monitoring, verifying and evaluating the implementation of the agreement, it was in fact US Secretary of State Condoleezza Rice's efforts which brought to a successful end five months of negotiations. See *The Economist*, 17 November 2005; *Haaretz*, 16 and 17 November 2005.
5 Quoted in 'Bush on Democracy in the Middle East', *Washington Post*, 6 November 2003.
6 'President Bush Discusses Iraq Policy at Whitehall Palace in London', Office of the Press Secretary, the White House, 19 November 2003. Online. Available: http://www.whitehouse.gov/news/releases/2003/11/20031119-1.html (accessed 8 January 2006).
7 The ENP's principal operating mechanism is the Action Plan, which rigorously regulates relations between the European Union and each neighbour. The bilateral Action Plans create the mutually agreed basis for aid and cooperation. Unlike the Euro-Med Partnership, ENP Action Plans identify political commitments for neighbours which will be measurable through benchmarks and

conditionality. Specific political and security commitments on terrorism and WMD proliferation form part of the agreements.

8 CIA National Intelligence Council discussion paper, from the December 2003 Commonwealth Conference: 'The Middle East to 2020'. *MERIA News*, 8 (2), February 2004.

9 Robin Wright, 'US Readies Push for Mideast Democracy Plan', *Washington Post*, 28 February 2004.

10 *Arab News*, 17 January 2003.

11 The Washington-based IFC is linked to the World Bank and exists 'to promote … sustainable private sector investment in developing countries as a way to reduce poverty and improve people's lives'. See http://www.ifc.org/about (accessed 8 January 2006).

12 Quoted in *Arab News*, 17 January 2003.

13 Author's conversations with officials from Egypt, Iran, Iraq, Jordan, Saudi Arabia and the UAE.

14 To address such fears, US Secretary of State Colin Powell told the US-funded Al-Hurra Arabic satellite television station that 'I agree with the Egyptians and the Saudis that reform can not be imposed from outside, and that it has to be accepted from within. The initiative must be acceptable to all the countries in the region'. Quoted in Gamal Essam El-Din, 'Asserting Home-grown Reforms', *Al-Ahram Weekly*, 4–10 March 2004.

15 Quoted in Wright, 'US Readies Action'.

16 Quoted in El-Din, 'Asserting Home-grown Reforms'.

17 Khaled Ezzelarab, 'Everyone Else Wants Reform', *Cairo Times*, 26 February–3 March 2004.

18 'The Wrong Way to Sell Democracy to the Arab World', *New York Times*, 8 March 2004. He further added that:

> There are other reasons to be wary of the administration's plan. Democracy, impatiently imposed, can lead to unintended consequences. If the Palestinians were able to choose a leader in truly free elections, might they not opt for the head of Hamas? If free elections were soon held in Saudi Arabia, would Crown Prince Abdullah, a reformer, prevail over Osama bin Laden or another militant Islamic leader? If not genuinely accepted and reinforced by traditions of constitutionalism, democracy can degenerate into plebiscites that only add legitimacy to extremism and authoritarianism.

19 Gamal Essam El-Din, 'Reform and Reformulating', *Al-Ahram Weekly*, 19–24 February 2004.

20 In terms of a sequence of events, in January, American and European officials met in Washington to work out the project's details. For EU diplomats the meeting had clarified an ambitious post-Iraq war idea being debated by the US administration. It was German Foreign Minister Joshka Fischer who announced on 7 February 2004, however, that the US–EU GMEI was based largely on linking the existing NATO Mediterranean dialogue with the European Union's Barcelona process (the former includes Israel, Egypt, Jordan and four North African states, while the latter also adds Syria and Lebanon). Fischer announced in several briefings that NATO would offer a security partnership, while the Barcelona process would lay the foundation for an economic partnership and a free trade area beginning in 2010.

21 Glenn Kessler and Robin Wright, 'Arabs and Europeans Question "Greater Middle East" Plan', *Washington Post*, 22 February 2004.

22 To understand the context for these attacks, consider the following:

> Please know ye, may God have mercy on you, that fasting on the 10th day in

the month of Muharram [the first month of the new Hegira year] atones for the sins of the two previous years. Fast on that day and also on the day before or after it. This is the tradition of your Prophet Muhammad, May the peace and blessings of God be upon him. He fasted on this day to thank God for saving Moses and his people and drowning the Pharaoh and his people. *It is a strange paradox that this happy occasion has been transformed by a Muslim faction [that is, the Shia] into continuous mourning and ceaseless wailing, in a picture that clearly shows ignorance of religion and following misleading persons without a good reason. O Ye, correct the path to God and follow the guidance of the prophet* (emphasis added).

This undisguised attack on the Shia was delivered by Shaykh Salih Bin-Mohammad Al Talib in the holy mosque in Mecca and carried live on Saudi Arabian TV1 on 27 February 2004 (Foreign Broadcast Information Service, 27 February 2004).

23 At two Hudson Institute conferences ('Saudi Vulnerability: The Source of Middle Eastern Oil and the Eastern Province' in April 2002, and 'Oil, Terrorism, and the Problem of Saudi Arabia', in June 2002) this strategy was the main focus of the discussions.

24 Note in this context the comments made by the Saudi Foreign Minister, Prince Saud al-Faisal, in New York: 'we [the US and Saudi Arabia] fought a war together to keep Iran out of Iraq after Iraq was driven out of Kuwait [in 1991]. Now we are handing the country over to Iran without reason.' Quoted in *The Daily Star*, 22 September 2005.

25 UNSC Resolution 242 was passed in 1967 following the Six Day War and was intended to provide a solution for the conflict in the Middle East. This resolution called for the withdrawal of Israeli armed forces from territories occupied during the Six Day War, in exchange for the 'termination of all claims or states of belligerency and respect for and acknowledgment of the sovereignty, territorial integrity and political independence of every State in the area'. Similarly, Resolution 338, passed in 1973 in the midst of the Yom Kippur War, called for the termination of the ongoing armed battle and for negotiations to begin between Israel and her Arab neighbours on the land-for-peace premise of Resolution 242. Both resolutions are regularly and routinely condemned by pro-Israeli groups as illustrating the UN's anti-Israeli bias. See, for example, the website of the Anti-Defamation League. Online. Available: http://www.adl.org/international/Israel_un_resolutions.asp?m_flipmode = 3 (accessed 8 January 2006).

26 NATO is charged with providing advice for ICI partners on defence budgeting and planning, defence reform, civil-military relations, military-to-military cooperation to promote inter-operability and joint operations in the war on terrorism. Its mission, as in Iraq and Afghanistan, seems to be to assist in capacity-building in order to partner NATO in counter-terrorism operations, WMD interdiction, and countering clandestine arms and security-related trafficking. In the 'regime changed' countries NATO is now providing military training.

7 Security strategy and the 'Russia problem'

Luke March

Is contemporary Russia still the Churchillian 'riddle wrapped in a mystery inside an enigma'? Is it a riddle the West has even come close to unravelling? Significant doubts could be forgiven: 15 years after the fall of the Berlin Wall, Russia's relationship with the West evokes some unsettling historical echoes. Tensions have occurred over a whole spectrum of issues, from the demarcation of borders with Estonia to Russian 'peacekeeping' in its neighbouring states. Competing notions of electoral legitimacy in Ukraine in November–December 2004 appeared to substantiate a new East–West divide most clearly, an occurrence almost unthinkable during Russian 'democratisation' a decade before. The Russian–Ukrainian gas dispute in January 2006 even raised the prospect of a major disruption to European energy supplies, a threat which had never surfaced even during the Cold War.

Do the West and Russia's respective security strategies reflect such anxieties and concerns? If so, have they developed appropriate mechanisms for overcoming their differences? In this chapter, we first identify the basic security premises underlying the Europe–United States–Russia triangle, in particular analysing the interests and values that underpin the notion of strategic partnership. We analyse Russia's place in the American and European conceptions of security. We then look at the Russian perspective, seeking to analyse Russia's general points of agreement and divergence with EU and US security agendas. The latter sections consider whether and how strategy is translated into practice in the security relationship between the three actors.

Both the NSS and ESS indicate fundamental problems in the EU and US relationship with Russia, and demonstrate that both find it extremely difficult to deal with a resurgent state whose aspirations to be a great power grow simultaneously with a diminution in its commitment to democracy. The NSS exhibits a tension between hard-nosed realism, seeing Russia as a great power partner in a global balance of power aimed at fighting terrorism, and a continuing idealism in its commitment to global democratisation. The European Union's idealism means that it treats Russia as a neighbouring European power, which can be potentially 'Europeanised', yet must contend with the reality that contemporary Russia is also a power of similar scope, which demands treatment as a traditional great power.

Russia has grown adept at playing on these contradictions. It interprets the NSS as justifying its own acts of pre-emption and anti-terrorist activities; it attempts to play on European divisions between those countries favouring Russia geo-politically and those wishing to assert human rights concerns. Ultimately, despite lip-service towards common democratic values, Russian foreign policy is simply not converging with European and US strategy. Churchill would have recognised how important (often short-term) 'national interest' is to contemporary Russian calculations. As a result, the Russia–transatlantic 'partnership' is based neither on normative consensus, nor strategic agreement on global challenges, but is increasingly a relationship based on short-term pragmatism, with deeper forms of cooperation increasingly problematic.

America from Mars, Europe from Venus, Russia from Pluto?

The US view of Russia

Russia receives a prominent, although brief, mention in the American NSS. It lists Russia as one of three 'potential great powers' (with India and China), which are envisaged as playing a pivotal role in creating a global 'balance of power that favours human freedom' created around a consensus over basic principles. But the detail proves more ambiguous. The NSS is cautiously optimistic about a Russia 'in the midst of a hopeful transition' towards democracy. Mutual relations have gone from 'confrontation to cooperation', Russia is 'a partner in the war on terror', and has (it is said) moved beyond Cold War approaches to a realistic appraisal of emerging shared interests and problems. However, although the NSS no longer views Russia as a strategic adversary, neither is it presented as an ally or friend (as are Europe and Canada). Significantly, almost the final words devoted to Russia in the NSS contain a warning about divisive issues such as the Russian elite's distrust of the United States, Russia's uneven commitment to 'the basic values of free-market democracy', and its poor record at combating WMD proliferation. Such admonishments are ominous, given the overall theme in the NSS of the international projection of American power. US encouragement of the great powers is strongly conditional: 'today' they are on the same side, but the United States will strongly resist aggression from other great powers, and will fight terrorists and tyrants to encourage democratic change 'when openings arrive', a statement which clearly presages America's controversial role in providing financial and (primarily) moral support for the 'coloured revolutions' of 2003–5.

Is the ambiguity of the NSS towards Russia a question of tone or substance? Probably both. On one hand, the optimism towards Russia as a potential strategic partner reflects a realist view of an interest-based partnership that was apparent in the strong Putin–Bush relationship initiated in Ljubljana in June 2001. Prior to this, the Bush administration had all but ignored Russia, promoting initiatives unilaterally and with scant regard to Russian interests and sensibilities, most obviously shown by withdrawal from the Anti-Ballistic Missile (ABM) Treaty in 2001, and promotion of 'Son of Star Wars' ballistic missile defence (Light 2003: 69–84). In Slovenia, Bush famously 'looked into Putin's soul' and found someone with whom he shared personal rapport, experiences and elements of a worldview. The relationship was cemented by Putin's audacious response to 9/11, when he was the first foreign leader to contact Washington, and offered support both tangible (by consenting to US forces operating in Central Asia) and moral (in supporting the view of a global 'war against terrorism').

While on the face of it a remarkable turnaround, the NSS reveals greater continuities with the Clinton administration's policy of democracy promotion in Russia, which had ostensibly been discredited by the deterioration of US–Russian relations in the late 1990s and the 'Who lost Russia?' debate in the United States in the run-up to the 2000 elections. During this period, the Clinton administration was attacked (and not just by Republicans) for a foreign policy allegedly too focused on interpersonal relationships with a corrupt elite (the 'Bill and Boris [Yeltsin] show'), and a selective application of democratic conditionality that ostensibly oversaw a *regression* in democratisation (Cohen 1999: 37–55). Nevertheless, even if the NSS does not specifically mention the controversial methods by which the United States promoted Russian democratisation in the 1990s, particularly through promotion of the 'Washington consensus' and fraternisation with Russian liberals, then it certainly reiterates the 1990s mantra that Russia is experiencing a transition to democracy that the United States can positively affect through an 'internationalism that reflects the union of our values and our national interests'.

The European Union and Russian security

At first glance, there is little to distinguish the ESS approach from that of the NSS, except that the ESS has even less to say about Russia, which in turn makes it somewhat more ambiguous. There is a general interest-based approach with a subtext of idealism. The European Union will help Russia with WTO accession and desires closer cooperation and a strategic partnership based around 'respect for common values', while seeking to extend the 'benefits of economic and political cooperation' to the European Union's Eastern neighbours. Russia is clearly valued, because it is placed on a par with both the United States and NATO as a partner in multilateral responses to global threats and peacekeeping such as in the Balkans and Middle East. Unlike the NSS, the ESS says nothing explicit about Russia's role in combating terrorism (which might be construed as ambivalence towards Russia's own Chechen war), yet nor does it replicate the NSS's potentially interventionist line towards Russia's internal development.

The ambiguity and omissions in the ESS have a number of possible causes. First, simply because it is a shorter document designed to present an agreed European approach it omits the most contentious issues. Since the European Union is a multilateral, multilevel organisation, it is unsurprising that documents other than the ESS flesh out the European Union's vision of its partnership with Russia. But as these documents themselves reveal, the ambiguity also goes to the heart of the European Union's Russian policy.

The 1999 EU Common Strategy on Russia supplements (but does not replace) its 1994 Partnership and Co-operation Agreement, which largely dealt with technical issues of facilitating trade and economic cooperation.[1] The Common Strategy is noteworthy for an emphasis on Russia's domestic democratic transformation and Europeanisation that is far more intense than in either the NSS *or* the ESS: this is repeatedly stressed in the first few pages and is the first of four 'areas of action' for relations. The other areas are: aiding Russia's transformation to a 'social market economy'; an enhanced security dialogue, principally through bilateral ties; cooperation in the OSCE (Organisation for Security and Cooperation in Europe) and WEU (the Western European Union); and joint measures regarding energy security and soft security issues such as the environment, crime and immigration. The same philosophy appears to underpin both the Common Strategy and the 2004 European Neighbourhood Policy (ENP) applied to other states to the European Union's east: that is, integration without institutions, supposedly offering all the benefits of membership without a formal seat at the table.

The European Union's more recent documents (such as the 2001 Country Strategy Paper 2002–6 and the 2005 Roadmaps for the 'Common Spaces'[2]) mute this emphasis on democratic transformation, but it remains fundamental. The former document largely focuses on EU–Russia economic cooperation in anticipation of enlargement. The latter's main innovation is that, unlike earlier proposals, it is to be negotiated in tandem with Russia, rather than being a policy designed by the European Union and presented to Russia as a fait accompli. Compared with the Common Strategy, the areas for cooperation are more specific and practical, with abstract democratic idealism and Europeanisation downplayed in favour of a detailed agenda of cooperation. For instance, the 1999 area of action entitled 'Consolidation of democracy' becomes the 'Common space of freedom, security and justice' focused on combating crime and terrorism.[3] However, the democratising aspect is still present in several references to the 'common values' (democracy, human rights and the rule of law) supposedly underpinning EU–Russia relations. Despite the growing realism, these documents still exhibit uncertainty over whether to engage Russia as an equal strategic partner (as Moscow wants), or to lock Russia into a 'core–periphery' approach, treated as an object for the export of EU norms, but without any prospect of membership (Averre 2005).

EU and US attitudes to Russia, as expressed through their chief strategic documents, are clearly points on a spectrum rather than polar opposites. The European Union's vision is more liberal institutionalist and interventionist, optimistic about the gains of mutual cooperation, and explicitly focused on a broader range of security agendas beyond hard security and the fight against terrorism. Nevertheless, this vision (although it is more comprehensive, with a greater concern for institution building and the social aspects of market transformation) echoes the United States' early 1990s democratisation agenda, which, as we have seen, is not altogether excised from contemporary US security discourse.

However, Europe and America clearly understand the notion of 'common values' differently. For the United States, these mean commitment to a democratic future in general and a shared understanding of global challenges. For the European Union (as explicitly stated in 1999, but implicit also in the 2005 aim of building 'a new Europe without dividing lines' around a 'rich shared heritage'), common values still imply at least partial Europeanisation. This approach is problematic: not only are Europeanisation and democratisation highly contested within Russia itself, as we now examine, but as a result this approach commits Russia to an agenda it is increasingly unable to fulfil, making mutual disappointment and misunderstanding all but inevitable.

Russia's security strategy

Russia's security vision was codified in three documents published in 2000: its National Security Concept, and the Foreign Policy Concept and Military Doctrine that supplement it.[4] Although Putin called for these documents to be revised to reflect the post-9/11 world in 2002, no new versions had appeared by early 2006, thus arguably reflecting 'total indecision' over strategy as well as Russia's habitually sluggish policy process (Felgenhauer 2005). Such as they are, they remain the best available guides to the foreign policy consensus that emerged beginning with Evgenii Primakov's stint as Foreign Minister from 1996 to 1998. Nevertheless, discussion of Russian security policy must go far beyond these documents. Their impact on actual conduct is debatable, given the lack of transparency and divergence of the formal and informal that often characterises Russian politics.

We can identify marked differences from the ESS and NSS on a number of key points. Most notably, the key security threats are seen as emerging from Russia's *internal* weakness – its economic decline and weak state power contribute to internal political instability and the spread of crime and terrorism. Second, Russia's view of the outside world is nakedly realist: there is no mention of common values, but Russia can join a 'community of interests' with other states in combating global threats, principally arms proliferation, conflict settlement and international terrorism. Although it is in Russia's interest to develop democracy and seek multilateralism in international politics, the underlying logic of international relations is still competitive, thus leading to an implicit anti-Westernism. A particularly dark and revealing passage in Russia's 2000 National Security Concept warns of 'attempts to create an international relations structure based on domination by developed Western countries ... under US leadership and designed for unilateral solutions (including the use of military force) to key issues in world politics'. NATO is accused of being in the vanguard of this destabilising process, while unnamed states are accused of attempting to weaken Russia's global and regional influence and violating international law, with foreign special services allegedly operating increasingly on Russian territory. Russia's aim of becoming a global great power is repeated several times.

There is much in these documents to support Bobo Lo's (2003) view of a marked continuation of a Soviet worldview, with the primacy of national interests and hard security fetishised, and a zero-sum, siege-mentality view of international relations packaged in greater multilateralism. However, we must be cautious, since these concepts are clearly deeply marked by the trough in Russia–West relations in the late 1990s. As Dov Lynch (2003) notes, 1999 marked a 'moment of truth': profound Russia disillusion with perceived NATO/US unilateralism and domestic economic problems led to a revived strategic alignment with the West alongside re-assertion of Russian sovereignty. In particular, Vladimir Putin's emergence as the key Russian foreign policy actor (a role Yeltsin never fully attained) and his 'risky Westwards turn' post-9/11 was initially understood as a dramatic departure from previous Russian foreign policy thinking (O'Loughlin *et al.* 2004: 3–34). In fact, security thinking under Putin displays more continuity than change. Putin's world vision, as set out in his Mission Statement of 1999, was a more realistic and internationalist, less alarmist, but ultimately still *realist* vision of Russia's future, which again focused attention on overcoming Russia's domestic crisis, maintaining domestic sovereignty and autonomous development (Putin 2000: 209–19). However, the so-called 'Putin doctrine' also implied a more realistic appraisal of Russia's external power projection, and a foreign policy more 'multivector' than 'multipolar'. This meant a global line 'based on pragmatism and on ensuring our national interests', but no longer seeking to 'balance' with countervailing anti-Western alliances against perceived US/Western unilateralism where this conflicted with Russian interests.[5]

A more substantive change was the insistence that Russia, while being a global 'great power', is European, rather than Eurasian, as the foreign policy consensus under Primakov had espoused. Although this may reflect the sincere views of Putin and other 'Petersburgers' in his administration, it is a highly problematic claim (Morozov 2003). Certainly, it makes sense as pure pragmatism. Declaring Russia 'European' recognises the multiple realities of geography, identity, security and trade. The majority of Russia's population inhabits European Russia, and a slim majority of the population see themselves as European. Above all, the European Union is already Russia's single largest trading partner, and the most vital partner for long-term economic stability.

However, Russia's conception of European-ness is paradoxical and not one that most Europeans would themselves share. It is an instrumental concept of shared interests in a common space rather than any community of values. For instance, Russia insists that Europe is wider than the European Union, and that the European Union has no monopoly over the definition of what is European. However, Russia continues to demarcate itself from the United States: it is never explicitly 'Western' and, as noted above, 'the West' is often identified as a threat.

Moreover, Russia under Putin has become more assertive about its own value system. In effect, Russia pursues an autonomous path governed by a melding of democratic and native traditions, which involves an instrumental acceptance of some democratic institutions without accepting the liberalism that underpins them (see Putin 2000: 214). This philosophy is behind the Russian elite's assertion that it is building a 'managed' or 'sovereign' democracy.[6] To the degree that Russia ascribes to European values at all, it is arguably a modern Europe of Westphalian sovereignty and national interests, rather than the post-modern liberal universalism espoused by the European Union. Nevertheless, this 'European-ness' is more than just skin-deep. For all Russia's modern political history it has defined itself in reaction to Europe, but not completely apart from it. Despite Russia's increasing military and economic cooperation with Central Asia and China, the concept of Asia does not exert the cultural influence that Europe does (Ronin 2001). Indeed, although Russia gravitates towards China when it seeks to score points against the West, and the arms and energy trade cements an increasing bilateral relationship, public opinion and key figures such as Defence Minister Sergei Ivanov (allegedly) regard Chinese growth with suspicion.

To what degree does the United States–Europe–Russia triangle rely on common strategic assumptions? The main problems are increasingly posed as a so-called 'values gap' reportedly separating an increasingly nationalistic-authoritarian Russia from the West.[7] This view may be overstated, but only slightly. True enough, values and interests cannot be so clinically delineated. Indeed, the NSS asserts that it reflects 'the union of our values and our national interests'. Nevertheless, there is little in the way of a strategic partnership – Russian and Western interests and values simply do not coincide enough. At times, Russia appears to share a worldview far closer to the United States than the European Union, ostensibly agreeing with Robert Kagan (2002) that the US and EU security agendas are as far apart as Mars and Venus. Certainly the United States under the George W. Bush administration has adopted a more hard-nosed realist foreign policy with a conservative-nationalist assertion of state power and national interests, focusing on hard security matters, involving the exercise of military power, a retreat from arms control and a 'war on terrorism'. This is a comprehensible worldview to the Russian security elite, who also share a realist preoccupation with military threats and state sovereignty. Most expressed a clear preference for a Bush win in the 2004 US presidential election, fearing that John Kerry might re-activate the liberal interventionism of the early 1990s.

However, as Dannreuther (2004: 16) notes, Kagan's polemics involve 'a mix of insights and questionable generalisations', underplaying both the United States' liberal traditions and Europe's military-security pretensions. In turn, these commonalities in the EU and US security visions still ensure shared values, whilst Russia's refusal to accept these commonalities has unquestioningly made it an often uncomfortable interlocutor. The Russian approach underestimates the importance of liberalism to the United States agenda. The NSS certainly prioritises common security interests relative to the ESS, but these shared interests are also seen as contingent upon agreement over liberal values ('freedom'). Most US thinkers would deny Russia's claim that its 'democracy' is somehow exempt from globally understood democratic norms. As the departing US Ambassador to Moscow Alexander Vershbow pointedly said in summer 2005: 'I do not like it when "democracy" is used with adjectives.'[8]

Given their physical proximity, the EU–Russia cooperation agenda is potentially far broader. Nevertheless, the European Union's worldview poses more problems for Russia than does that of the United States. The more post-modern and liberal internationalist European security agenda, focused on soft security issues addressed through multilateral and multilevel governance, and with a strong integrationist slant, makes the European Union a problematic and complex partner for Russia, especially given that they are very different actors – Russia a 'state strongly defensive about its sovereignty and territoriality' and the European Union 'an association where sovereignty is pooled and territoriality diluted' (Lynch 2004: 112).

Overall, shared assumptions over the desirability of Russia's democratic transformation mean that US and EU security policies towards Russia hardly come from different planets. Rather, it is the Russian approach to security that increasingly reflects a different worldview. On paper, the US approach to Russia is more realistic in its assessment of the possibilities for and limits to joint cooperation. The EU approach, in contrast, fundamentally overestimates the normative bases for long-term partnership. However, neither approach appears able to deal with a resurgent state that operates according to short-term national interest, adopts integration only selectively, and, like China (as Alyson Bailes notes in the following chapter), is adept at 'cherry-picking' from the transatlantic security agenda those issues which best serve its own interests, speaking the same language, but imbuing it with very different meanings.

For example, the NSS was positively received in Russia for its prioritisation of the war on terrorism and its emphasis on unilateral pre-emption (Wilhelmsen and Flikke 2005). It is likely that when new versions of Russia's 2000 concepts do appear, they will make both elements central to Russian security strategy to serve the purposes of operations in Chechnya, a campaign which itself originally looked to NATO's 1999 intervention in

Kosovo for justification. Indeed, the 2003 Military Modernisation Strategy had already stipulated Russia's right to launch pre-emptive military strikes against military threats within its borders and to destroy terrorist bases anywhere in the world (Hansen 2004). While insisting on its European-ness, Russia seeks to redefine it, rejecting EU conditionality as a unilateral infringement on sovereignty, and has watered down the mention of shared values in EU–Russia agreements (Schuette 2004). Russia's 1999 Strategy on the European Union notably insists on Russian sovereignty as the basis of mutual relations, while denying the need to join the European Union.[9] However, Russian strategy is only imperfectly Machiavellian: attempts to redefine 'Europe' underestimate the strength of the European Union's self-image as the custodian of European values, and so are never likely to succeed.

In sum, this absence of basic shared understandings in the United States–Europe–Russia triangle makes the emergence of a long-term strategic partnership deeply problematic. In essence, the transatlantic partnership has consistently misread Russia, while Russia misreads the West. As we turn to focus on how the relationship has evolved in practice, these points become abundantly clear.

A problematic 'partnership' in practice

The 'war on terror'

Dealing with the terrorist threat is ostensibly one of the most visibly successful strands of Russia–West relations, but the practical achievements have been meagre, with frictions never far from the surface. 9/11 allowed Putin to link the domestic conflict in Chechnya with the wider war on terrorism, and the United States has publicly never seriously questioned this link, gratefully accepting Russian support and downplaying public criticism of human rights abuses, while broadly accepting Putin's repeated assertions that Russian sovereignty precludes international meddling in Chechnya, and that the interests of regional stability take precedence over individual rights. Human rights activists have, with some justification, asserted that this has given Russia a free hand in Chechnya, with little Washington reaction to long-running problems, such as the increasingly blatant distortions of the democratic process at successive 'elections' of the pro-Moscow authorities, and credible reports of their systematised violence. Washington has been supportive of the official Moscow line at key junctures, such as the Dubrovka Theatre siege in November 2002, or the assassination by Russian security forces of the rebel Chechen leader Aslan Maskhadov in 2005. Nevertheless, disquiet has grown markedly. US academic and journalistic opinion has been far more sceptical about whether Russia's ends in Chechnya justify the means, or will indeed exacerbate regional instability. Although Russia has remained a US partner in the war on terror, its perceived democratic backsliding has made its contribution ever more counter-productive (Mendelson 2004).

The European Union has been much more reluctant than either the United States or Russia to see combating terrorism as a 'war' for which military means are appropriate or desirable, and during which civil liberties may play second fiddle, despite sympathy for the problems confronting the Russian state. Nor has the European Union really accepted Putin's claim that the Chechen problem is part of the wider problem of international terrorism. This position is consistent with the ESS, which (in contrast to the NSS) notes that terrorism has domestic roots as 'part of our own society'. While Russia shares some European concerns about US unilateral responses to terrorism, continued strong criticism of Russia's operation in Chechnya from the European Commission, European Parliament and Council of Europe remain a running sore in mutual perceptions. However, the Commission's attempts to come up with a common critical position on Chechnya have repeatedly been thwarted by key member states (including Germany, France, Italy and the United Kingdom) breaking ranks. The EU position is not helped by the insensitivity of spokespersons such as Dutch Foreign Minister Bernard Bot (speaking for the Dutch EU presidency), who demanded, during the September 2004 Beslan events, that the Russian authorities provide an explanation for them, provoking a furious Russian response. Certainly, one might contrast Russia's sympathetic response to 9/11 with the Europeans' standoffish response to a terrorist atrocity of potentially similar psychological impact.

Moscow's accusations of Western 'double standards' have been far more difficult to avoid since the war in Iraq. Russia consistently opposed the war, and was happy to side with 'old Europe' in insisting on the continuation of the UN inspections regime and acting as a champion of international law. However, Moscow preserved cordial relations with the United States by signalling its intent far in advance, and by adopting a less confrontational approach than either France or Germany. In the longer run, however, the war has certainly helped to strengthen Russia's moral claim in Chechnya – abuse of prisoners, reliance on local warlords, and elections of less than spotless legitimacy are now reported in Baghdad as often as in Grozny, and criticism of Russian conduct as somehow an exception from the general conduct of a 'just' war has been far harder to maintain.

Nevertheless, Russian domestic conduct is a significant factor in the worsening of Russia–West relations. Putin's consolidation of power has been accompanied by increasing centralisation of the political system and by the 'securitisation' of domestic and foreign policy. According to Buzan *et al.*, securitisation occurs when issues are presented 'as an existential threat, requiring emergency measures and justifying actions outside the normal bounds of political procedure' (Buzan *et al.* 1998: 22). In Russia, this process is partly a direct response to specific security threats (in particular those posed by the Chechen war), but is accentuated by the Soviet tradition of securitising everyday issues, and the increasing electoral success of 'patriotic' or overtly nationalist forces (such as the pro-presidential 'United Russia' and 'Motherland' blocs in 2003 (see Bacon *et al.* forthcoming)). The administration has promoted a securitising discourse that has continually sought to restrict social and political (particularly media) freedoms, ostensibly in the name of state security but arguably also to increase state power.

Symptomatically, although many Western observers sympathised with Russia's predicament over Beslan, Moscow's response was less comprehensible. In addition to a host of more minor security measures, Putin announced the wholesale replacement of gubernatorial elections with an appointment system. Even if one avoided criticising this for its anti-democratic potential (and many saw it as a decisive lurch towards authoritarianism) and focused on its security rationale, it was hard to believe it would not compound the problems of an already over-centralised, paranoid and out-of-touch administration (Petrov 2004). Official reaction to Beslan from Putin and the deputy head of the presidential administration Vladislav Surkov betrayed remarkable continuities with Soviet conspiratorial thinking, by implying that outside forces sponsored international terrorism in the interests of keeping Russia weak, and by equating liberals with fascists, and terrorists as existential challengers to the Russian state (Lynch 2005).[10] Whilst Beslan clearly provoked a heated emotional response, anti-Westernism became an integral part of the Putin administration's domestic legitimacy, despite its pragmatic international face, further hindering the promotion of a coherent strategy.

Global security versus global democracy

The 'balance of power that favours freedom', as heralded in the NSS, has been more problematic in practice than theory. Whilst West–Russian relations are no longer dogged by the most intractable issues of the immediate post-Cold War era, Russia's position in the international system is still controversial.

On the face of it, international harmony is institutionalised. Putin dropped Russian opposition to NATO expansion, the leitmotif of Russian foreign policy in the 1990s, for three main reasons. First, unlike Yeltsin, he saw little reason in wasting effort on opposing a fait accompli even to score domestic points. Second, the NATO–Russia Council increasingly gave Russia a voice at the NATO table, even if not a veto. Third, NATO's lack of any pivotal role in the war against terror showed that Russia's former fears about NATO becoming a global threat were exaggerated.[11] Another success for Putin's multivector approach was Russia's full acceptance into the G-8 in 2002 after years of quasi-membership.

However, Russia's domestic de-democratisation caused deep dissatisfaction in the United States with Bush's tactics and strategy towards Russia. The perception was that the relationship had 'drifted', with little substantive engagement beyond the personal chemistry of the incumbent presidents (Kuchins *et al.* 2005). US policymakers' views were deeply divided. Some downplayed Russia's domestic changes and proffered a more active interest-based engagement.[12] The dominant view sees Russia as increasingly dictatorial and 'breaking away from the core democratic values of the Euro-Atlantic community'.[13] The West should unite to prevent further democratic backsliding by engagement and encouragement, or even by punishing Russia with trade sanctions or expulsion from the G-8.[14] The OSCE's uncharacteristically strong criticism of Russian elections in 2003–4, and Freedom House's downgrade of Russia to 'not free' status in December 2004, provided grist to the mill of such views. Condoleezza Rice's appointment as Secretary of State saw a limited return to a more critical democratisation agenda, but Bush's public stance was noticeably softer.

The human rights dimension has further complicated Russia's relations with the European Union. Prior to Putin, the European Union had largely been ignored as a significant foreign policy actor. It was seen as predominately an economic bloc, whilst most attention was devoted to bilateral relations with the United States and NATO. However, Russia's foreign policy concept of 2000 mentioned the European Union as a main partner for the first time, and Putin devoted increasing attention to the European Union's growing foreign policy aspirations. But Russia's overall dim view of the European Union's external political muscle has been reinforced by its own experience: whenever the Commission or Parliament upbraided its human rights situation, some European state would invariably break ranks, prioritising their geo-political interests over a common position. However, whenever Russia has confronted a more united European Union, it has encountered a far less agreeable negotiating partner, for instance over Kaliningrad, where the European Union successfully insisted on a visa regime (in all but name) for Russian citizens crossing EU territory.

Without doubt, EU enlargement has increased the potential for conflict with Russia, as the EU rhetoric of 'common spaces' and 'neighbourhoods' in an area that Russia long defined as an area of its *own* special interest makes clear. An additional problem is the political contribution of 'new Europe'. States such as Estonia and the Czech Republic naturally bring a US-centric and Russo-phobic history to bear on EU discourse, whilst larger new members like Poland have aspirations to become regionally significant players. Disputes between the Baltic states and Moscow over Russia's wartime role, and demands for 'repentance' for Stalinism during the 60th anniversary of the World War II victory celebration in May 2005, indicated that enlargement had given the European Union's normative arguments an additional dimension.

Both occupants of the 'new neighbourhood' can be accused of pursuing competition in the region. Russia, and indeed some of the other former Soviet states of Eastern Europe, view the European Union as more interested in creating a zone of stability on its borders and exporting its norms than in giving its neighbours any real share in how the European Union itself is run. While Russia has always sought to be a regional hegemon in the NIS, greater EU activism has prompted a more assertive, zero-sum approach. Russian policymakers increasingly see the European Union as 'just a new kind of empire': one that aims to isolate Russia and drive it from its sphere of interests.[15] There is some substance to this view: Russia lacks the 'soft power' that proves so attractive to potential future candidates such as Moldova and Ukraine, and it is difficult to see how rapprochement with the European Union can co-exist with membership in the Russian-dominated Commonwealth of Independent States (CIS) and its affiliated structures. It was partly the fear that Ukraine under Viktor Yushchenko would secede from the projected Common Economic Space (the free trade area incorporating Russia, Ukraine, Kazakhstan and Belarus, proposed in 2004) that drove Moscow to intervene so heavily in favour of his rival for the Ukrainian presidency, Viktor Yanukovych, in November 2004. Whilst the portrayals of the resulting 'Orange revolution' as a bipolar East–West dictatorship–democracy conflict were clearly overplayed, in a real sense Ukraine's long-term geo-political direction was at stake.

A year later, the long-term effects of the Orange revolution were unclear. On the one hand, there was evidence of greater realism: European Union–Russia summits in 2005 went out of their way to suggest 'business as usual', while Moscow insisted that it intended 'normal relations' with neighbouring republics. On the other hand, such statements need parsing – 'normal' in such a context most likely means raising energy prices to world market levels, threatening disloyal neighbouring states like Ukraine in the process, and imposing tougher visa regimes on other EU-leaning states like Moldova and Georgia. There were several signs of a more interventionist policy emerging. In 2005, Kremlin spin doctor Gleb Pavlovsky led several voices proposing a radical change of policy towards the CIS, aiming to foster pro-Russian forces (including civil society and opposition forces) as a mirror image of US-backed democratisation efforts. Domestically, the Putin administration took measures (such as restrictions on foreign-funded non-governmental organisations in November 2005) which were designed to combat the 'orange threat' (symptomatically viewed as a product of US–EU foreign policy rather than the democratic wish of NIS populations), which simultaneously threatened to extinguish Russian civil society altogether. Such divisions should not be overplayed. If Peterson and Dannreuther are right (see Chapter 1) that the European Union and the United States are now revolutionary powers, Russia is a status-quo power, not neo-imperialistic but post-imperialistic, beating a grudging retreat and without (at least yet) a post-imperial model for dealing with its neighbours. Moreover, EU paroxysms over its Constitutional Treaty and budget, and domestic problems in Ukraine, mean that the European Union's external power projection will be limited for the medium term. Nevertheless, the utterly divergent conceptualisations in the West and Russia of the 'coloured revolutions' and issues like Belarus bode extremely poorly for future harmony.

Military and nuclear cooperation

One area where United States–Russian dialogue is still (relatively) active is in the military security sphere. This is despite a poor start. Bush's unilateral withdrawal from the Anti-Ballistic Missile Treaty and missile defence proposals threatened the Gorbachev–Reagan legacy of incremental arms dialogue, and in theory threatened to produce further nuclear proliferation (by making the United States invulnerable to attack and fuelling further defensive nuclear build-ups by states including China). However, the 2002 Russo-American Strategic Offensive Reductions Treaty (SORT) allowed Russia and the United States to manage the arms reduction on their own terms and timetables, despite its lack of legal guarantees and verification mechanisms.

Globally, Russia has a shared interest with the United States in avoiding proliferation, and it has proved an active player in the six-party talks to neuter North Korea's missile programme. However, it has often undermined these interests with short-termist actions. The European Union and the United States have long been irritated by arms sales to Syria, and Russia's help in constructing the Iranian nuclear re-processing plant at Bushehr has been a source of particularly deep concern. Russia has belatedly grown concerned itself, and joined the European Union and the United States in pushing Iran towards inspections by the International Atomic Energy Authority (IAEA). Bush's invocation of the 'axis of evil' in 2002 made Russia's previous conduct much more suspect: certainly CIA reports of Russia's involvement in Iraq's oil-for-food scheme revealed that a concern for international law was probably not the only motive for Russia's caution about toppling Saddam Hussein.

Russia's military dialogue with the European Union is far weaker, however, with discussions, for example over initiatives such as European missile defence, proceeding at glacial pace. Although Russia initially welcomed the European Security and Defence Policy (ESDP) for its potential to increase bilateral EU–Russia security ties and act as a bridge to NATO, Moscow has become much more sceptical of its effectiveness (Lynch 2003). Most hard security discussion (such as constraining shipments of WMD) has (ironically) occurred with NATO, with the European Union barely involved. Among the chief reasons are that Russia prefers counter-terrorist dialogue with the United States and does not see the European Union as serious about terrorism. Once more, fundamentally different values are at fault: the European Union prefers soft-security dialogue and long-term preventive solutions, while Russia tends to see soft security as an issue for richer countries, with its response focused on shorter-term militarised solutions. Despite small steps (for example in human rights dialogue), cooperation over the main soft security threats (such as AIDS) has been minimal (Monaghan 2005).

Indeed, in several aspects Russian–EU cooperation has worsened, with Moscow's view of joint activities in crisis management and peacekeeping increasingly distrustful (particularly as expressed through the OSCE). Prior to Putin, Russia had generally welcomed the OSCE as a multilateral security forum where US influence could be diluted and the Russian voice amplified. However, particularly since Russia fell foul of the OSCE's electoral benchmarks in December 2003, it has become increasingly critical of the OSCE's democratisation agenda, suggesting it return solely to a security focus. This has coincided with Russian threats to the OSCE budget that have effectively paralysed the organisation (Donovan 2005).

Economic constraints

'Economisation' has been key in Russia's foreign policy. This has two elements: the reassertion of the administration's control over the 'commanding heights' of the energy industry such as Gazprom and Yukos, and the potential for these industries to play a greater role in Russia's leverage on its neighbours and indeed the European Union. The Union now relies heavily on Russian energy imports, as the Russian cut-off of supplies to Ukraine over its bilateral dispute in early 2006 demonstrated. The other prong of Russia's 'economisation' strategy is the emphasis on economic modernisation. Russia is keenly aware that 'great power status' is impossible with an economy smaller than Portugal's, and that its membership in global economic clubs is a key to this.

This economic concern remains (as it was throughout the 1990s) an important constraint on Russia's potential anti-Westernism, since alliances with China, still less with states like Belarus, simply do not give the economic dividends that accrue from access to Western markets. The Russian elite recognises that without integration in the global economy and foreign capital 'our country's road back to recovery will be long and hard' (Putin 2000: 217). Economic need still drives cooperation with the European Union, as does the fear that Russia will be excluded by the emergence of new trading barriers at the Schengen border. Nevertheless, the imprisonment of Mikhail Khodorkovskii showed clear ambiguities in trying to play by global market rules whilst promoting increasingly unfree domestic economic and political policies; it is not clear whether the damage to Russia's international image and foreign investment was offset by the benefit accrued from making an example of Russia's chief tycoon. WTO entry would improve Russia's economic image, but negotiations over entry remain tortuous, with the lack of liberalisation of energy, banking and services all issues for the West, and key industrial and farming sectors within Russia very wary of what WTO membership might mean for them.

Conclusion

Does the transatlantic alliance even have a strategy towards Russia? One could easily conclude that it does not. Despite their different emphases, both the NSS and the ESS reveal some common assumptions, including Russia's importance as a strategic partner and its convergence towards liberal values. But both of these grounding assumptions appear misplaced. Russia is simply not converging towards 'Western' interests or values, and so to base policy towards it on that assumption will involve a near-permanent misreading of Russia's intentions that is no basis for productive engagement.

Why do the NSS and the ESS get Russia so wrong? Clearly the idealism present in both security doctrines, but expounded in most depth in the European Union's strategy towards Russia, is integral to a view of the world influenced very much by liberal internationalism and ideas of the democratic peace. Both strategies are clearly still legacies of the doctrine of democratisation, which dominated discourse towards Russia until the millennium, and in 2002–3 had not yet been seriously shaken by events in Iraq. But it is also true, and our brief overview of the conduct of mutual relations bears this out, that EU and US policies towards Russia suffer from an acute lack of coordination, which Russia only too readily exploits.

Again, the security strategies are perhaps children of their time, when US–EU relations were at a nadir, and the European Union's foreign policy vision was vitiated by the conduct of its constituent states. Relations with Russia were not a priority for a United States dealing with 9/11 and a European Union coping with deepening as well as widening; nor were relations with the West the focus for a Russia concentrating on internal consolidation and the Chechen conflict. All of the three actors were largely focusing on domestic concerns, and none really needed each other. But it is also true that, perhaps following the tradition of Communist double-speak, Russia, like China, is adept at quoting back to the West what it wants to hear when it wants to hear it, and cloaking its national interests behind an ostensibly common discourse ('terrorism', 'sovereignty', 'democracy' and so on), which in fact has a nationally specific subtext. Putin's strategy has involved defusing a host of significant West/Russia tensions, including over NATO enlargement, intervention in Kosovo, and Afghanistan (where US support for Pakistan and Saudi Arabia undermined regional cooperation over the Taliban and the Islamist threat). However, Russia's ostensibly pro-Western foreign policy has been accompanied by an increasing reversal of domestic democratisation. The relative optimism of both the NSS and the ESS towards Russia reflects the former improvements but fails to engage with the latter deterioration.

It is easy to paint Russia as a reactionary, neo-Soviet or anti-Western power. But Russia has certainly not renounced its policy of integration with the West. Rather, it is pursuing a policy of selective engagement that aims to consolidate Russia's domestic sovereignty as a prelude to the resumption of great power status. This involves engaging with the European Union over issues of regional borders and trade, and with the United States over global security problems. Economic weakness will limit Russia's ability to do anything else – although Russia fears the West, it fears isolation from the West still more, and certainly the idea of 'Russia on the periphery of an ever more powerful Europe' (Lynch 2004: 101). Whilst domestic liberalisation, as Putin openly declares, is no longer a near-term Russian priority, it would be unwise to write off its democratic potential altogether. Generational turn-over and economic development might begin to coax a political culture, which currently often appears both to emulate and hate the West simultaneously, towards the former tendency.

It is also far easier to criticise Western policy towards Russia than it is to identify concrete solutions, which, as Derek Averre (2005: 25) remarks, will require from the West a 'high-wire act of some delicacy' between a more realist interest-based, and more liberal idealist approach. To choose one rather than another might make sense conceptually, but would in practice be very problematic. A purely realist approach that would concede that Russian state sovereignty prevails over human rights concerns at least proceeds from more sober assumptions of limited partnership. However, it risks giving Russia a free hand in its self-declared sphere of interest, which involves con-doning a creeping authoritarianism that is increasingly unpalatable to Western audiences and, as in Chechnya and Uzbekistan, is threatening the very regional security that it claims to secure. A more activist liberalism risks (as in the 1990s) being seen as patronising: it treats Russia as an object of Western democratisation rather than an equal partner, and raises expecta-tions which Russia is unable to fulfil, thereby potentially provoking a coun-ter-productive negative reaction within Russia. The United States and the European Union are beginning to grapple with this unenviable choice, but until the nature of the choice is seriously explored in both the United States and the European Union's official security discourse, it is hard to see how realistic strategies will emerge to deal with what is an increasing Russia 'problem'. Nor, without greater coordination over practical action between the United States and the European Union, and before that within the European Union itself, is any common 'solution' likely to be effective.

Notes

1 See European Council, 'The EU Common Strategy on Russia', 4 June 1999, Brussels. Online. Available: www.delrus.cec.eu.int/en/p_244.htm (accessed 8 December 2005).

2 The relevant documents are European Commission, 'EU/Russia: the Four "Common Spaces"', DG External Relations, Memo 103 (18 March 2005), Brussels. Online. Available: http://europa.eu.int/comm/external_relations/russia/intro/memo05_103.htm (accessed 5 December 2005); European Commission, 'Final Road Maps', DG External Relations, 2005, Brussels. Online. Available: http://europa.eu.int/comm/external_relations/russia/intro/index.htm#comm

(accessed 12 December 2005); European Commission, 'Russia: Country Strategy Paper 2002–2006' and 'National Indicative Programme 2002–2003', DG External Relations, Brussels. Online. Available: http://europa.eu.int/comm/external_relations/russia/csp/index.htm (accessed 12 December 2005).

3 The other common spaces are the 'Common Economic Space', the 'Common Space of External Security' and the 'Common Space on Research, Education and Culture'.

4 *Kontseptsiya natsional'noi bezopasnosti Rossiiskoi Federatsii* (*Concept of National Security of the Russian Federation*, hereafter NSC) at http://www.scrf.gov.ru/documents/decree/2000_24_1.shtml; *Kontseptsiya vneshnei politiki Rossiiskoi Federatsii* (*Foreign Policy Concept of the Russian Federation*) at http://www.scrf.gov.ru/documents/decree/2000_x.shtml; *Voennaya doktrina Rossiiskoi Federatsii* (*Military Doctrine of the Russian Federation*) at http://www.scrf.gov.ru/documents/decree/2000_706_1.shtml (all accessed 12 December 2005).

5 See the Russian Foreign Minister, Sergei Lavrov, quoted by Federal News Service, Moscow, 19 January. Online. Available: http://www.fednews.ru/ (accessed 6 December 2005).

6 See V. Frolov, 'Surkov's Sovereign Democracy', *Russia Profile*, 5 August 2005. Online. Available: http://www.russiaprofile.org (accessed 5 December 2005).

7 See, for example, E. Verlin, *Nezavisimaya gazeta*, 15 January 2004, p. 2.

8 Alexander Vershbow, 'Demokratiya ne nuzhdaetsya v prilagatel'nykh' ('Democracy does not need adjectives'), *Novaya Gazeta*, no. 52, 21 July 2005. Online. Available: www.novayagazeta.ru (accessed 6 December 2005).

9 *Russia's Middle-Term Strategy towards the EU (2000–2010)*. Online. Available: http://www.delrus.cec.eu.int/en/p_245.htm (accessed 6 December 2005).

10 See also V. Surkov, *Komsomolskaya pravda*, 29 September 2004, p. 4.

11 See N. Poroskov, 'Looking for the Enemy', *Russia Profile*, 14 July 2005. Online. Available: http://www.russiaprofile.org (accessed 6 December 2005).

12 'An Open Letter to the President of the United States of America George W. Bush and the President of the Russian Federation Vladimir V. Putin', in *Johnson's Russia List* 9060, 14 February 2005. Online. Available: http://www.cdi.org/russia/johnson/9060-3.cfm (accessed 5 December 2005).

13 'An Open Letter to the Heads of State and Government of the European Union and NATO', 28 September 2004. Online. Available: http://www.freedomhouse.org/pdf_docs/russiastatement.pdf (accessed 5 December 2005).

14 See the range of views reported in S. Dinan and J. Sparshot, 'Senators Seek to Sanction Russia', *Washington Times*, 15 February 2005. Online. Available: http://www.washingtontimes.com (accessed 5 December 2005).

15 Fyodor Lukyanov quoted in 'Taking on the Bear: Russia's Awkward Position in Europe's Jigsaw', *The Economist*, 7–13 May 2005.

8   China and security strategy

Alyson J. K. Bailes

After December 2003, one of the traditional American complaints about the European Union had to be considered time-expired: that it 'does not have a strategy'. The adoption of the Union's new security strategy, however, still left open the way for Americans – or others – to accuse Europeans of lacking a strategy on, or having an insufficiently strategic grasp of, more specific external policy issues. In 2004–5 the most frequent such aspersion related to the People's Republic of China.

Officials and analysts alike in the United States reacted, in particular, to the European Union's declared plans to lift a European arms embargo on China (imposed at the time of the Tiananmen Square massacre in 1989) with three specific charges. First, the Europeans were only interested in profit from the China trade – including but not limited to defence sales. Second, they underestimated the threat of China's growing military strength. Third, Europeans underestimated the risk of China using force to make good its claims against Taiwan – a risk that many had seen as heightened by Beijing's adoption of a new 'Anti-Secession Law' in March 2005.[1]

Some European commentators echoed the criticism,[2] adding that the European Union was sending a false normative signal by rescinding a measure imposed on human rights grounds when China's record in the latter field was still so poor. Official Europe's defence of its own case in response was somewhat vitiated by the tendency of different states to tell different stories. Several argued that the embargo would be replaced by a more modern, strict and universal arms transfer constraint in the shape of a re-modelled EU Code of Conduct (originally adopted in 1998; see Bauer and Bromley 2004). Others said that lifting the embargo would make little difference, not just because the measure itself had been so vague but because China's real interest in state-of-the art European weapons was as limited as Europe's willingness to supply them. (EU leaders had anyway agreed at the December 2004 European Council that lifting the embargo should not result in 'an increase of arms exports from EU Member States to China, neither in quantitative or in qualitative terms'.) Others again met the US argument head-on: Europe had no cause to treat China as a strategic adversary and could best reduce any general threat it posed by cooperative engagement. At the same time, some EU members who had been lukewarm on raising the embargo got even colder feet in the face of the American vocal displeasure – which extended even to threats, in Congress, of retaliatory sanctions against US–European arms collaboration.[3] Such internal wavering, plus the US campaign, and similar complaints received from Japan, were enough to push EU implementation of the proposed measure onto the back burner, where it remains as of the time of writing (early 2006).

On the face of it, this episode was tailor-made to prove the US case. EU states had no concerted policy rationale to offer for their actions, let alone a joint 'selling strategy' that would have identified and tackled US (and Japanese) worries in advance. The arguments they did provide publicly were inconsistent, suggesting either the denial of strategic realities or a perverse – from the US viewpoint – reading of them. Behind such a wispy smokescreen, it was only too easy to see crude profit motives lurking. Yet some features of the story fit less comfortably with the verdict of a total European 'train-wreck'[4] on this topic. Why did the United Kingdom, so loyal to the United States on other divisive security issues in 2003–5, and certainly no strategic novice in Asia, argue so strongly at first – to the US audience as well – for shifting to the universal instrument of a Code of Conduct? Why did the United States itself export as much as $31 million worth of defence supplies to China in 1999 compared with EU supplies totalling $39 million that year?[5] Was the United States' own strategic community any more united in its take on China and did the Americans have a strategy that actually *worked* better in these first years of the twenty-first century?

As 'Yugoslavia' was once an abstracted crux in Sino-Soviet ideological disputes of the communist days, 'China' may be taking on a referential value in US–European strategy debates after Iraq. This use of China as shorthand stands apart from, and sometimes clashes with, the realities of how each side engages in practice with this massive partner. Although scant justice can be done here to the manifold levels of the issue, the discussion that follows will try to slice it in several different ways: theory and practice, regional and global perspectives, substance and style.

The focus will be on EU–China relations – since this is currently the most controversial and probably the least researched leg of the triangle – but with frequent comparative references to the US–China case. We begin with the European Union's 2003 Security Strategy (ESS) and the US National Security Strategy (NSS) of 2002 as starting-points for asking how fully, and credibly, Europe's strategy is articulated at the level of concept and high policy. Then the real-life factors will be reviewed that seem to shape EU and US handling, respectively, of China in itself and in its region and in the world. Finally, the European Union's current engagement with China will be examined from three viewpoints. First, the thesis that the European Union has a strategically challenged, 'it's the economy, stupid' approach. Second, the possibility that EU strategy is informed by security considerations, but different ones from the American strategy. Third, that problems of style and process apply to the European Union's external action more widely than the case of China alone. The tentative conclusion may already be revealed: that any EU 'strategy' is at best an inchoate, non-joined-up one, but that this partly reflects the West's (or the Northern Hemisphere's) general failure to get to grips with the phenomenon of *strong* developing states.

Contrasting strategies: handling emergent powers

The word 'China' appears twice in the text of the European Union's December 2003 security strategy.[6] The section 'An international order based on effective multilateralism' makes approving reference to China having joined the WTO. Then in the penultimate section under the sub-heading 'Working with partners', after separate paragraphs explaining the importance of the United States and Russia respectively, the following statement is made: 'In particular we should look to develop strategic partnerships with Japan, China, Canada and India as well as with all those who share our goals and values, and are prepared to act in their support.'

The expression 'strategic partnership' is applied in the ESS only to the four nations mentioned here, plus Russia. If we assume that Canada was mentioned out of courtesy (because it was not covered elsewhere), the adjective 'strategic' coupled with the rest of the quoted sentence implies that Europe is placing these remarkably heterogeneous 'partners' in a special class because of their power and regional importance, including in two cases their permanent UN Security Council membership, even if they do not (all) share the same 'goals and values'.

So far, so logical. But what is missing is an explanation of what the proposed strategic partnerships are *for*. In the case of Russia, the strategy's section on 'Building security in our own neighbourhood' explains that transnational threats like terrorism or pollution cannot be controlled in the wider European space without Russian involvement, and Russia has a role to play (at least, through benign restraint) in the Balkans and Middle East. But there is no corresponding discussion of the specific geo-politics and threat profile of the East Asian region, other than repeated mentions of North Korea as a proliferation issue. The strategy's whole security vocabulary outside the direct European neighbourhood zone is, in fact, generic. Threats come from the instability of weak states, conflict phenomena, bad governance, terrorism, proliferation and so on. The remedies are efficient multilateral rule-making bodies and improvement of governance, trade and development. The reader confined to this single document could only conclude that China is of interest to the European Union as a potential partner for applying these remedies to these threats, and – by inference – for conflict prevention in relation to North Korea. But just the same may be inferred from the text about Japan. No hint is given that China itself might be part of the problem, or that China and Japan are not a simple and happy dyad. If this starts to look like a 'strategy-free strategy', it should be noted that it reflects a larger area of omission or suppression in the entire document. The EU strategy never uses the words 'enemy', 'adversary' or 'opponent'. The only classes of problem states it recognises are: (a) 'weak' ones plagued by conflict; and (b) 'countries ... outside the bounds of international society' (whom the European Union offers to embrace should they repent). There is no place left for *functional* states *within* international society that offer some kind of security or strategic challenge – possibly because the drafters were bending over backwards to avoid placing the United States in that light?

For comparison, the US National Security Strategy (NSS) has five separate references to China. The last of them has six paragraphs exclusively on this subject, and strikes a generally positive note: 'We welcome the emergence of a strong, peaceful and prosperous China ... The United States seeks a constructive relationship with a changing China.' It also notes problems to be overcome on the way, including China's democratic shortcomings, human rights, and the US commitment to Taiwan (on which more below). The feature most in contrast to the European Union's treatment is the statement (also echoed in the NSS introduction) that 'In pursuing military capabilities that can threaten its neighbours in the Asia-Pacific region, China is following an outdated path that, in the end, will hamper its own pursuit of national greatness.' This theme of military excess has been regularly underlined by other US policy documents: notably the Pentagon's 2005 annual report which suggested China's military spending that year (including subsidies to industry and science) could total three times its declared defence budget of $29.9 billion (US Department of Defense 2005).

The NSS treatment of China does tend to make the ESS look incomplete at best and strategically naïve at worst – even allowing for the two documents' different lengths. On a second reading, however, questions may emerge about America's own strategic coherence. It takes two to make a strategic competition and it can hardly be denied that in practice the United States treats China as a strategic rival to itself, as well as to (say) Russia, Japan or India. The United States tends to see conflicts of interest with China wherever it looks, in the trade and financial as well as the security and defence fields, and it instinctively frames its strategy in terms of reaction and denial: to prevent China gaining clout as a regional strategic power, let alone 'breaking out' as a global one. Yet to achieve this it offers neither a deal based on reciprocal self-restraint and non-military 'national greatness' on both sides, nor a set of inducements designed, as it were, to 'buy China off'. On the contrary, other parts of the NSS make brutally clear that the United States intends to maintain its present global dominance by military means and will claim freedom to use those means, even in the most novel and controversial ways, to ward off all threats to that ambition. The US military budget in 2004 was $455 billion and independent calculations consider it to be some 13 times larger than China's (Sköns *et al.* 2005).[7]

The United States seeks to contain China specifically with its own military strength in the Asia-Pacific region and by toughening the defence capacities (and doctrines) of other regional players. Expecting China on this basis to forswear its 'military capabilities', to give up the option of force and to rely for its own and its people's future purely upon the influence and appeal of its economic, social and political qualities looks more strategically naïve than any vision in which the Europeans have yet indulged. It is more likely that China will continue to play the old competitive game at least for as long as the United States does and encourages other Asian powers to do so; and a China that rises to global-power status in this fashion will be the nastiest, not the easiest, incarnation of a future China for the world to deal with.

The adversarial 'containment' approach to China has in fact often been challenged by other elements within the US elite. The four first articles in a specially themed edition of *Foreign Affairs* in autumn 2005 were devoted to arguments that the United States could best avoid 'losing China' a second time by adjusting more graciously to its rise. Nor has the latest Bush administration's bite on China been consistently as tough as its bark.[8] As so often, however, the problem is that it is hard to detect a clear European alternative for handling China, or indeed for any other emerging strategic power not circumscribed (as Russia arguably still is) by the Euro-Atlantic region's relative strategic stability. The European Union's approach to such players often only seems explicable by unspoken and unexamined, if not necessarily irrational, habits and assumptions.

Both Europe's own history of peace-making and integration since World War II, and its nations' memories of regional power balance in imperial times, predispose Europeans when they first look at another region to seek out the largest local power and pursue all possible chances of turning it into a partner and a centre of stability. Some of them may hope that such regional leaders combining power with (at least minimal) respectability will contribute to a 'multipolar' world system that imposes – among other things – a certain discipline upon the United States. Many more Europeans would reason more simply that if the largest power in a region is not stable and cooperative, the region as a whole cannot be; and that such a regional system could at best be frozen in an unproductive 'Cold War' state of containment and deterrence, missing out on its due role in globalisation.

Three specific characteristics of the European Union encourage this kind of calculation. First, the European Union finds it easier to engage with other regions that have their own system of working multilateralism. Second, it has a dismal record of helping in more divided and disorganised regions (like the Middle East). Third, the European Union lacks the kind of power to engage in balancing and containing transactions on its own account. Trying to promote stable regional cooperation regimes centred upon the largest player (and to 'school' these players by persuasion and example) is not just a philosophical but a practical dictate for European diplomacy (Gowan 2004).

By contrast, the United States more naturally sees each region's largest player as its foremost rival. It typically reacts by working with the second-largest or smaller players for purposes of containment (and as sites for forward basing). It often dreams of pushing the rival state back to a lower level of power rather than leading it towards a virtuous 'post-Westphalian' form of existence.

Contrasting strategies: engagement in East Asia

The argument can be made more concrete by looking at East Asia more closely. The United States not unreasonably treats China policy also as a function of its other defined commitments and interests in the neighbourhood. These include military basing arrangements and wider strategic alliances with both Japan and South Korea, commitments to Taiwan under the Taiwan Relations Act,[9] a second-echelon US military presence in other parts of the Pacific such as the Philippines, strong ties to Australia for both regional and global security purposes, and – of course – a vision of the People's Democratic Republic of Korea (North Korea) as a possible direct threat to the United States as well as to its neighbours. The United States itself is part of the Asia-Pacific regional system. It is engaged in its dynamic economic (and cultural) interactions but also exposed to all the consequences of the area's ambivalent power balances and persisting security challenges. In the simplest terms, Washington thus has to deal with China as a strategic proposition on at least four levels: China versus the United States' regional allies, China impacting on the United States itself in the regional context, China impacting on the United States through more globally mediated processes (such as trade and finance, proliferation, energy and intellectual property), and China impacting on the whole world system and on how the United States sees its own place in it.

For Europeans, only the last two global levels of strategy really apply. Not only is Europe physically detached from the region, its last colonial possessions and post-colonial defence commitments have dwindled rapidly, the handover of Macau in 1999 being one of the latest staging-points. No European nation has defence commitments in 'front-line' states and territories like Japan, Korea or Taiwan. Remaining formal relationships such as those of the United Kingdom in Southeast Asia (the Five-Power Defence Arrangement) have lost salience with the rise and enlargement of ASEAN (the Association of Southeast Asian Nations). Recent apparent exceptions – the decision of Portugal to send forces for the peace mission in its former territory of East Timor, and EU mediation and peacekeeping in Aceh – actually underline another point: that Asia for Europeans is also a region coloured by the memories of empire and imperial collapse. As everywhere, it is a perspective that tends to make Europeans blame themselves for at least some of the region's scars, and make them think twice about any action there that might look coercive or hegemonic. The deals done over Hong Kong and Macau have given Europeans recent experience of solving acute problems with China by peaceful negotiation, and predispose them to see the ideal solution for Taiwan as one similar in spirit and perhaps even in detail. While relatively unengaged on North Korea, Europeans would also see the solution there more in terms of diplomatic horse-trading and eventual détente, and may perceive positive value in China playing a steering role (and in Beijing–Seoul détente), not least because the ultimate fantasy of German-style Korean reunification could hardly work without Chinese acquiescence.

These are all factors that, aside from mere powerlessness, might steer Europeans away from viewing China as a strategic opponent. But there is at least one more – aside from 'multipolar' thinking – that may subtly support notions of China as a strategic friend. For the latter and larger part of the Cold War after the Sino-Soviet split, China helped to contain from the east the Soviet threat that always loomed over European territory more intimately than over North America. Because of the way in which, notably, it divided Moscow's forces and strategic attention it was often, only part jokingly, referred to in Europe as the '17th member of NATO'. Even in today's profoundly changed setting, the human tendency (first remarked on by the historian Lewis Namier) to see the next-but-one large power as a helpful balance to the next-door·one could be at work subliminally, at least in Europe's more Russo-sceptic minds. The facts show anyway (see next section) that China now weighs more heavily and positively than Russia as a trade, investment and technological partner.

Is it just 'the economy, stupid'?

The thesis of overwhelmingly economic motives in Europe's China strategy rests first on statistics. Since the early 1980s EU trade with China has increased 43 times over, and in 2004 stood at a total of €174.7 billion. That made China Europe's second-largest trade partner after the United States, and the European Union China's single biggest export market (Barysch 2005: 35).[10] (For comparison, Russia is the European Union's fourth-largest export market and third-largest source of imports, and Japan comes fifth and fourth respectively.[11]) The structure of trade also underlines the value of the relationship for European governments. While 'machinery and electronics' accounts for about half the value on each side, Europe has found a fertile market in China for cars (40 per cent of all car sales in China are currently of European brands as against 10 per cent from the United States) and mobile phones, and also for large-scale construction services and retail activities. On the import side, clothing, shoes, leather goods and miscellaneous manufactures together account for over a third of Chinese sales, while they are insignificant in European sales to China (Barysch 2005: 37–9). While competing with European producers, such supplies also promote consumer choice and satisfaction within Europe, an aspect that was politically important not least for Central Europeans in the hard transition from communism (Bailes 1990). This pattern is not, in fact, dissimilar from Europe's interplay with its larger and more sophisticated overseas dominions in the late imperial age, and it helps strengthen the impression that Europe has (relatively speaking) 'hopped over' the former Soviet area to try to develop China as its new-age economic hinterland.

Does this bulky economic tail wave the strategic dog for Europe – especially when contrasted with the United States – or make the Europeans 'soft' on China? This view starts looking simplistic when the relationship is examined more closely. First, Europe is hardly unique in its addiction to the Chinese market. US trade turnover with China in 2002 was $97.2 billion to the European Union's $86.8 and US imports from China grew faster than the European Union's that year. The European Union's stock of direct invest-ment in China amounts to some 7 per cent of the Chinese total ($34 billion at the end of 2002) but the United States' share is higher at 17.5 per cent ($78 billion), and also outstrips those of Japan, Hong Kong and Taiwan.[12] If intra-European Union trade is set aside, in 2002 the European Union received 7.5 per cent of its total foreign imports from China, while the figure in the United States was 11.1 per cent, and for Japan 18.3 per cent (IMF quoted by Barysch 2005: 43). The United States notoriously depends on Chinese (and other Asian) banks and investors for support of the dollar and for sustaining its present huge current-account and domestic budget imbalances, which in turn are one of the ways it achieves a higher growth rate than Europe. There is no comparable macro-economic way in which China could hold Europe to ransom. If the United States, nevertheless, is not commonly portrayed as 'kow-towing' to Beijing for economic reasons, it may be because Washing-ton's style has been rather to put the onus for the problems on China and press Beijing, more or less belligerently, to solve them through changes in its own policies. The more frequently combative American approach has not – to date – been proven to work any better than that of the Europeans.[13] Still less does it guarantee that the United States will cope better than Europe with the longer-term hazards that China-dependence brings for its welfare and influence.

Second, the European Union and individual European states cannot be happy about the China trade as long as it remains as sharply unbalanced as it has been since the 1980s. Consider €126.7 billion in imports from China in 2004 against only €48 billion in EU exports (Barysch 2005: 35). Europe well knows, moreover, that this imbalance is not just about competitiveness and popular demand but is artificially boosted by China's own policies and actions. Despite supporting China's WTO entry, the European Union has long held out against re-classifying China from a 'transition economy' to 'market economic status' – which would allow China to share more fully in the benefits of WTO membership – and only agreed during the EU–China summit of September 2005 to offer a 'road-map' on how much China must still do to earn the title. Precisely because of European Union firms' close engagement, Brussels is all too well aware of the broad problem of con-tinuing state control and manipulation in the Chinese economy, as well as specific abuses such as disregard for intellectual property, obstacles to the free import of services, inadequate company law and investment protection, judicial partiality and abusive resort to red tape.

The European Union has tried to use its economic leverage, and its vote in world forums where China is a *demandeur*, to apply pressure on all these points. It has launched more anti-dumping actions against China than against any other partner (34 up to the time of writing; see Barysch 2005: 42). Since the turn of the twenty-first century it has become more alert to the general threat of Chinese competition with its own producers, as a function of advancing (global) trade liberalisation; improvement of Chinese producers' range and quality; the particular interests of new Central European members whose industries are more directly competing with China's; and general worries about low growth and sluggish employment in the eurozone. The so-called 'bra wars' crisis over a surge of Chinese textile exports in 2005 was, thus, less of an isolated unpleasantness than a straw in the wind. The domestic US agitation against Chinese competition that has been a fact for some time, and helps to explain the administration's often aggressive tone towards Beijing, is more likely than not to find a growing echo in Europe as time goes on. It is also likely to ensure that even if EU–China relations were purely trade-obsessed, they would not be over-harmonious.

There is, however, still an important transatlantic difference in how all of this translates into overt policy. In process terms, lead responsibility both for negotiations and for sanctions in the relevant fields has long resided with the European Commission. Its rights have steadily expanded – for instance, recently to the conclusion of civil aviation agreements. This means that the Europeans speaking with China on trade are not those who 'own' European strategic interests and tools, making it less likely that these different aspects of relations will be handled in concerted or trade-off fashion (see more on this below). The Commission itself has no – literal – 'big guns' and can get tough only within the confines of orderly, civilian, international negotiation. For reasons already touched on above, compromise deals that make some acknowledgement of Chinese interests and that save Chinese 'face' can come to be seen in Brussels as optimal rather than a *pis aller*. After securing a set of self-imposed restraints from China on its booming textile exports to the European Union in June 2005, the European Union's Trade Commissioner, Peter Mandelson, openly criticised the United States for tackling its own parallel problem through unilateral import quotas, thus hinting perhaps at a more general cultural contrast across the Atlantic: 'The US has chosen to act first and then talk later, which might make the talking slightly more difficult because China might react in a different way.'[14]

The rest of EU strategy

In 1995 the European Commission attempted for the first time to set out a long-term EU strategy on China.[15] Some seven of the 17 pages of its paper (including summary) were devoted to economic and other practical forms of cooperation. The general tone was set in the opening pages:

> Europe must develop a long-term relationship with China that reflects China's worldwide, as well as regional economic and political influence ... The EU is eager to see China sharing in the opportunities and responsibilities at the heart of the international community as China opens up to a freer flow of ideas and cooperation, both in the key Asian region and globally.

While the need for the European Union to be strong and coherent in getting its message across was noted, three of four guiding principles proposed for EU–China relations presupposed *shared* interests – in global and regional security, 'other global issues' and global economic stability – and only the fourth was potentially zero-sum: a concern with competitiveness. As for the active goals for EU policy, the first was defined as:

> to promote a dialogue on regional and global security issues which encourages full Chinese engagement in the international community through accession to all the key international instruments governing non-proliferation and arms control.

Elsewhere, the paper argued that opening China to the 'free flow of trade, investment, people and ideas' was the strongest single hope for democratisation. This logic was presented as giving the European Union further reason to draw China into international processes, as well as supporting bottom-up improvements in governance and the rule of law. Despite a reference on the first page to China's 'military-political strength', however, no prescriptions were offered on defence and only one paragraph suggested the European Union should use its influence to promote peaceful solutions to the nuclear challenge on the Korean peninsula and territorial disputes in the South China Sea. It must of course be remembered that defence and (traditional) security matters were not part of the European Union's own competence at the time (many still are not), and many states would have been scandalised by the Commission – in particular – trying to pontificate about them.

In October 2003 the European Council endorsed a 17-page Commission report updating the analysis of the EU–China relationship under the title 'A maturing partnership: shared interests and challenges in EU–China relations'. This time, only nine out of 26 pages were devoted directly to economic issues and practical cooperation. The paper noted how China's strength, and the European Union's strategic ambitions, had both grown since the 1995 paper was written. The conclusion remained, however, that:

> The EU and China have an ever-greater interest to work together as strategic partners to safeguard and promote sustainable development, peace

and stability ... Europe thus has a major political and economic stake in supporting China's successful transition to a stable, prosperous and open country that fully embraces democracy, free market principles and the rule of law ... Dialogue and cooperation should continue to constitute the main EU approach to improving the human rights situation in China, although this should not exclude expressing comments and observations in other appropriate fora.

Several dimensions of non-military security were identified in which China and the European Union might cooperate on the basis of 'shared responsibilities', including anti-terrorism and non-proliferation. No more was said than before, however, on Taiwan or on regional issues other than the specific European interest in Hong Kong and Macau. In short, even in the year (2003) when the European Union was working on the ESS, its detailed strategy for China remained focused on the *bilateral* and *global* levels of interaction with a yawning gap over Asian regional power politics in between.

What does Europe actually do with China in the security field? Global and functional security comes up under the European Union's 'political dialogue' with Beijing, while specific (non-military) aspects may be identified for practical cooperation under sectoral dialogues and agreements. Themes covered in the former setting have included non-proliferation (including technology control and export control), anti-terrorism, international crime, smuggling and piracy, and controls on illegal migration and people-trafficking. China's increasing engagement in UN peace operations (Gill 2004) makes global conflict prevention and management a relevant topic, together with issues particularly linked to intra-state conflict such as small-arms control. As an example, the EU–China summit of December 2004 at The Hague (led on the European side by the then Dutch presidency together with representatives of the Commission and Council Secretariat) signed a Joint Declaration on Non-Proliferation,[16] an agreement on joint research into the peaceful use of nuclear energy, and an agreement on customs cooperation, while also agreeing to prolong the bilateral Science and Technology Agreement dating from 2000 – four topics that all carry obvious relevance for the (broadly conceived) security agenda of today.[17]

Here, however, an interesting definitional point arises: what does the European Union and what do Europeans have in mind by 'security' when dealing with China? It is by now commonplace that European definitions, priorities and even values in this sphere may not be identical (if they ever were) with those of the United States. Thus for Europe the themes of climate change, environmental depletion, energy policy and population control are eminently strategic ones, and the value of Chinese cooperation in these fields is such as to be worth foregoing other Chinese concessions or even overlooking some Chinese offences to get it. Europe must rate very highly, for example, any Chinese move to implement international rules and targets like those of the Kyoto Protocol (a new joint declaration on climate change was the hot story of the 2005 EU–China summit), while the United States refuses to join the Protocol itself. The same contrast could be drawn in several arms-related fields, such as the Comprehensive Test Ban Treaty. On the other hand, Europe has been much more relaxed than the United States about China's recent shopping-spree on oil and gas concessions (including in Iran and other problematic countries), understanding this as part of how the market works and as preferable to China burning more dirty coal. Nor does the European Union seem to regard the subject of its scientific and techno-logical relations with China in a primarily or even largely strategic light. An exemplar is the European Union's October 2003 agreement with China on cooperation in the European Union's *Galileo* satellite navigation pro-gramme,[18] an enterprise about which the United States had security-related qualms to start with, and in which it was certainly not happy to see China intimately involved. (The European Union for its part contended that this agreement includes adequate 'fire-walls' to avoid China exploiting the military spin-off from *Galileo* technology). After June 2001 a joint EU–China office in Beijing worked to promote research cooperation, citing among its target areas biotechnology, the environment, information tech-nology (IT) and nano-technologies – three out of four of which had major security implications. European companies were eager to engage in joint technology development and other cooperative ventures with Chinese partners in fields such as aerospace, telecommunications and IT, materials science and advanced machine tools, in part because they fear that simply selling the goods or techniques involved to China would result in China over-taking them and stealing their markets in the next phase of development. All these fields, however, are of great potential relevance to the development of Chinese military technology and, in some cases, even to weapons of mass destruction (Anthony 2005).

One field in which the European Union as such has not yet dabbled in cooperation with China is 'hard' military activity. The strategy paper on the European Union which China itself produced in 2003 (on which more below) included a section calling for high-level military exchanges, a strategic security dialogue mechanism, training and defence studies cooperation as well as the earliest possible lifting of the EU arms embargo. Up to now it has been left to EU nations to decide whether to respond, and some of them have gone quite far. 'Softer' interactions such as military liaison, accepting Chinese candidates for defence educational and training courses, and discus-sions on peacekeeping and military modernisation are now widespread. France has also carried out no less than 12 naval port visits to China since 1980 and six EU nations plus Turkey and Ukraine have accepted inward Chinese naval visits. The French and British navies have held joint exercises with their Chinese counterparts, and China has admitted European obser-vers to some of its ground-force and amphibious exercises (Gill 2005). All this makes it harder, on the one hand, to interpret the European interest in raising the arms embargo as an 'ignorant' commercial one, but, on the other hand, also to believe in European claims that there is no serious interest in China as a defence industrial partner.

Conclusion

At this point, it may be timely to revisit the EU arms embargo débâcle from a deeper understanding of the European Union's would-be strategic logic. The 1989 embargo was a political decision made in a still fairly inchoate phase of the Common Foreign and Security Policy and leaving much leeway – which was duly exploited – for national interpretation. The subsequent Code of Conduct contained far clearer and more elaborate rules, including a detailed section clearly drafted with Taiwan in mind that prohibits doing damage to regional security by providing weapons that might be misused 'to assert by force a territorial claim'. The European Union has, in fact, in recent years sent a consistent message to Beijing that the Taiwan issue should not be resolved by force (Barysch 2005: 69–71). Adoption of a beefed-up Code would standardise EU practice, enhance transparency, and shift at least some responsibility for enforcement (especially if made legally binding) from states to the centre in Brussels. On all these grounds it should better serve a strategically conscious and responsible EU policy on China – and indeed on all arms customers – than any old-style embargo could do.

Even leaving aside the link between the embargo and human rights, however (and the European Union is now confronting that issue more formally and frontally elsewhere), the European Union's handling of this episode highlights a cluster of problems that arise over the expression and execution of any joint European strategy almost regardless of its inherent quality. First come the well-known generic handicaps to EU unity and coherence in external action:

- the diverging interests and wishes of EU member states, which lead them among other things to talk a different talk to outsiders;
- the division of responsibility and action between national capitals and the centre, with the latter still particularly weak in competence (in every sense) on strategic matters; and
- the compartmentalisation in Brussels of different parts of the EU policy *acquis* and resulting action programmes, without – so far – any adequate central mechanism to ensure strategic consistency across the board.[19]

In the Chinese case, factors like these make it easier to understand (inter alia) how the placatory bias and economic interests of larger European powers can swamp more critical voices; how the security angle on hi-tech transfers may be persistently overlooked; and how hard it is to apply tough cross-sectoral trade-offs and leverage against China through a collective European channel.

A second point more specific to China is that the formal documents underpinning the EU–China relationship are still overwhelmingly economic/ technical in nature, and the mechanisms of dialogue have been tailored to serve such interactions rather than straight talking on security (see Barysch 2005: 8–10). The main working-level instrument is an EU–China Joint Commission designed and staffed to deal with trade issues, and in the past the most frequent high-level contacts have been with the President of the Commission on the European Union side. Since 1998 there have been annual EU–China summits at Heads of Government level, with ministerial meetings between times in the 'troika' format (EU Council Presidency, Commission, and the 'High Representative' for the CFSP, Javier Solana). A more 'strategy-friendly' structure has been proposed by a recent European Policy Centre study (see Cameron *et al.* 2005), but the EPC prescription still does not offer a single bilateral forum to work on and seek joint solutions to the different dimensions of security-related cooperation. The European Union has talked of negotiating a more strategic 'framework agreement' but this means getting China to agree on the definition of troublesome issues – no easy task – before they can even be addressed.

Third, although many Europeans like to recognise a kind of matching sophistication in themselves and the Chinese elite, in practice they are woefully easy targets for China's skill in divide-and-rule tactics and double-speak. The unusual gesture made by Beijing in publishing its own EU strategy paper after the first edition of the ESS in 2003 may have mirrored in part a sincere recognition of the importance of the integration phenomenon and of Europe's growing weight (not least because of enlargement) in the strategic balance. It was also, however, a prime example of the Chinese elite's ability to 'play back' to a given interlocutor the language as well as ideas that the partner finds most congenial – while behaving in a flatly con-tradictory way towards, say, Taiwan or Japan or on the home front. David Shambaugh (2005) has drawn (if perhaps over-drawn) a connection here with the fact that Europe collectively has rather few 'China wonks', that even fewer of them have a policy-framing role in Brussels, and that EU policy may consequently base its judgements too often on what it sees reflected (as it were) from China's surface.

An obvious remedy, if this is a real problem, would be for the European Union to concert more with the United States and with other players who either see different parts of the Chinese reality or interpret them differently. As announced by Javier Solana and US Secretary of State Condoleezza Rice at their May 2005 meeting, the European Union and the United States have in fact agreed to launch a direct dialogue on China, and two sessions have already been held at senior official level. Such a mechanism should at least help to ease such EU–US frictions as are worsened by misunderstand-ing, and to dig back towards the ground-rock of common strategic interest that plainly still connects the United States and European sides. Neither wishes China to tyrannise its own people, to start wars in its region, to act as a deal-breaker and bully at a global level or to fall below even Western levels of responsibility in stewardship of its share of the global commons. Perhaps a more open recognition of the asymmetry of both brawn and attitude with which Europe and the United States address the challenge could encourage more thinking about the *complementarities* of their respective impacts on China, and less fretting about historically and geographically fated differences. While 'nice cop, nasty cop' would be too crude a metaphor, it makes as little sense to expect the European Union to defend Taiwan as for Washington to teach Beijing the skills of multilateralism. A recent RAND study by mixed US and European experts (Gompert *et al.* 2005: 51) suggested in this spirit of agreeing-to-disagree that 'Europe should not undercut the United States and the United States should not exclude Europe in dealing with the emergence of China'. In the practical world, however, the European Union will not be able to carry its side of even such a limited accommodation without sustained progress in its external and internal coherence and – this author would suggest – a greater effort to talk to and understand China's Asian neighbours as well.

Seen from a broader perspective, however, neither US aggressivity nor European accommodation offers a convincing answer for handling states that were called 'third-world' in the twentieth century, but are now both dominating and outgrowing their regions and doing so with minimal overt use of military power. The old labels of 'regional' and 'global' power tell us nothing useful about the China or, indeed, the India phenomenon of today, whereby still developing economies can buy up major Western companies, penetrate others through the provisions of outsourced services, and hold the fate of the dollar hostage. US-style containment and hectoring cannot alter the degree of reverse dependence the West has already entered into with such emerging giants, but neither will soothing and appeasing tactics keep them tucked away in their corners. The European Union's experimentation with new forms of give-and-take partnership under a shell of global regulation may be messy both in thinking and execution. Yet, as UK Prime Minister Tony Blair said at the September 2005 EU–China summit (when talking of China's trade challenge): 'There is, of course, a case for managing change. What there is not is a case for resisting change.'[20] The European approach is still far from a strategist's strategy. But that it will ultimately be what works cannot be excluded.

Notes

1 See Anti-Secession Law adopted by the PRC People's Congress, Beijing, 13 March 2005. Online. Available: http://english.people.com.cn/200503/14/eng 20050314-176746.html (accessed 11 June 2005).
2 For example, see Lawrence Freedman, 'A Failure of European Diplomacy', *Financial Times*, 18 April 2005, p. 15; Chris Patten, 'Why Europe is Getting China so Wrong', *Financial Times*, 26 September 2005, p. 23.
3 'Pressure Mounts as Ministers Discuss EU Embargo on China', *Financial Times*, 15 April 2005, p. 4.

4 An expression often used in US circles but also used by a European Ambassador in Beijing in conversation with the author in May 2005.

5 Over the whole period 1989–2004, however, the US total of $32 million in deliveries was outstripped notably by France ($202 million) and Italy ($64 million). In principle these sales should have been limited to non-warlike items and spare parts for earlier deliveries. See the SIPRI arms transfers database http://www.sipri.org/contents/armstrad/atchi_taidata.html (accessed 2 February 2006), expressed in notional dollar values at constant (1990) prices.

6 For comparison, there are five references to Russia, two to the Korean Peninsula/North Korea, one to ASEAN and one to Japan.

7 Estimates of Chinese military spending are bedevilled not just by Chinese non-transparency but by the issue of how to convert exchange rates. 'Purchasing power parities' are often used in US writings and indicate the higher quantity of goods that a given budget can buy in China, but they fail to allow for lower quality.

8 For example, Washington has preferred to multilateralise talks on the North Korean nuclear menace under Chinese leadership, rather than deal with Pyongyang bilaterally, and it has done much to restrain provocative behaviour by Taipei. There is also some tension between its containment goals and the Pentagon's plans to move US troops back from forward locations in East Asia, including South Korea and Japan. The themed issue of *Foreign Affairs*, with the single word 'China' presented in very large bold red type on its cover, appeared in September/October 2005.

9 See (US) Taiwan Relations Act, 1 January 1979, text at http://www.taiwan documents.org/tra01.htm

10 Figures for trade in the first four months of 2005 showed China overtaking the United States to become the European Union's largest partner as a result of differential growth in EU imports. See Ralph Atkins, 'China Poised to Overtake US on Exports to EU', *Financial Times*, 21 July 2005, p. 4.

11 Figures taken from the European Union's website. Online. Available: http://europa.eu.int/comm/trade/issues/bilateral/countries/japan/index_en.htm (accessed 8 January 2006).

12 Chinese government figures for trade and investments quoted in the annex to a European Commission policy paper endorsed by the European Council on 13 October 2003, available at European Commission EU–China portal. Online. Available: http://europa.eu.int/comm/external_relations/china/intro/index.htm (accessed 8 January 2006).

13 When China announced a small revaluation of its currency in July 2005, some commentators gave credit to US Treasury Secretary John Snow who had blocked Congressional pressure for a tougher line on the perceived undervaluation of the renminbi (see Andrew Balls and Alan Beattie, 'US Treasury Welcomes Currency Reform', *Financial Times*, 22 July 2005, p. 2; Martin Wolf, 'Though Precedents are Ominous, China's Rise to Greatness Need Not Bring Conflict', *Financial Times*, 15 September 2005, p. 11).

14 Quoted in 'Be More Conciliatory, Mandelson Tells US', *Financial Times*, 13 June 2005. Ironically, Mandelson's initial deal hurt European consumer-goods importers too much and had to be renegotiated in September, adding to the growing EU strategic lexicon the notion of a pyrrhic victory.

15 All of the policy papers to which this section refers may be found at the Commission's portal for documents on EU–China relations: http://europa.eu.int/comm/external_relations/china/intro/index.htm (accessed 2 February 2006).

16 Text online. Available: http://www.fmprc.gov.cn/eng/zxxx/t173749.htm (accessed 8 January 2006).

17 EU–China summit agreements of 8 December 2004. Online. Available: http://

europa.eu.int/rapid/pressReleasesAction.do?reference=MEMO/04/284&format
=HTML&aged=0&language=EN&guiLanguage=en (accessed 8 January 2006).
18 Cooperation Agreement on a Civil Global Navigation Satellite System (GNSS)
– *Galileo* between the European Community and its Member States and the
People's Republic of China, 17 October 2003.
19 The draft EU Constitutional Treaty would have tackled this with (inter alia)
a long-term European Council President, and an EU 'Foreign Minister', but
the way ahead for these reforms seemed blocked after the negative French and
Netherlands referendums in 2005.
20 B. Hall and George Parker, 'China–EU Near Import Deal', *Financial Times*, 6
September 2005, p. 1.

9 Security strategy and the arms industry

Chad Damro[1]

Introduction

Defense industries are vital components of national security strategies because they supply the military capabilities through which strategy is implemented. The United States' National Security Strategy (NSS) and the European Security Strategy (ESS) both suggest an important role for military capabilities. While neither security strategy directly mentions its respective defense industry, they do both stress the need to develop military capabilities for use as strategic assets. This demand for capabilities is crucial for understanding the interaction between security strategy and the transatlantic defense industry.

This chapter explores the factors that determine demand in the United States and the European Union for military capabilities and the ways in which they may influence government policy and supply-side strategies.[2] The NSS and ESS reveal important insights into the factors that drive US and EU demand for military capabilities. They converge on the need to develop capabilities to address 'new threats'. While the need for new capabilities requires new military technologies and hardware, the United States and Europe differ significantly on how to fulfill this need. The United States tends to prioritize defense spending and 'transformation' as ways to increase its military capabilities. The United States outpaces Europe's capabilities as reflected in its consistently higher levels of military spending and research and development (R&D) expenditures. The notion of 'transformation' requires modifications to existing US national military doctrine, force structure and military acquisition to meet the challenges of new threats.

The European Union's circumstances generate different priorities. While the European Union is also striving to meet the challenge of new threats, it faces a considerable gap with the United States in military capabilities (Biscop 2004a; Cooper 2004a). Obstacles to increasing defense spending have led the European Union to prioritize increasing the efficiency of its defense spending through institutional change.[3] In particular, efficiency gains have been sought by creating three new institutions to enhance European industrial collaboration: the Organisation Conjointe de Coopération en matière d'Armement (OCCAR), the Letter of Intent (LoI) and the

European Defense Agency (EDA). These institutional changes are being pursued both within and outside the European Union's framework as means to increase Europe's capabilities to meet the challenge of new threats. Thus the European Union is addressing its need for military capabilities by developing new institutions instead of striving for parity in defense spending and 'transformation' of existing national defense institutions.

This chapter employs a basic tenet of neorealist theory – the importance of relative capabilities – to determine and explain variation between US and EU security strategies. The empirical record is clear on the importance of relative capabilities: a gap exists between US and European military capabilities, and any increase in this gap will make interoperability problems more likely in the future.[4] The European Union's prioritization of institutional change may be redirecting energy and resources in a manner that actually expands the gap with the comparatively more efficient and consistently better-financed United States. The European Union's institutional efforts at industrial collaboration will have to generate significant efficiency gains, or risk expanding a capabilities gap that will likely reduce the ability of the European Union to address new threats, and determine the limits of any future European security strategy.

The chapter is organized as follows. A first section discusses the two concepts central to the argument: new threats and military capabilities. The chapter then reveals how the NSS and ESS both address the challenge posed by new threats. The following section investigates the current state of US and European defense and R&D spending. The disparities reflect current levels of capabilities and suggest future incentives in the transatlantic defense industry. The next section elaborates the United States' prioritization of defense spending and transformation as ways to increase its capabilities. The European Union's response to the capabilities gap – specifically, institutional changes designed to increase efficiency in Europe's defense spending – is then examined. The chapter concludes with a summary of findings and speculates on the long-term impact of the EU and US security strategies for the United States and European arms industries.

The analytical concepts and argument

This chapter identifies two concepts – new threats and military capabilities – as the factors that most determine the dynamics of US and EU security strategies and the contours of the transatlantic defense industry. The two concepts are linked in the central argument of the chapter to reveal the implications of a potentially expanding capabilities gap between the United States and Europe.

The NSS and ESS agree on the existence of *new threats*, and thus signal a shared concern with the changing priorities of international security. However, they do not necessarily agree on their nature. The NSS emphasizes the emergence of new threats from 'rogue states and terrorists' and their predilection to use weapons of mass destruction. For its part, the ESS lists the new threats of terrorism, proliferation of weapons of mass destruction, regional conflicts, state failure and organized crime. The first two of these new threats reflect similar concerns in the NSS. While the precise nature of new threats does not correspond exactly between the NSS and ESS, it is crucial to note that both strategies emphasize new threats in the first place. This convergence leads both the United States and the European Union to evaluate their capabilities and pursue changes to their security policies and defense industries accordingly.

Capabilities are also prominent determinants of US and EU security behavior. Indeed, it has been argued that the most important differences between states are differences of capability, not differences of function (Waltz 1979). These relative capabilities reflect differences of power and help to determine state behavior. The extent of disparity between EU and US relative military capabilities is discussed below. For now, it is important to point out that this chapter is concerned with military capabilities. While other capabilities – for example, natural resources, population size, diplomatic resources, economic power – can be important in determining state behavior, military capabilities often prove decisive (either through their exercise or credible threat) in determining security strategy (Robertson 2001: 793; Waltz 1979).

New security threats are increasingly pressuring governments and industry to develop military capabilities that offer high-tech solutions, increase projection capacity, bolster intelligence resources, and improve aerospace and satellite capabilities. Such new programs typically depend on significant levels of military-related expenditures on R&D. Disparities in such national expenditures – such as exist between the United States and EU member states – can create gaps in capabilities between allies. Such capabilities gaps exacerbate interoperability problems and undermine the potential for operational coordination.[5] Ultimately, capabilities gaps can reduce the ability of allies to coordinate their responses to the new threats that, ironically, increasingly require international coordination in order to be resolved.

The security strategies and new threats

The NSS argues that the security environment has undergone 'profound transformation' since the collapse of the Soviet Union and the end of the Cold War. It argues that today's security environment is 'more complex and dangerous' because of 'the nature and motivations of these new adversaries [rogue states and terrorists], their determination to obtain destructive powers … and the greater likelihood that they will use weapons of mass destruction against us'.

The NSS goes on to assert that the challenge of 'new threats' will be addressed by cooperation with allies and increases in US defense capabilities. Foremost among these allies are the members of NATO. However, the NSS argues that NATO needs to develop 'new structures and capabilities'. In particular, NATO

> must build a capability to field, at short notice, highly mobile, specially trained forces whenever they are needed to respond to a threat against any member of the alliance ... we must ... take advantage of the technological opportunities and economies of scale in our defense spending to transform NATO military forces ... maintain the ability to work and fight together as allies even as we take the necessary steps to transform and modernize our forces.

Thus, while identifying the importance of cooperating with NATO allies, the NSS implicitly acknowledges the capability (including technological) gap that exists between the NATO partners. The issues of defense spending and force modernization also figure highly in the NSS plans for NATO.

The NSS focuses attention on the need to increase the United States' own military capabilities to combat new threats. According to the NSS, the United States must prepare for more deployments like Afghanistan by 'developing assets such as advanced remote sensing, long-range precision strike capabilities, and transformed maneuver and expeditionary forces'. The NSS also cites the need for force projection capabilities in order to 'ensure US access to distant theaters, and protect critical US infrastructure and assets in outer space'. Noting the importance of technology, the NSS states that 'innovation within the armed forces will rest on experimentation with new approaches to warfare, strengthening joint operations, exploiting US intelligence advantages, and taking full advantage of science and technology'. Such an emphasis on innovation again reveals the United States' desire to develop new technologies as a means to increase the capabilities necessary for addressing new threats.

Similarly, the ESS reveals Europe's desire to combat 'new threats' and to increase its own capabilities to meet them. The ESS also reveals Europe's preference for and commitment to institutional changes to meet these security threats. It starts with the premise that 'large-scale aggression against any Member State is now improbable. Instead, Europe faces new threats which are more diverse, less visible and less predictable.' According to the ESS, the European Union must address these 'new threats' by becoming more active, more capable and more coherent. Such objectives will entail new policies that will require adjustments in the supply of military capabilities.

As for the requirement to become *more active*, the ESS identifies the need for a new strategic culture and more effective use of current EU defense spending: 'we need to develop a strategic culture that fosters early, rapid, and when necessary, robust intervention. As a Union of 25 members, spending more than 160 billion Euros on defence, we should be able to sustain several operations simultaneously.' This culture is described entirely in terms of military objectives and strategic needs.[6]

In order to become *more capable* of combating new threats, the ESS argues for institutional adjustments that will foster industrial collaboration. It also calls for increases in defense spending as well as more efficient and effective defense spending:

> Actions underway – notably the establishment of a defence agency [the European Defence Agency, or EDA] – take us in the right direction. To transform our militaries into more flexible, mobile forces, and to enable them to address the new threats, more resources for defence and more effective use of resources are necessary. Systematic use of pooled and shared assets would reduce duplications, overheads and, in the medium-term, increase capabilities.

Thus the ESS does hint at the need to increase defense spending. However, as will be shown in the next section, the Union and its member states' spending records suggest this has been mostly lip-service, while priority has been placed instead on institutional initiatives such as the EDA as a means to increase the efficiency of defense spending.

The ESS also notes the need to become *more coherent* in order to address new threats. Coherence requires better coordination among supranational and intergovernmental political authorities. The ESS highlights the number of different instruments that have been created through the European Union's Common Foreign and Security Policy (CSFP) and the European Security and Defense Policy (ESDP). Coherence also requires better coordination in areas of non-traditional military significance: 'the challenge now is to bring together the different instruments and capabilities: European assistance programmes and the European Development Fund, military and civilian capabilities from Member States and other instruments'. Thus, in its drive for more coherence, the European Union again stresses the importance of capabilities for its security strategy.

The ESS identifies a number of ways in which the European Union can increase its capabilities. Unlike the NSS, the ESS does not seem to prioritize, at least in comparative terms, increased defense spending and technological innovation as the primary means through which to address new security threats.

The demand for EU and US military capabilities

The gap between EU and US military capabilities reflects their relative levels of military and R&D expenditures. The high levels of US expenditures indicate the high political priority the United States places on defense spending. While some of the EU member states do spend a fair percentage of their public budgets on the military, expenditures are quite uneven across the Union, and, as a whole, EU military expenditure falls far short of total US expenditures. In addition, EU expenditures are often inefficient because of duplications and overlaps in Union supply.

Figure 9.1 shows the military expenditures of the United States and the EU member states from before the end of the Cold War through 2004. It demonstrates considerable and (generally) consistent disparities in military spending throughout this period. These disparities lead to dramatic differences in relative capabilities. The trend is not simply two straight lines, but an actual, overall divergence in the amounts of defense spending, especially since the end of the 1990s. The divergence appears to continue despite the European Union's recent enlargement in 2004.

In addition, and more importantly for future military capabilities, huge disparities in military spending on R&D are now historically engrained features of US and EU spending patterns. These differences define the future constraints and opportunities of the supply-side. Figure 9.2 identifies total expenditures across four different years for the United States and EU member states. It reveals starkly how wide the disparity between European and American spending on military R&D had become even *before* the massive increases in US defense spending under the post-2000 George W. Bush administrations.

Military R&D is probably the most alarming measure of the potential for future divergence in EU and US security strategies and defense capabilities. The now considerable disparities between US and EU member states' spending on military R&D suggest further divergence in the capabilities gap that already exists.[7] While the European Union and the United States agree that they are intent on addressing new threats, the United States appears far

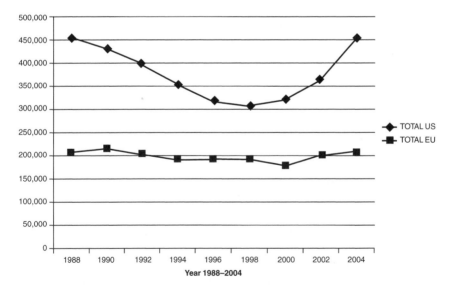

Figure 9.1 European and US military expenditures (US$ million), 1988–2004.

Source: SIPRI's FIRST Database. Online. Available: http://first.sipri.org (accessed 13 August 2005). The figures displayed are calculated in constant US dollars at 2003 prices and exchange rates.

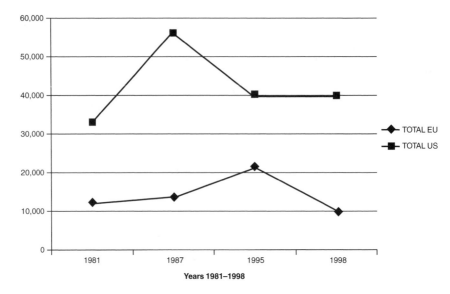

Figure 9.2 European and US expenditure on military R&D (US$ million),
1981–1998.

Source: SIPRI's FIRST Database. Online. Available: http://first.sipri.org
(accessed 13 August 2005). The figures displayed are calculated in constant
US dollars at 1998 prices and exchange rates.

more committed to addressing them with new military technologies. If problems of interoperability exist with current technology, then they will only increase in the future unless the military R&D gap closes.

It is also worth noting that the United States is unlikely to transfer its military technologies to Europe in a display of generosity to close the capabilities gap among allies. According to a recent report, 'The US is resisting Europe's call for it to relax its grip on technology and allow its transfer to American allies' (Huband 2005). It is most likely that future military technologies will also be guarded in a similar fashion by the US government.

The US response: spending and transformation

The United States' response to new threats seems to be fundamentally characterized by a desire to increase defense spending (including R&D expenditures) and to transform outmoded and costly Cold War-era ideas and weapons. This section elaborates the US strategy of spending and 'transformation' and the types of capabilities that are likely to be demanded from the transatlantic defense industry in the future.

Taken together, the NSS and continued increases in US defense spending reflect a new doctrine of armed force 'transformation' that has been promoted most prominently by the US Secretary of Defense, Donald Rumsfeld. The philosophy of transformation requires changes from Cold War US military doctrine, and force structures and acquisitions to meet the new threats of the twenty-first century. In a speech at the National Defense University in Washington, Rumsfeld (2002) argued that US defense strategy must be focused on achieving six 'transformational goals':

- First, to protect the US homeland and military bases overseas.
- Second, to project and sustain power in distant theatres.
- Third, to deny US enemies sanctuary, making sure they know that no corner of the world is remote enough, no mountain high enough, no cave or bunker deep enough, no vehicle fast enough to protect them from American reach.
- Fourth, to protect information networks from attack.
- Fifth, to use information technology to link up different kinds of US forces so that they can in fact fight jointly.
- Sixth, to maintain unhindered access to space and protect US space capabilities from enemy attack.

To achieve such transformational goals, the United States has elected to increase spending on new capabilities. But the US strategy is not only to purchase new capabilities:

> In addition to new capabilities, transformation also requires rebalancing existing forces and existing capabilities by adding more of what the Pentagon has come to call low-density, high-demand assets, which is really a euphemism, in plain English, for 'our priorities were wrong, and we didn't buy enough of what we need'.
>
> (Rumsfeld 2002)

Thus, transformation does not simply require more spending. Instead, in an echo of the European Union's position, the United States also promotes better spending. As Rumsfeld (2002) has argued, the Pentagon must shift investment to what are considered more valuable programs:

> as we change investment priorities, we have to begin shifting the balance in our arsenal between manned and unmanned capabilities, between short- and long-range systems, stealthy and non-stealthy systems, between shooters and sensors, and between vulnerable and hardened systems. And we need to make the leap into the information age, which is the critical foundation of our transformation efforts.

The leap into the information age portends a reliance on new technologies to improve intelligence, surveillance and reconnaissance. Significant sums have already been dedicated to such new technologies across successive annual US defense budgets. Specific transformational initiatives include the Predator and Global Hawk Unmanned Aerial Vehicles; the army's Stryker Interim Armored Vehicle, Non-Line-of-Sight (NLOS) cannon system and Future Combat System; the navy's Littoral Combat Ship and Broad Area Maritime Surveillance; and the air force's Multi-sensor Command and Control Constellation (MC2C). Dramatic changes in US defense spending seem to have followed from this doctrine of transformation. For example, the White House's 2003 budget request for defense spending represented 'a 12 percent real increase above current spending and a dramatic 14 percent increase above the Cold War average spending – to fund a force structure that is one-third smaller than it was a decade ago' (Hellman and Baker 2002).

The United States' prioritization of spending on defense and R&D suggests a further expansion in the capabilities gap with Europe. Similarly, the United States' focus on transformation may also increase the capabilities gap unless similar changes are sought by European governments. As will be discussed in the next section, however, Europe does not seem to be prioritizing spending or similar transformational initiatives. Rather, it seems to be prioritizing the creation of completely new institutions for industrial collaboration among independent states.

The European Union: institutional change and industrial collaboration

As the ESS asserts, in order to make the European Union more capable, the member states will need to increase defense spending and, in particular, the efficiency of that defense spending. Given recent trends in spending and political obstacles to increasing defense spending (including public opposition), the European Union is prioritizing institutional change and industrial collaboration as the most realistic means to increase its military capabilities and to meet new threats. Such institutional developments would help to 'reduce duplications, overheads and, in the medium-term, increase capabilities'. This section is particularly interested in the EU/European efforts to increase military capabilities through the Organisation Conjointe de Coopération en matière d'Armement (OCCAR), the Letter of Intent (LoI) and the European Defense Agency (EDA).[8]

These three institutional changes have occurred quite recently considering that the European Union is now almost five decades old. Since its beginnings, defense procurement has been one of the policy areas that remained outside the Union's extensive economic collaboration. This anomaly is often traced to Article 223 of the Treaty of Rome (1957) which allowed states to protect their 'essential interests' when they were connected to 'the production of or trade in arms, munitions and war materials'. As Leonard (2005: 15) argues, most Member States have claimed a blanket exemption for defence supplies, even extending in many cases to the provision of soldiers' boots and rucksacks. It is a rarity for the supply of any goods for the military to be put out to open tender and even when competitive bidding is permitted it is seldom widely publicised on a cross-border basis.

While such behavior does little to create a climate of collaboration in European defense procurement, certain members of the European Union did begin changing their ways in the mid-1990s (Schmitt 2005).

The institutional development of OCCAR took place outside the European Union's framework. France, Germany, Italy and the United Kingdom established OCCAR in November 1996 with the goal of enhancing collaborative armament programs among its members. According to the OCCAR convention, membership is open to other states as long as they accept OCCAR's principles and take part in a 'substantive collaborative equipment programme involving at least one OCCAR partner'.[9] OCCAR employs its own staff, places and manages contracts, and follows its own set of management procedures. To date, OCCAR has been involved with projects such as the Franco-Italian surface-to-air anti-missile system family (FASF), the German-Dutch armored utility vehicle (BOXER), the Franco-German TIGER helicopter and short-range optical/radar-guided surface-to-air missile (ROLAND), the British-Franco-German long-range battlefield radar system (COBRA), and the Airbus all-weather, day/night tactical and strategic airlifter (A400M). After recently adding Belgium and Spain, OCCAR now includes seven states that are all EU members.

OCCAR's greatest contribution to the European defense industry could be its renunciation of the principle of *juste retour*. The prevailing European approach to defense industries, *juste retour* awards defense contracts on the basis of government bargaining instead of market competition, with each state's industries receiving a politically derived 'fair share' of contracts. As a result, the role of states remains very important compared to industry, and 'contracts take longer and involve duplication' (Salmon and Shepherd 2003: 191). Thus, OCCAR's renunciation of *juste retour* promises to increase industry's role in decision-making while reducing government involvement, which could increase efficiencies in defense spending. However, the significance of this policy shift should not be exaggerated because it will be the most difficult objective for OCCAR to implement (Capuano 2005: 71).

The Letter of Intent (LoI) – officially known as the Framework Agreement Concerning Measures to Facilitate the Restructuring and Operation of the European Defence Industry – was also established outside the European Union and is independent of OCCAR. Signed in July 1998, the LoI created a framework that was intended to spur restructuring in the European defense industry. Three EU member states and central actors in the European defense industry initiated the process that led to the LoI. In December 1997, France, Germany and the UK agreed that the restructuring of the European defense industry was in their vital political and economic interest (Mörth 2003: 83). This political initiative was 'interpreted as a reaction to the industry and its demand for political activities to enhance the creation of transnational defence companies' (Mörth 2003: 83–4). In the summer of 1998, Europe's six largest arms producers – France, Germany, Italy, Spain, Sweden and the United Kingdom – decided to launch the LoI to increase the prospects for their defense companies of collaborating and for governments to organize joint projects.[10] As Salmon and Shepherd (2003: 191) argue, these states were the logical choice to sign the LoI because '[n]inety percent of the defense reorganization in Europe in the previous ten years had taken place in those six states. They accounted for 80 percent of armaments procurement in Europe and 90 percent of the armaments industrial capacity.'

The LoI sets the following objectives:

- to establish a framework to facilitate industrial restructuring in Europe;
- to ensure timely and effective consultation over issues arising from the restructuring of the European defense industrial base;
- to contribute to the achievement of security of supply for defense articles and defense services;
- to bring closer, simplify and reduce, where appropriate, national export control procedures for transfers and exports of military goods and technologies;
- to facilitate exchanges of classified information between the parties or their defense industry under security provisions;
- to foster coordination of joint research activities to increase the advanced knowledge base and thus encourage technological development and innovation;
- to establish principles for the disclosure, transfer, use and ownership of technical information to facilitate the restructuring and subsequent operation of the defense industry; and
- to promote harmonization of the military requirements of their armed forces.

The LoI has received mixed reviews. Salmon and Shepherd (2003: 192) argue that these six states have at least shown the will to succeed by agreeing to the LoI in the first place. However, more recently, Keohane (2004) has concluded that 'the Letter of Intent has not had much impact'.

Since the late 1990s, the European Union itself has become more directly involved in efforts to institutionalize military industrial collaboration. At the Cologne European Council in 1999, the Union signaled its determination to increase military capabilities when it declared that 'the Union must have the capacity for autonomous action, backed by credible military forces, the means to decide to use them, and the readiness to do so, in order to respond to international crises without prejudice to actions by NATO'.[11] As a result, the Union set out to create a new, so-called European Security and Defence Policy and began the process of reviewing its defense industry capabilities.

At the end of 2001, the Laeken Council launched the European Capabilities Action Plan (ECAP) to identify shortfalls in European defense capabilities and recommended solutions to those shortfalls.[12] The solutions would be based on national decisions aimed at rationalizing member states' defense efforts. The ECAP identified 38 capability shortfalls and submitted its recommendations in May 2003. A few months earlier, the Brussels European Council had decided to look into the possible creation of an 'intergovernmental defence capabilities development and acquisition agency within the EU'.[13] Thus the momentum from ECAP and the idea of a European Defence Agency (EDA) provided impetus within the European Union for institutional change.

In November 2003, the Council decided to prepare for the establishment of an EDA in the field of defense capabilities development, research, acquisition and armaments. By July 2004, a Joint Action of the Council of Ministers had established the Agency.[14] It became operational in 2005, with a small initial staff, a clear work program and a budget of about €20 million.[15] The EDA is designed 'to help EU Member States develop their defence capabilities for crisis-management operations under the ESDP'.[16] Its stated purpose is to produce better military capabilities, stronger European defense industries and better value for European taxpayers. According to the agency, it will achieve its goals, first, by encouraging EU governments to spend defense budgets on meeting tomorrow's challenges; and, second, by helping EU governments to identify common needs and promoting collaboration to provide common solutions.[17] According to Biscop (2004a), the EDA is also intended 'to promote defence-related [research and technology] and the restructuring of the European defence industry'.

The EDA's main 'shareholders' are those states participating in the agency, which includes all 25 EU member states except Denmark. Its key 'stakeholders' include the Council and European Commission, as well as third parties such as OCCAR, LoI and the Western European Union. According to the EDA, NATO and non-EU states are also 'important interlocutors'.[18]

As the two most active new institutions, the relationship between the EDA and OCCAR will be crucial in determining the extent to which these new initiatives will contribute to EU capabilities. OCCAR's Executive Director Nazzareno Cardinali is quick to note the amicable relationship he hopes to forge with the EDA:

> We are in working contact with the [EDA], and I have already had several meetings with the Agency's Chief. We are working towards a goal of common understanding so that OCCAR should be considered the preferred partner of EDA for managing cooperative programmes. The

two organizations are complementary, and it would be wise to avoid duplication of effort.

(quoted in Capuano 2005: 72)

Cardinali concludes on a recurrent theme in Europe's recent institutional changes: 'We have to make sure that our relationship with EDA is stable and moves forward, becoming effective and efficient' (Capuano 2005: 73).

Institutional initiatives hold promise for Europe in its efforts to increase its military capabilities to meet new threats. The extent to which OCCAR, LoI and EDA will operate in a stable and effective manner will determine the efficiency gains that follow from proposed industrial collaboration. These efficiency gains will determine the European Union's ability to address new threats and to close the capabilities gap with the United States.

Conclusions

This chapter has investigated the factors that determine the EU and US demand for military capabilities and the extent to which they may influence government policy and supply-side strategies. The analysis has focused on the linked concepts of new threats and military capabilities to understand current security strategies. This final section provides a summary of the findings and speculates on their implications for the future of the transatlantic defense industry.

The United States has taken a series of strong political decisions to counter new threats with large expenditures to transform and modernize its military capabilities. The country is also pursuing a comprehensive transformation of its outmoded Cold War military doctrine, force structures and acquisitions. This strategy and its associated levels of investment will compel defense firms to develop new technologies to supply the United States' growing demand.

The European Union also requires military capabilities to counter new threats. To address its needs, it has not engaged in comparatively significant budgetary allocations to defense spending and/or military R&D expenditures. Rather, it has decided to focus its energy on increasing the efficiency of its defense spending. It has adopted a strategy that prioritizes internal institutional changes. Europe's strategy to seek 'institutional efficiency gains' differs from America's 'transformation' in that the United States is promoting changes to existing national military doctrine, force structure and acquisition, while Europe is creating completely new institutions for industrial collaboration among independent states. These new institutions – OCCAR, LoI and EDA – are intended to promote industrial collaboration as a way to reap efficiency gains in defense spending and also to overcome the obstacle of public opposition to increased defense spending.

This strategy may have serious implications for future European security policy as it diverges from the US strategy. By not prioritizing increases in defense spending and R&D expenditures, the European Union may actually cause a further drop in its military capabilities relative to the more efficient and consistently better-financed United States. The European Union will have to reap massive efficiency gains from its institutional collaboration if it hopes to close the capabilities gap with the United States. Without such gains, the European Union's strategy will expand the gap in the long term.

This EU–US capabilities gap does not foreshadow a complete and automatic split in transatlantic military cooperation. But it does suggest a certainty that will drive policy: as the capabilities gap increases in the future, US–European interoperability problems will increase and their military forces will encounter greater obstacles to operational coordination. For practical purposes, the United States and the European Union will have to rely less on allied military coordination to combat new threats. Such an outcome becomes problematic because the very nature of new threats often requires that they be addressed through international coordination.

The inconsistency between US and EU priorities does not necessarily dictate transatlantic divergence in their respective defense industries. However, these different priorities and an expanding capabilities gap will likely create different market-based incentives for both US and European defense industries. The increasing likelihood of interoperability problems in the field will likely create, in the long term, a de facto mandatory division of labor in the fight against new threats. *In extremis*, European and US defense firms may choose to specialize in supplying one market or the other. One potential outcome of such a scenario is that incentives will increase significantly for defense firms to gain and increase access to and investment in foreign markets. In particular, without substantial R&D investment, European firms may face increased incentives to supply lucrative but potentially hostile markets in China and the Middle East where demand will remain for the European military capabilities that will be unnecessary and even obsolete in the US market.

Notes

1 The author would like to thank Emily Rueb for research assistance on this chapter.
2 For more on developments in the supply-side of US and European defense industries, see Schmitt (2005), Kapstein (2004), Center for Strategic and International Studies (2003), Guay and Callum (2002), and Adams *et al.* (2001).
3 For a similar argument, see Biscop (2004a) and Schmitt (2003).
4 It should be noted that the argument here is *not* that Europe is driven by a need to 'balance' with the US in the neorealist sense. (I am grateful to Jolyon Howorth for his thoughts on this point.) Rather, Europe will seek to close this capabilities gap for practical purposes in order to decrease the likelihood of current and future interoperability problems. On the European Union's fear of a technological capabilities gap with the United States, see Mörth (2003).
5 Interoperability problems are often cited when differences in military hardware reduce the ability of allies to coordinate their forces in the field. More recently,

concerns have also been expressed that military tactics and new technologies, such as the United States' network-centric warfare (US DOD 2001), can create even greater interoperability problems among allies.

6 For more on the importance of capabilities for developing strategic culture, see Cornish and Edwards (2005).

7 For more on the US lead in science and technology, see Paarlberg (2004).

8 For more on these and other institutions of EU armaments policy, see Schmitt (2003). The Western European Union (WEU) may be considered an early institutional attempt to increase efficiency in European defense spending. The European Union's 1992 Maastricht Treaty declared that the WEU would examine further cooperation in the field of armaments with the aim of creating a European armaments agency. The WEU generated two bodies involved in armaments cooperation that existed under different guises: the Western European Armaments Group (WEAG) and the Western European Armaments Organisation (WEAO). The WEAG/WEAO activities are now largely subsumed in the EDA's work program. As Salmon and Shepherd (2003: 188) argue, these WEU-related bodies produced limited results because 'they became yet another forum for discussion. They lacked real decision-making powers (taking non-binding decisions by consensus) and the members lacked political commitment.' Most of the functions of the WEU were absorbed by the European Union itself after 2002.

9 OCCAR Convention. Online. Available: www.occar-ea.org/C1256B0E0052F1A C/vwContentFrame/N254SMVV967SLEREN (accessed 16 August 2005).

10 It should be added that the United Kingdom signed a major agreement for similar purposes with the United States in 2000: the Declaration of Principles, a UK–US agreement to promote Defence Equipment and Industrial Co-operation.

11 Presidency Conclusions, Cologne European Council, 3–4 June 1999, Annex III. Online. Available: http://europa.eu.int/european_council/conclusions/index_en. htm (accessed 2 February 2006).

12 Presidency Conclusions, Laeken European Council, 14–15 December 2001, Annex II. Online. Available: http://europa.eu.int/european_council/conclusions/ index_en.htm (accessed 2 February 2006).

13 Presidency Conclusions, Brussels European Council, 20–21 March 2003, Conclusions, paragraph 3. Online. Available: http://europa.eu.int/european_council/ conclusions/index_en.htm (accessed 2 February 2006).

14 See Council Joint Action 2004/551/CFSP of 12 July 2004 on the establishment of the European Defence Agency. Online. Available http://europa.eu.int/european_ council/conclusions/index_en.htm (accessed 2 February 2006).

15 Details from the EDA's website. Available: http://www.eda.eu.int/background. htm (accessed 16 December 2005).

16 For more on the financing of ESDP military operations, see Scannell (2004).

17 For details, see the EDA website. Available: http://www.eda.eu.int/ (accessed 16 August 2005).

18 See note 17.

10 Security strategy, ESDP and non-aligned states

Annika Bergman and John Peterson

Before 2004, the idea that all member states of the European Union should move together at one speed and form a coherent bloc was a powerful 'religion' of European integration. Of course, there were always anomalies, such as the Schengen agreement, the Social Chapter, and monetary union, where sub-groups integrated faster than others. But all were presented as inclusive and open to all other EU states (who met certain criteria) and thus first steps towards truly common policies in a single, ever closer Union. Ultimately, agreement on a *single* European Security Strategy (ESS) in 2003 could be cited by true believers as demonstrating that the 'single bloc' thesis still lives.

Clearly, the 2004 enlargement challenged the credibility of this religion's theology. Yet, even before that, the notion of a single-speed European Union was always a political cover for a rich series of intra-European divisions. Some were long-standing: net contributors versus net recipients, the original EEC 6 versus everyone else, Europeanists versus Atlanticists, and so on. New divisions emerged over time to overlay old ones: northern versus southern states, big versus small, and, most recently, 'old' versus 'new' Europe'. Of course, having so many lines of division between groups of states with different memberships produces cross-cutting cleavages, thus leaving no state permanently isolated and protecting the European Union from permanent splits.

By the same token, states with similar international orientations, including non-aligned states, often want the same things in EU politics, but more because their interests and visions overlap than because of any conscious effort to coordinate them. In the broadest sense, all EU member states are allies, arguably 'permanent' ones. But all value flexibility in alliance-building on EU policy questions to the extent that there seem to be few permanent alliances between EU states. The wider point is that we are wise to avoid being seduced by the religion of the European Union as a single bloc.

Paradoxically, a schism that was, at one time, one of the most fundamental and divisive of all in Europe – between NATO members and non-members – is more significant in terms of sheer numbers now than ever before, yet rarely a source of rifts in EU policy debates. When Cyprus and Malta joined the Union in 2004, the number of non-aligned (or militarily neutral) member states rose to six. Questions naturally arise about the precise meaning of non-alignment in a post-Cold War world, especially when any member state of the European Union is, in key respects, obviously 'aligned' with 24 others. Still, it is striking and rarely remarked upon that nearly one-quarter of the European Union's membership now have national interests and normative objectives that differ in important respects from those of militarily allied states. Focusing on this internal EU divide, as opposed to others, offers productive insight into the Union's own concept of security, and how it differs from that expounded in the US National Security Strategy (NSS).

This chapter examines the ESS, the European Security and Defence Policy (ESDP) and transatlantic relations from the perspective of the non-aligned members of the European Union. We argue that both the ESS and ESDP have been shaped in important respects by the shared policy priorities of the non-aligned, a view at odds with the assumption that EU policy debates on matters of high politics are dominated – even monopolised – by large member states. Our thesis helps explain why states including Austria, Finland, Ireland and Sweden have been so sympathetic to the development of the ESDP and the ESS despite their policies of non-alignment.

The evolution of the ESDP illustrates how the content and objectives of the ESS matter in practice. Both are centred on conflict resolution, crisis management, multilateralism, and the pursuit of international peace and order. As always, it is fiendishly hard to prove precise causation in EU policy debates, or to show which member states, or groups of them (or which EU institutions), had how much influence on which agreement. But the ESS and ESDP are broadly consistent with the strategic cultures of the non-aligned states, which themselves have been enthusiastic supporters, even occasionally leaders, in the emergence of the European Union as a strategic actor.

We also examine the role of non-aligned states in EU–US relations. Two arguments are developed, both of which seem counter-intuitive. First, despite their non-membership of NATO, all of the non-aligned EU states continue to view their state-to-state relationship with Washington as one of their most important bilateral relationships. Second, and notwithstanding the first point, all consider cooperation with the United States on key international issues to be a cardinal priority of EU foreign policy, and none are obstacles to it despite profound differences over Iraq, climate change, and the content of the NSS.

A more general thesis emerges when we consider the surprising impact of non-aligned states on core decisions of EU security policy and strategy. Specifically, membership in the European Union may motivate states to 'export' their own foreign and security policy priorities in a way that pushes the Union as a whole towards greater international activism. We cannot claim that the modest activity that the European Union has undertaken under the ESDP thus far proves the thesis. But neither has it rendered it implausible.

Small states, non-alignment and the ESDP

The intergovernmental nature of EU foreign policy – extending to ESDP as a policy instrument – means that the member states are the central actors in the decision-making process. An orthodox, realist-inspired, account of international politics would hold that it is mostly (if not exclusively) great powers that can exert any real impact upon the formation of European foreign and security policy, which itself is viewed as unimportant relative to national policies on matters of high politics. Seen from this perspective, the ESDP could be reduced to an expression of the large member states' power capabilities, national interests and general wish to 'multiply' their influence in the international system. Small EU states have no choice but to follow suit and accept that their lack of power, especially 'hard' military power, will seriously limit their ability to shape the ESDP. This view is broadly shared by proponents of liberal intergovernmentalist European integration theory (Moravcsik 1998), although it focuses primarily on economic cooperation and 'has not yet lent itself fully to the application to European foreign and security policy' (Tonra 2001: 28). A liberal intergovernmental account of the ESDP would, nonetheless, hold that it is the national interests of the large member states that largely dictate EU security and defence policy outcomes.

It is hard to deny that each member state's impact on the European Union's core decisions is determined in important respects by its financial capacity and human resources. However, EU decision-making is governed by powerful norms that are hardly the norms of raw, power politics (see Peterson and Bomberg 1999: 53–9). Perhaps paradoxically, one norm associated with decision-making arrangements that are as 'purely' intergovernmental as those by which the ESDP and ESS have been derived is that outcomes must respect, or at least not do violence to, the priorities, values and norms of *all* member states, large or small, aligned or not (see Tallberg and Elgström 2001).

In a sign of how different divisions between EU states overlap and cross-cut, all six non-aligned states are 'small', with populations of less than nine million.[1] Despite the strict intergovernmentalism of EU foreign and security policy, there is clear evidence of convergence and parallel pressures that arise from Europeanisation – 'the political and policy changes caused by the impact of membership in the European Union on the member states' (Wong 2005: 135) – in this realm as in others. At the same time, it is difficult to speak of a 'non-aligned bloc' in the European Union because of the diversity of states that might potentially constitute one.

Consider, for example, that Sweden ranks (by most measures) as one of the six most powerful EU states in military terms, spending considerably more (1.8 per cent in 2003) of its total gross domestic product on defence than Finland (1.4 per cent), Austria (1.0 per cent) or Ireland (0.5 per cent).[2] Sweden invests a higher share of its defence budget on research and development than any EU state besides Spain, France or the United Kingdom (and more in absolute terms than Italy or the Netherlands; see Lindstrom 2005: 29–33). It has a modern, vibrant defence industry that has embraced globalisation and international cooperation with considerable vigour (see Bitzinger 2003: 53–8), and was one of six countries involved in the 1998 Letter of Intent on cooperation to restructure the European arms industry (see Chapter 9).

Of course, the non-aligned states share more in common than just their relatively small size. All (except Austria) are on the geographical periphery of the European Union. All share an interest, by virtue of their non-aligned status, in keeping the ESDP focused on the so-called Petersberg tasks – humanitarian, rescue and peacekeeping missions, along with crisis management (including 'peacemaking', a notion never really adequately defined[3]) – as opposed to evolving into a mechanism for collective security à la NATO.

Yet, when we scratch the surface of the European Union's non-aligned 'bloc', we find far more diversity in terms of orientation and interest than we might expect. For example, Sweden and Finland have at times worked together closely, particularly in placing crisis management firmly on the ESDP agenda. There is evidence of close Finnish–Swedish collaboration on policy towards NATO, with both inconspicuously using its Partnership for Peace framework to assimilate their defence force structures, planning to integrated European standards and jointly suggesting ideas in 2002 for reinvigorating NATO's Euro-Atlantic Partnership Council.[4] A leading Nordic defence analyst observes that 'the current saying is that Finland and Sweden have never been as close as now' (Huldt 2003: 7).

But close does not mean identical. If orientations and attitudes towards European security have converged, they have done so from very different starting points: Sweden's as a sheltered safe haven, protected by the buffers of its Nordic neighbours and friendly great powers, and Finland's as the European country most exposed to northern, foreign pressures (see Bailes 2003). It may seem wholly out of character, but Finland's unique geopolitical position means that, for example, it has not (thus far) ratified the Ottawa Convention banning the use of land-mines.[5] Sweden and Finland both contribute more than their share to peacekeeping, but Sweden through a general (even radical) post-2000 conversion from territorial defence to peace operations, and Finland through the creative modernisation of equipment available to several 'readiness' brigades while still maintaining a traditional, ground-force-heavy, territorial defence.

Non-alignment itself seems to mean rather different things in Stockholm and Helsinki. Finland moved quickly after the Cold War ended from its traditional position of 'neutrality' to a new designation of 'militarily non-allied'. Moreover, the durability of the new formulation was left open by repeated statements that 'under the prevailing circumstances' Helsinki was best able to guarantee its own and Europe's security by remaining non-allied. In contrast, only in 2002 did Sweden's main political parties agree a new national security concept stating that 'Sweden is militarily non-aligned' (literally alliance-free) and would seek 'to remain neutral in the event of conflicts within our vicinity', with no further qualification (Bailes 2003: 67–9; Ruhala 2003: 113). Thus, Finland has generally shown less concern about the 'militarisation' of the European Union or even (despite strong public opposition) the eventual possibility of NATO membership (see Sivonen 2003).

Nor should we be surprised if other non-aligned states give rather different answers to the questions: 'Against what are you supposed to be neutral?' and 'Which are the scenarios that will justify EU member states to step out of the solidarity line and say: Here ends our loyalty, we will go no further?' (Huldt 2003: 15). In 2001, Austria decided to rid itself entirely of neutrality in favour of a 'European solidarity' policy, and thus went further than either Sweden or Finland in declaring that its security and that of the European Union 'are inseparably linked'. For its part, Ireland has been reticent on moves to beef up defence industry collaboration (Bailes 2003: 61) and insisted on an explicit declaration that its military neutrality would not be compromised by the ratification (after a second referendum in 2002) of the Treaty of Nice (Edwards 2005: 56). The official Austrian position is that the question of joining NATO is 'left open', while presently Ireland's is that no Irish government would propose that the Republic join NATO (and both states would require successful referendums; see Ruhala 2003: 112). Neither Cyprus nor Malta are even members of NATO's Partnership for Peace, as are – with various degrees of enthusiasm – the other four non-aligned EU states.

Thus, seeking to divide EU member states into two neatly separated camps – NATO members and non-aligned – hides considerable nuance. Even on the 2003 Iraq war, while the EU non-aligned states all refused to sign up to the pro-United States 'coalition of the willing', the coalition itself drew support from both large and small member states, while the opposing camp was made up of European states of all sizes. Traumatically for Finland and Sweden, Denmark supported the invasion of Iraq and even contributed forces to 'Operation Iraqi Freedom' (Bergman 2006). The effect was to put paid to the once vaunted (especially around the 1995 enlargement) 'Nordic bloc' which, if Norway had joined, would have occupied one of four seats in a hypothetical European Union of 16 (see Peterson and Bomberg 1998; Grendstad 2001).

Just as simple divisions between EU states lack analytical purchase, variations in the EU policies of the non-aligned states and their larger partners on matters of European security are easily overemphasised. The success, at least in political terms, of the European Union's efforts to agree a security strategy and launch an embryonic defence policy reflects considerable convergence on security policy goals and priorities. The main contribution of the non-aligned to this convergence is their (largely) collective and distinctive strategic culture.

Strategic culture and the non-aligned states

Increasingly, it is accepted that defence and security policies cannot be decoupled from the wider social and political context in which they are constructed. Farrell (2002: 49) notes a 'culturalist' or constructivist turn in security studies and a new focus on ideational factors rather than power and national interests alone (see also Koenig-Archibugi 2004). A particular and, given the starting point, logical concern of such an approach is the idea of 'strategic culture', which involves 'a dynamic interplay between discourse and practice' (Neumann and Heikka 2005: 11) and assumes that it is the 'domestic system that explains particular beliefs about military power and reproduces these beliefs in national military institutions' (Farrell 2002: 50). Strategic culture has gained prominence both as a subject of academic inquiry (see Cornish and Edwards 2001, 2005; Howlett 2005) and as a practical concern for the European Union. The European Security Strategy acknowledges the 'need to develop a strategic culture that fosters early, rapid, and where necessary robust intervention'. In other words, the European Union requires 'the political and institutional confidence and processes to manage and deploy military force, coupled with external recognition of the European Union as a legitimate actor in the military sphere' (Cornish and Edwards 2005: 814).

As we have shown, there are significant variations in the non-aligned states' national defence policies, as well as interpretations of their roles within the ESDP. Yet, at least by the criterion of strategic culture, there is sufficient common ground to treat them as a distinctive group (Ojanen 2003). This is not to argue that the non-aligned states necessarily strive to be regarded as a collective force within the European Union. The point is that the non-aligned countries' security discourses and practices are framed in much the same language and emphasise the benefits of non-alignment.

To explain why, we might start with public opinion. As might be expected amongst countries that traditionally have resisted involvement in collective defence, there is uneasiness amongst the non-aligned with the idea of a European Union able to 'manage and deploy military force'. Yet, by the mid 2000s, clear majorities emerged in Austria, Finland, Ireland and Sweden in support of a common EU foreign policy and even – after the 2003 invasion of Iraq – in support of 'a common *defence* and security policy' (see Ojanen 2003).[6] Even clearer was public opposition to NATO membership, which was widely seen in the non-aligned states as inconsistent with the self-perception of peace-loving nations that promote security and justice in the international realm (see Sivonen 2003: 140–3; Munro 2005). A broad vision of the European Union as a security actor, framed by an affinity for multilateralism as well as the use of force only for self-defence and international peace operations, is shared by the non-aligned. Sweden, for instance, has no recent experience of inter-state conflict and a strong domestic consensus that the use of force should be confined to peace operations under the auspices of the United Nations and more recently the European Union and NATO. Yet the participation of Swedish forces in Operation Artemis in Bunia (Democratic Republic of the Congo), at the 'hard end' of the first ever EU-flagged military operation outside of Europe, gave Sweden credibility as a state that was prepared to use force at the service of humanitarian intervention when requested by the United Nations (Howorth 2005: 194).

More generally, Sweden together with Finland and the other Nordics has a long and respected track record in international (especially UN) peace operations. Sometimes referred to as 'superpowers of peacekeeping' (Salminen 2003: 181), these states have been the vanguard of developing post-modern militaries that play non-traditional military roles, a phenomenon that has begun to be replicated across the European Union as a whole. Majorities in nearly all European states now link values such as freedom and democracy directly with military power, and view missions to restore or keep peace as the paramount jobs of their national militaries. Across the European Union, around 80 per cent of citizens agree that their national militaries should aid other countries in the event of natural, ecological or nuclear disasters, or provide famine relief or remove landmines (see Manigart 2001).

Interestingly, international and regional crisis management provides both a channel through which Nordic states can 'export' their own norms and values (Bergman 2004) and a basis for strong loyalties to national militaries. For example, popular support for the Finnish military is exceptionally strong, as reflected in the fact that over 80 per cent of Finnish males continue to perform their military service in any given year (Sivonen 2003: 143). To the popular Nordic mind, a primary purpose of military power is to show to populations in crisis-stricken areas how Nordic societies have organised themselves to maintain peace and security.

Here, again, we must be careful not to gloss over important distinctions between non-aligned states. Eliasson (2004) distinguishes between the 'ideological neutrality' of Ireland and Sweden and the 'pragmatic and realist' neutrality of Finland and Austria (which was more or less imposed upon the latter after World War II). The stance of Sweden, the largest of the non-aligned, is directly linked to the strong advocacy of neutrality/non-alignment by the Social Democratic Party (SDP), which has been in government in Sweden for nearly all of the post-war period (Nilsson 1991; Eliasson 2004; Ferreira-Pereira 2005; Bergman 2006). Still, the tone and wording of current foreign and security policy discourses in all the non-aligned states tends to highlight their shared commitment to duties across borders and converging strategic cultures.

To illustrate the point, Finnish foreign policy historically has had a pronounced realist, pragmatic, Russo-focused bent (see Sivonen 2003). Yet the Finnish government has recently committed itself to reaching the UN recommended target for overseas development assistance (ODA) of 0.7 per cent of GDP by 2010 (Finnish Minister for Foreign Affairs 2003: 2).[7] Finland has also participated actively in international conflict mediation in Europe and beyond. Its former president, Martti Ahtisaari, played a vital role in ending ethnic cleansing in Kosovo in 1999 and may be the world's best-known international mediator.[8]

Ireland's strategic culture is framed by Article 29 of its Constitution which 'affirms its devotion to the idea of peace and friendly co-operation ... amongst nations founded on international justice and morality'. At first glance, it may appear that Ireland fits the mould of a traditional, pacifist, neutral state that is bound to inactivity by its 'triple lock' mechanism, whereby Irish troops may only be deployed in military situations under a UN mandate and with the approval of both the Irish government and parliament. However, Ireland (like Finland) has recently committed itself to raise its contribution to ODA to meet the UN target (Ahern 2004a). Moreover, Ireland and Austria's peacekeeping records may be less well-known than those of the Nordics, but both have participated actively in international peacekeeping and never viewed neutrality as an obstacle to such engagement (Neuhold 2003: 15), unlike (say) Switzerland. Amongst all EU member states, Ireland and Austria ranked behind only Poland, the United Kingdom and France in terms of their contributions of personnel to UN operations in 2004 (Lindstrom 2005: 101). It was perhaps a signal of Austria's arrival as a 'normal' EU state on matters of foreign policy that its former foreign minister, Benita Ferrero-Waldner (2004: 2), was chosen as EU Commissioner for External Relations in 2004, after identifying multilateralism, the combat of global poverty, the rule of law and the UN as the core values informing her own country's external relations.

More generally, the contribution of the non-aligned states to the European Union's strategic culture is visible in their broad vision of the European Union as a 'civilian' and 'ideological power' that promotes 'redistributive justice' and exports peace and order (Manners 2002). Put simply, the non-aligned states aspire to a different, more comprehensive, and higher quality of security than is implied by the mere absence of war between states. Their strategic cultures are built on notions of collective, comprehensive security, and more recently the concept of 'human security', which originated in UN Human Development Reports of the early 1990s and was a prominent theme at the 2000 UN Millennium summit. Human security is distinctive in taking 'the individual and his community as a point of reference, rather than the State, by addressing both military and non-military threats to his/her security' (Biscop 2005: 5). The aspiration to promote this broader concept of security leads to a strategic culture that is both normative and active on gender issues, global redistribution of income, and close cooperation with the UN. In a far cry from how they once watched from the sidelines as neutrals during the Cold War, the non-aligned states have found themselves using the European Union as a vehicle to push themselves, each other, and other EU allies towards global activism in the pursuit of a distinct normative agenda.

The non-aligned states and the ESDP

The non-aligned states' support for the ESDP can be traced to both general and specific factors. Generally, the ESDP reflects the core values of the non-aligned states' national security discourses and practices, which have also fed into the ESS. The European Union's security and defence policy has evolved from a set of ideas and aspirations to an actual set of actions according to a timetable that has suited the non-aligned states, and has even allowed them to shape its evolution at crucial junctures. Being present at the creation of the ESDP has given the non-aligned members a chance both to influence the ESDP to make it resemble their own security policies and to steep the European Union in their own self-image.

Here we focus mainly on Finland and Sweden's contributions since they have been particularly active and have influenced the ESDP above and beyond what might have been expected.[9] The mid 1990s brought an unusual degree of coordinated action between Helsinki and Stockholm, as shown most tangibly by their joint memorandum on security submitted to the 1996–7 intergovernmental conference (IGC). Tabled at a crucial point in the negotiations on what became the Amsterdam Treaty, the memo urged that the ESDP should focus on the Petersberg tasks (see Finnish Permanent Representation 1996). Joint Finnish–Swedish diplomacy demonstrated, in at least three ways, *nous* about EU decision-making that was both shrewd and unusual for any state new to the cut and thrust of Brussels bargaining. First, the Finns and Swedes 'got in early' and shaped the debate – arguing for the embrace of crisis management (as opposed to 'defence') – at a time when positions were still forming. Such a strategy is a wise one for any small state(s) in any EU policy discussion, particularly one (potentially) 'driven by the large and militarily most capable EU countries' (Eriksson 2003: 130). Second, on such a divisive set of questions, the Swedes and Finns found others receptive to falling back on the Petersberg tasks formula already agreed several years earlier (for the Western European Union), which had 'the merit among other things of minimizing substantive Treaty amendment in this field' (Bailes 2003: 61). Third, the Finnish–Swedish memorandum 'defined the middle ground in the IGC' and attracted support both from 'maximalists' keen to see the European Union become a primary European security organisation and 'minimalists' concerned about the sanctity of NATO (Sjursen 1998: 107). Crucially, the Finns and Swedes proposed an activist ESDP (well before it went under that name) but one that did not either threaten or replicate NATO.

Within two years of agreement on the Amsterdam Treaty, a major turning point in the development of the ESDP arrived in 1999 with Finland holding the EU Council Presidency. After Europe's military infirmity had been cruelly exposed in Kosovo, the 1999 Helsinki summit saw the Union agree to create a 60,000-strong rapid reaction force (RRF) that would be quickly deployable and protractedly sustainable. The same summit reached agreement on the so-called Helsinki Headline Goals, to increase EU military capacity, and produced breakthroughs on enlargement and Turkey. The Finnish chair could not take all the credit for a series of agreements that, together, led to suggestions that the European Union at Helsinki had finally grown up and 'found its place in the world'.[10] But an early assessment of the impact of the 1995 enlargement on the European Union had highlighted three main effects: the addition of three new states that strongly favoured further enlargement, the reinforcement of the importance of Brussels as a political capital, and an increase in the power of the Council Presidency (Peterson and Bomberg 1998). If nothing else, 1999 was a defining moment in Finland's relationship with the European Union, since it was when a country that had previously been 'Finlandised' reinvented itself as a leader in fleshing out European foreign and defence policy.

Subsequently, all four non-aligned states in the EU-15 committed more than their share of financial resources and troops and officers to the RRF (see Working Group VIII-Defence 2002: 21), despite delays in its operationalisation, as well as to KFOR, the 35-nation peacekeeping force in Kosovo which, in a sign of changing times, operated under the command of NATO. All the non-aligned except Ireland contributed to the Union's Concordia operation in the Yugoslav Republic of Macedonia in 2003. As indicated, Sweden was a key participant in the European Union's Artemis operation in the Democratic Republic of Congo, which operated under French command. Austria was a prominent participant in Operation Althea, through which the European Union took over peacekeeping in Bosnia from NATO in 2005 (see Lindstrom 2005: 95).

Meanwhile, Sweden accepted the leadership of one (of a total of 15) of the European Union's battle groups, whose membership included Estonia, Finland and (even) Norway. Stepping forward to be the 'framework nation' for a battle group might seem like an odd thing to do for a non-aligned state. However, it is very much in line with the current defence discourse of Sweden, which stresses the significance of rapid reaction to international crisis (Bergman 2004).

More than anything else, however, Sweden and Finland have been associated with the development of a European civilian crisis management capacity, which they consider to be one of 'the Union's most important challenges' (Lindh and Tuomioja 2000: 2). This view is driven by the diverse range of diplomatic means at the European Union's disposal, and the conviction that they could be more effectively used in order to execute effective conflict resolution and peace support (Hjelm-Wallén 2003: 7; Freivalds and Tuomioja 2003; Ferrero-Waldner 2004; Finnish Prime Minister's Office 2004; McBean 2005). The final decision to add a civilian aspect to the Union's crisis management mechanism was taken during the Swedish Presidency of the European Union in 2001, and embraced police and judiciary cooperation, combat against international organised crime as well as anti-terrorism measures. Together with Germany, Sweden has been at the forefront of calls for a European Civilian Headline Goal by which civilian rapid reaction groups consisting of specialists in policing, judicial training, and post-war reconstruction are created (see Strömvik 2005).

Explaining non-aligned state activism

However much they differ, the normative objectives of the non-aligned states and those of other EU member states have converged markedly. Austria, Finland, Ireland and Sweden now broadly support further military integration to make the European Union a more effective provider of conflict resolution in its immediate vicinity and beyond.[11] Of course, none wishes to transform the European Union into a traditional military alliance. Rather they envisage the ESDP as a powerful instrument in the deployment of the European Union's civilian and normative powers (Tewes 2002: 10; Manners 2002). The Swedish Ministry for Foreign Affairs (2003: 1) is clear on this point, viewing the RRF as an important mechanism by which the European Union can 'prevent injustice and safeguard human rights'. In effect, the non-aligned states have become defenders of a new, modernised conception of the European Union as a civilian power, deploying (if necessary) post-modern militaries whose main task is to bring 'civilisation' to the 'international environment' (Tewes 2002: 11).

Divergences with the European Union at large

Thus far, the ESDP that has emerged is one with which all member states can live. Still, the question of whether the European Union will always offer sufficient room for divergences in member states' strategic cultures remains a live one. Sooner or later, non-aligned EU states are likely to have to decide how far they are prepared to go in endorsing the move towards a fully integrated defence policy. All, to a greater or lesser extent, have expressed concern with the possible adoption of an obligatory 'mutual defence arrangement' (Cowen 2003a: 1), although respecting other member states' wishes to go ahead with such a proposal.

Sweden and Finland also voiced scepticism about the proposal, put forward in the Constitutional Draft Treaty of the European Union, to allow for so-called structured defence cooperation, in which sub-groups of EU states could undertake their own defence projects. A shared view in Stockholm and Helsinki was that flexible defence integration might have a disintegrative effect on the European Union as an international actor (see Freivalds and Tuomioja 2003). Yet, in a sign that the non-aligned do not constitute a bloc, the issue did not seem to evoke the same level of concern in Austria (Hajnoczi 2005: 11). Also indicative was the Irish foreign minister's visit to Sweden, Finland and Austria in early 2005 to try to construct a common 'non-aligned front' – apparently unsuccessfully – on the danger posed to Irish neutrality by the battle groups initiative.[12]

In sum, the non-aligned consider it their duty to be active participants in European crisis management and peace support. However, they are not yet prepared to sacrifice their non-alignment at the altar of the ESDP. For now, circles are still able to be squared. For example, all four non-aligned in the EU-15 were able to declare unconditional support for the idea, launched by the Convention on the Future of Europe, for an EU clause of 'deeper solidarity' according to which each would be obliged to assist any member state subject to a terrorist attack or natural disaster (Lindh and Tuomioja 2002: 2). All were active supporters of the European Council declaration following the Madrid bombings of 11 March 2004 that committed all member states to aid each other in similar circumstances with 'all the instruments at their disposal, including military resources' (see Missiroli 2005). Neither provision was considered a threat to non-alignment, since they did not involve defence of other EU states' national borders (see McBean 2005: 31). Future clauses that do are neither unimaginable nor welcome from the point of the non-aligned.

The European Security Strategy

The ESS seeks to give the Union a strategy, within which the ESDP is one (of many) instrument(s). The main stated purpose of the ESS is to make Europe 'ready to share in the responsibility for global security and building a better world'. The support of all non-aligned EU states for the ESS was unequivocal. While there is no yardstick by which we can measure their specific impact on the ESS, its discursive patterns bear close resemblance to their own security discourses. The first chapter of the ESS is devoted to global challenges – poverty, infectious diseases, drought and famine, violent conflict – most of which affect today's Europe only indirectly and none of which are strictly matters of 'defence'. The final wording of the ESS highlights effective multilateralism, cooperation with the UN, and value-based internationalism. In particular, the ESS pledges to aid the UN in its effort to 'assist countries emerging from conflicts' and to aid 'short-term crisis management situations'.

The ESS preference for a broad approach to conflict resolution also strikes a chord with the security strategies of the non-aligned states. Although Helsinki stated its wish for a stronger emphasis on the root causes of conflict (Raik 2004), Finland welcomed the focus of the ESS on comprehensive security and its potential 'to strengthen the Union as a global actor' (Finnish Prime Minister's Office 2004: 48). Austria would have preferred an ESS more focused on Russia and disarmament – issues at the centre of its security and defence policy (Reiter and Frank 2004) – but still was wholehearted in its support for the ESS.

In the words of the Irish prime minister, 'the EES very much reflects the European Union's and Ireland's commitment to a comprehensive approach to security' (Ahern 2003: 3). The Irish view is that the ESS is fully compatible with Ireland's preference for a 'holistic approach to security, going beyond purely military matters ... the United Nations, conflict prevention' as well as a 'rule-based international order' (McBean 2005: 27). Arguably, Ireland's main contribution was made during its EU Presidency in 2004 after the actual adoption of the ESS. The Irish prime minister, Bertie Ahern (2004b: 1), was an enthusiastic supporter of the ESS during the Irish Presidency and committed his country to 'accelerating implementation of the European Security Strategy Recommendations on Terrorism' and enhancing the European Union's role as a provider of 'effective multilateralism' (Ahern 2003: 3–4).

For its part, Sweden was deeply involved in the development of the strategy, not least by organising and hosting the final of three seminars that preceded the adoption of the ESS in December 2003. The Stockholm seminar gathered national experts and academics and gave them a unique opportunity to comment on the final wording of the ESS. Notably, the ESS was revised from earlier drafts towards a text that was less muscular in tone and more distinct from the NSS, particularly in its insistence that new security threats arising from terrorism and WMD should not obscure the imperative to deal with '"old threats", such as regional conflicts, or the need to address the root causes of threats' (Biscop 2004b: 19).

Sweden also was the main engine behind the adoption of a separate EU Strategy Against Proliferation of Weapons of Mass Destruction, a concept introduced by its foreign minister, Anna Lindh, in spring 2003 (Strömvik 2005: 218). An important first step was the publication in a leading Swedish newspaper of a jointly authored editorial by Lindh and her Greek counterpart, Giorgios Papandreaou, in April 2003 under the title 'How We Avoid a New Iraq'.[13] It provoked a significant amount of exchange and policy work on non-proliferation involving the EU Council Secretariat, national officials and experts, before the Union's WMD strategy was adopted at the same time as the ESS in December 2003. Two tangible effects were non-proliferation clauses contained in a Partnership and Cooperation agreement signed with Tajikistan, and Association Agreements agreed with Syria and Mauritania in 2004 (Ahlström 2005: 41). More generally, in an interesting illustration of how one state's activism encourages that of others, Stockholm's impulse on WMD proliferation could be viewed as planting the seeds for the diplomacy led by France, Germany and the United Kingdom (the so-called EU-3) to try to negotiate limits to Iran's nuclear development programme (see Kile 2005).

More generally, the focus of the ESS on UN-led multilateralism, fair and free trade, global development, good governance, rule of law and human rights shows a desire to conceptualise international security in the broadest terms. The non-aligned states thus managed to export to the European Union their concern to make Europe noticeably more global and internationalist in its outlook. Another side of the same coin is that EU member states outside the non-aligned bloc appear to have moved closer towards a specifically non-aligned conception of good international conduct. The ESS 'builds on a "European way" in international relations' in its insistence on 'a comprehensive security strategy' that 'looks beyond the traditional confines of security policy' (Biscop 2004b: 32). It also provides a new 'D-drive', pushing the European Union towards international activism with its focus on disasters, diseases and disruptions, even as it mostly skirts traditional questions of 'defence' (Missiroli 2005).

In short, the adoption of the ESS appears to mark a convergence in EU member states' conception of security. In particular, 'the ESS was born at a time when leading EU states were seeking reconciliation both with each other and across the Atlantic' (Bailes 2005: 23). In the section which follows, we examine how and what non-aligned states contribute to the European Union's evolving relationship with Washington, especially in the aftermath of the United States-led intervention in Iraq.

The non-aligned states and transatlantic relations

The impact of the non-aligned states on the European Union's relations with Washington is heavily nuanced and resists simple caricatures. To illustrate the point, a crude (and somewhat wild-eyed) analysis of the European Union's defence ambitions by an American lawyer complains that:

> Austria, Finland, Ireland, and Sweden all were neutral during the Cold War, and do not belong to NATO ... None of these countries [along with France] has a history of cooperation, let alone coordination, with Washington on pressing security matters such as counter-terrorism, Afghanistan, and Iraq.
>
> (Cimbalo 2004: 114–15)

All of the non-aligned, of course, were opposed to the 2003 Iraq war (see Menon and Lipkin 2003).

Yet, however much Sweden and other non-aligned states seek to make the European Union more effective and active globally,[14] all continue to view US–EU relations as a way to avoid 'great power domination of Europe' and all place a high priority on their own bilateral relationship with Washington. In Stockholm's case, the imperative arises from the (perceived) unsolved problem of Russia, policy cooperation with the United States in the Baltic region, the tendency for Swedes to think universally (so Sudan is as important as Ukraine), and the inclination for Baltic and (to a lesser extent) Nordic states with diasporas in America to be instinctively pro-United States. Here and in other non-aligned national capitals, two views tend to co-exist somewhat uneasily. One accepts that the European Union needs to punch closer to its collective weight in Washington: 'We all know that the strength of the European Union is its magnetism. We need somehow to enhance our magnetism in the US, too.' The second accepts that strengthening US–EU relations is a worthwhile aim but contends that 'the real issues should be done bilaterally': that is, between Washington and European national capitals.

If these two views seem paradoxical, consider that however much the Bush administration's policies – as reflected, for example, in the NSS – have posed particular difficulties for the non-aligned states, all continue to place transatlantic relations at the centre of their security policies (see, for example, Swedish Government 2004: 9; Persson 2004). As Austrian foreign minister, Ferrero-Waldner (2003: 9) argued that 'in terms of creating and maintaining peace in the world, transatlantic relations indubitably play the most substantial role'. As EU Commissioner, her line became: 'we have no more important partnership than with the US'.[15] Helsinki's consistent view has been that only the European Union and the United States working together can tackle the challenges of global poverty, disease, weapons proliferation, religious fundamentalism and terrorism (see Tuomioja 2004). The Irish position is that 'what was true before our differences over Iraq is equally true today – ongoing and pragmatic cooperation between Europe and the United States is indispensable' (Cowen 2003b: 2).

None of this is to deny that tensions exist over how relations with the United States are conducted by the European Union. Another reason why non-aligned national capitals continue to want to tackle the 'real issues' bilaterally is that national foreign ministries complain that they feel a sense of being placed at the periphery of the EU–US dialogue by the European Union's institutions and thus feel a low sense of ownership of it (see European Commission 2005). Even if all EU member states agree that a sound and well functioning transatlantic relationship is the best guarantor of international peace, there are clear divergences in European attitudes towards US foreign policy under the current American regime. Prominent amongst them are ones that flow from how deeply embedded in non-aligned states' foreign policies are their instinctive support for international law, UN-led multilateralism and the role of diplomacy in conflict prevention, as opposed to any natural opposition to the United States. More generally, the support of the non-aligned for transatlantic solidarity in meeting new threats arising from the convergence of terrorism and WMD proliferation is no weaker than that of states who are formally military allies of the United States. By the same token, there is no evidence of will amongst the non-aligned to obstruct the EU–US dialogue.

Conclusion

We began by suggesting that the theology of the 'European Union as a single bloc' was always something of a myth, even before the 2004 enlargement and divisions over relations with Bush's America challenged it as never before. We have cast light on the specific security concerns of non-aligned states, which now count for nearly one in four members of the European Union.

Our assessment provides a distinctive angle on the internal dynamics of the development of the European Union's security policy. We have argued that, whatever new divisions have emerged, there is little or no evidence to suggest that one of the most politically salient old divisions – between NATO members and non-aligned states – has troubled agreement on the ESS or the development of the ESDP. It might actually be the case that states such as Sweden and Finland, with less at stake in the international distribution of power, can exercise proportionally more impact upon the European Union's strategic culture than their larger partners. In the language of realist theory, their actions are less likely to be judged with suspicion by other states as designed to achieve 'relative gains'.

We also have detected a tendency for the non-aligned states overtly to frame their European defence commitments in light of their global duties (Bergman 2004). Rather than obstructing the development of the Union's crisis management capacity, the non-aligned members have actively pushed the European Union to become more capable and active as a manager of crises. Restrictions arising from non-alignment can be transformed into opportunities by which non-aligned states can provide mediation in conflict and civilian crisis management, without having to face the obvious restrictions imposed by NATO membership. Phrased differently, we might say that non-alignment is a peace strategy in its own right, rather than an impediment to international and regional conflict prevention. Going one step further, a plurality of foreign policy traditions may be an asset for the European Union rather than an obstacle, providing all members adhere to a set of core values for European foreign policy (see Smith 2004).

Our analysis leads us to three observations about alliance strategies in the European Union more generally. First, the non-aligned do not really qualify as a bloc even if they want many of the same things much of the time. Second, while life in the new EU-25 needs further investigation, it is remarkable how rarely we can identify permanent alliances between states across policy debates. Third, EU membership seems, fundamentally, to have the effect of encouraging member states to push the Union as a whole to be more activist, using the European Union's institutions and processes as a multiplier of what national capitals wish to achieve in international politics. It is hard to imagine how another framework could be used to encourage, say, Sweden to be more concerned about the problems of the Mediterranean region or (say) Spain to be more concerned about the anti-democratic drift of Putin's Russia.

As for the ESDP specifically, nothing that the European Union has agreed or done under its rubric has yet forced the non-aligned to make hard choices between preserving their non-alignment or abandoning it to become full participants in a collective EU security guarantee. There has been no deployment of hard military power in a way that clearly violates the Union's status as a 'civilian power'. By the same token, hard choices concerning relations with the United States have been avoided, or at least deferred, because

'ESDP [was not] created to deal with a specific, visible threat, as was the case with NATO' and, at least for now, 'there is no member state for which ESDP is central to its defence or security policy' (Cooper 2004b: 189). The secret to the success of the ESDP and the ESS, insofar as the Union has mostly moved at one speed on both, is that the United States is still considered a key – perhaps *the* key – partner in guaranteeing national security for all EU member states, including (implicitly, if not explicitly) the non-aligned. Those alarmed about NATO's long-term decline imagine that the European Union might eventually develop a 'powerful federal national security apparatus' (Cimbalo 2004: 113), which might conflict sharply with the norms and values of non-aligned states. But the European Union remains a very long way away from having one. Until it does, the Union is likely to continue to allow enough space for variations in states' attitudes towards the ESDP, while ensuring that there is sufficient convergence to strengthen the European Union's crisis management capacity on a global stage, and consensus on the need for a true alliance with the United States. The non-aligned have thus far played a game of squaring circles skilfully. The game is unlikely to become any easier for them to play.

Notes

1 As a cautionary note, both Sweden, and to a lesser extent Finland, view them-selves as 'medium-sized states', and we have found that officials from both states often press this point vociferously.

2 Despite recent cuts in its defence spending, Sweden continues to invest a higher than EU average share of its GDP in defence. Cyprus and Malta have only token military budgets (although Cyprus signed up to a 'Balkan battle group' for peace-keeping and humanitarian operations with Bulgaria, Romania and Greece in late 2005) and have had little discernible impact on debates surrounding ESDP. Thus, our focus in this chapter is on the European Union's other four non-aligned states.

3 The Petersberg tasks were agreed in Petersberg, near Bonn, in 1992 as the primary military jobs of the Western European Union (WEU), which itself was created via the Brussels Treaty of 1948. The Amsterdam Treaty (1997) declared that the European Union would 'avail itself' of the WEU if military instruments were needed to carry out conflict prevention or peacekeeping. See Rees (1998).

4 The Euro-Atlantic Partnership Council was launched in 1997 and contained 46 member states by 2006: the 26 members of NATO plus 20 'partners' involved in Partnership for Peace, which promotes exchange between NATO and non-NATO forces, to promote transparency, modernisation and inter-operability. Austria, Finland, Sweden and Ireland are all participants (Cyprus and Malta are not).

5 The current official position is that Finland will join the Ottawa Convention in 2012 and eliminate all anti-personnel mines in its arsenal by 2016. Finnish officials take pains to insist that there are no land-mines deployed on Finnish territory. See testimony of Timo Kantola, Counsellor, Permanent Representation of Finland to the European Union at hearings held on 'Landmines Information Day: the European Parliament for a Mine-Free World', 16 June 2005, available from: www.europarl.eu.int/hearings/20050616/joint_hearing/kantolin_intervention.pdf (accessed 24 November 2005).

6 See, in particular, results of the Eurobarometer survey of April 2003, which saw support for an ESDP shoot up by five points or more on previous poll results in Austria, Ireland and Sweden. Online. Available: http://europa.eu.int/comm./public_opinion/index_en.htm (accessed 26 November 2005).

7 All member states in the 'old' EU-15 agreed in May 2005 that they would meet the UN target for ODA by 2015. But Finland was in the vanguard by pledging to meet the target five years earlier and doing so several years earlier than other EU states.

8 Ahtisaari now heads his own non-governmental organisation called Crisis Management Initiative, which acts as the secretariat for the 'Helsinki process', a joint initiative by the Finnish and Tanzanian governments billed as a 'search of novel and empowering solutions to the dilemmas of global governance'. In 2005, Ahtisaari served as special UN envoy to the 'final status' talks on the future of Kosovo. Online. Available: http://www.ahtisaari.fi/ (accessed 8 January 2006).

9 Actually, the same might be argued about Austria and Ireland. The first ever informal Council of EU Defence Ministers was held under Austria's (first ever) 1998 Council Presidency. Bilateral US–EU declarations on counter-terrorism and counter-proliferation, which helped sustain cooperation on homeland security policy, were agreed in 2004 under an Irish EU Council Presidency.

10 See Simon Taylor, 'Union Comes of Age in Helsinki', *European Voice*, 16 December–5 January 2000, p. 10.

11 Swedish and Finnish support for the ESDP coincides with the internationalisation of their armed forces and their participation in the PFP, as well as numerous regional defence initiatives in the Baltic Sea region (see Stålvant 2003).

12 See EUObserver, 'Call for Neutral Countries to Work Together', 26 January 2005. Online. Available: http://EUObserver.com (accessed 8 January 2006).

13 'Så undviker vi ett nytt Irak', *Dagens Nyheter*, 10 April 2003. Online. Available: http://www.regeringen.se/sb/d/1354 (accessed 27 November 2005).

14 To illustrate the point, a visit by one of us to Stockholm in early 2005 to gauge views on the narrow question of how well the 1995 New Transatlantic Agenda (NTA) EU framework for relations with the United States was working found nearly all interviews focusing on foreign policy and ESDP, matters almost entirely untouched by the NTA itself. A total of 15 interviews were undertaken 8–10 February 2005 with officials and academics. Several quotes in the paragraphs that follow are taken from them. For full text of the study see European Commission (2005).

15 Online. Available: http://europa.eu.int/comm/external_relations/us/revamping/index.htm (accessed 8 January 2006).

11 Measuring up

The strategies as strategy

James H. Wyllie

The advanced industrial states of North America and Europe have rarely experienced as long a period of established peace within their region as they presently enjoy. Yet within the European Union, and between the United States and some of the leading founder members of the EU, there has been a profound, and often bitter, debate about the quality of security enjoyed by the West and the appropriate strategies required to sustain that condition (see Applebaum 2003; Broughton 2003; Daalder and Kagan 2004). Arguably, the security debate reached its apex – in terms of bitterness – in early 2003 after the United States-led invasion of Iraq. The Iraq war began almost exactly halfway between the unveiling (September 2002) of the US National Security Strategy (NSS), and the European Council's endorsement (December 2003) of the European Security Strategy (ESS). Both have been promulgated as serious, coherent responses to the security challenges of the current era. Investigation of how and in what circumstances the United States and the European Union intend to use force, or avoid the use of force, in addressing new security challenges provides an indication of their global strategic and political compatibility now and over the short to medium term. This chapter offers such an assessment.

Security dynamics and strategy

In the classic realist tradition, the protection of the community from 'the ever-present threat of conflict' is the objective of strategy (Baylis and Wirtz 2002: 6). To date, such order as exists 'within modern international society is precarious and imperfect' (Bull 1978: 52). In all but the rarest exceptions, states cannot abrogate responsibility for their own protection. It is the strategies which governments devise which deliver whatever degree of security is attainable. Security may be a 'contested concept' (Buzan 1991: 35), but without a serious commitment to national security the other achievements and values of the state become vulnerable.

Undoubtedly, assessing one's real security condition is a constant challenge for states, not least because there is a distinct psychological dimension to notions of security. On the whole, security is negative in nature in that it stops nasty things happening to core values, and it is often difficult to prove that nasty things were going to happen anyway. Nonetheless, while states may often be uncertain as to the level of national security they enjoy, in times of jeopardy and attack they certainly know when they feel unsafe. Clearly, security is an inexact concept. Identifying all the relevant variables is problematic; measuring them even more so. Traditionally, military considerations are deemed the most important. However, military superiority alone does not provide a high level of relative security. In the modern world a strong, vibrant technological and economic base is essential to provide advanced military hardware and software and the means to pay for it. A legitimate political system and a popular consensus in support of a security policy are vital for a robust, durable level of security against a wide spectrum of threats. A holistic view of security would argue that as well as defence policy and most foreign policy, elements of domestic policy such as social welfare and education have crucial national security functions. This is a view particularly popular in many West European societies. Indeed, all states have their own national security cultures which are reflections of their histories and strategic circumstances (see Kagan 2003).

Security, however, is a condition, not a framed set of objectives and inflexible strategies. To be effective, national or collective security policy must be allowed to be dynamic. Just as power is a relative concept, and meaningless unless related to countervailing power, then so is security. Security is different depending upon the threat to which it is related, and the level and severity of threat posed by other states and non-state actors may change constantly, and often rapidly. If, when measured in objective capabilities, a state is relatively weak, then diplomatic arrangements with other states which share a mutual view of how the international system should be shaped may be pursued. Formal alliances, informal coalitions, collective security agreements and balance of power manoeuvres all have particular visions of security as the goal. According to classical realist theory, such security regimes survive so long as the interests of the members correspond. When they diverge in a serious manner, alliances and other collective security arrangements disintegrate and balances of power change as partners are changed (Walt 1997: 163). Changing circumstances may even drive states to risk war for reasons of national security. It should not be assumed that security always equates with peace. States facing existential threats may perceive war-making as an opportunity to deflect enemies and establish longer-term security (Mearsheimer 2001: 32–3). Historically, nearly all states have seen independence and well-being as more important than the absence of war (Bull 1978: 18). Perceptions of national security do not always coincide with sustaining the status quo.

Recent times have witnessed a particularly dynamic character to the condition of international security. The Cold War model of containment of quantifiable threats with timely recourse to warnings, and to last-resort coercion as the threat emerges, is no longer feasible. There is now a transnational geography of security where national frontiers no longer define threats, as Germany's did for France between 1870 and 1945 and the Soviet Union's did for the West between 1947 and 1990. There are now major threats which, while exploiting the cover of states, are not of states nor aspire to be orthodox states. Where these hostile transnational groups have relationships with states, it is usually with radical anti-Western states, thereby compounding the uncertainty and unpredictability of the threat (Gaddis 2005: 4). Preparedness for an attack is a function not just of identifying an enemy, but also having some degree of warning. Security is a function of time, but the 'bolt out of the blue' attack is a key characteristic of modern mass terrorism. For reasons of religious fanaticism or political spite, such an attack could also be the characteristic of a rogue state facing political defeat and armed with WMD. There may be little time to identify the aggressor's target, take specific defensive measures, and deploy forces (Zelikow 2003: 25–6). Even assuming some time is available, the aggressor may often be difficult to locate and unwilling to negotiate. Al Qaeda, for instance,

> represents a transnational threat – one very different in kind from that posed by the IRA or even newer groups such as Hamas. Al Qaeda has potentially thousands of members and no interest in bargaining with the United States or its allies. Instead it seeks to cripple them, by inflicting mass casualties if possible, potentially with weapons of mass destruction.
>
> (Stevenson 2003: 77)

There is no question that these conditions of 'globalised insecurity' (Bertram *et al.* 2002: 142) place challenging demands on states. These challenges are reflected in controversies surrounding differing interpretations in international law about the legitimate use of force, not least anticipatory self-defence by states anxious about new forms of surprise attack. International law in this regard, including the pre-nuclear, pre-transnational mass terrorism UN Charter framework, has developed historically. Until recently, in custom as well as statute, the law has addressed states versus states, with conventional weapons. Custom is now changing and the evolutionary fusion of new custom with reformed statute to reflect the age-old principle that states have the sovereign right 'to use force to defend themselves effectively' (Arend 2003: 98) is underway, but by no means settled.

In an era of asymmetrical conflict, neither international law nor distance nor deterrence, together or separately, meet the requirements of national security against non-state and state adversaries who are intent on mass killing, eschew risk-adverse behaviour, and often advance ideological agendas beyond rational negotiation (Levite and Sherwood-Randall 2002–3: 81; Freedman 2003: 105). While Western military and economic superiority may provoke such adversaries, it is strategies utilising these strengths which address the new security conditions. The alliance bipolarity and nuclear balance-of-terror security architecture of the Cold War years obliged cautious, rational, strategic decision-making on the part of the competitive great powers, and the aim of strategy was often to avoid war. Caution and rational policy are clearly characteristics often absent from the West's current adversaries. Freed by changing circumstances from the demands of mutual deterrence, Western strategy can return to its traditional function of defeating the enemy and winning the war. Indeed, the nature and behaviour of the enemy does not allow for an alternative.

The security of states or collectives of states can never be absolute, but leaders need to make reasonable efforts to adapt strategies to meet prevalent demands. Strategy is derived from '*strategos*', the ancient Greek term for generalship. In modern times, the concept of strategy has moved beyond tactics and battlefield manoeuvre; but neither is it just a big plan or a world view. For nearly 200 years, strategy has been informed by the popularised Clausewitzian dictum that 'war is the continuation of politics by other means'. It is a specific mode of behaviour with serious and often costly implications. It is 'the use that is made of force and the threat of force for the ends of policy' (Gray 1999: 17). It is 'the art or science of shaping means so as to promote ends in any field of conflict' (Bull 1968: 593). The coherent use of coercion in the context of conflict is what strategy is all about, and to use the term otherwise is misleading and may have outcomes contributing to costly insecurities. For instance, wittingly or unwittingly, leaders may lead their publics to believe that threats have been rigorously assessed and forces procured and deployed to meet such threats when, in reality, all that has been declared is a preferred view of the world and how it should work, and this *Weltanschauung* has been labelled a strategy. At the end of the last century, the eminent strategic scholar Colin Gray (1999: 16) warned that often

> the noun and adjective, strategy and strategic, are purloined by the unscrupulous or misapplied by those who are careless or ignorant. Such sins or errors can have dire consequences in practice for a realm of behaviour that is, after all, about life and death, victory or defeat.

In the dark days of the Cold War, an even starker, but equally accurate, picture was presented: 'there is no other science where judgements are tested in blood and answered in the servitude of the defeated' (Brodie 1959: 21).

Strategy considers power capabilities, mainly but not exclusively military capabilities, and connects them to political ends. As such, a crucial function for any modern, viable strategy is to guide policymakers and the paying public, in detail, as to the strategic theories to be utilised, and the expensive military means required to convert the theories into action. These theories present a range of instrumentalities, such as deterrence, compellence or military intervention, which allows the best use of coercion by subordinating it to policy objectives outside the basic, crude violence of war (Moran 2002: 18). If this is done effectively, then strategy will also deliver a clear projection of foreign policy goals and the response enemies may expect if they transgress. To maximise its effect, a strategy should be rapidly applicable to most parts of the international system, it should not be too complicated or obtuse, it should be enthusiastically supported by those who promulgate it, and it should be accepted by the public as relevant rather than otiose. Ideally, it should be accepted in practice by allies, yet without undue constraints inhibiting unilateral or extra-alliance multilateral action when deemed necessary.

NSS: utilising force

The NSS is a strategy as defined above. It is the cornerstone of a US strategic programme launched between September 2002 and February 2003. Two supplementary components are the National Strategy to Combat Weapons of Mass Destruction (December 2002), and the National Strategy for Combating Terrorism (December 2003; see Newman 2004: 70–1). The threats posed by connections between surprise attack, terrorism and the proliferation of WMD, and the question of how to use power to address these conditions, are at the core of the programme. The NSS is candid and unambiguous about its purpose. In its introduction, the president makes it clear that it is the democratic and free enterprise model of society which will receive the support of American power, and that a range of strategic instruments will be used to fight terrorists and tyrants, to build good relations among the great powers, not least Russia and China, and to encourage free and open societies everywhere. Throughout the document, principles are clear and are linked to the power required to advance them. The 'logic of force' paradigm which has characterised US high foreign policy for 60 years – that idealism achieves little without the application of raw power – is the leitmotif of the NSS (Kagan 2003: 89–91). The rhetoric is robust: the NSS does not seek a quiet life. The mode is pro-active, the perspective is grand (Gaddis 2005: 2), and 'it is unapologetically global in its outlook' (Duke 2004: 468). The NSS exhibits conviction and brooks no compromise on values such as liberty and democracy, which it views as concomitant with US national security. It feels no restraints on tasks and no limits on time: 'the war against terrorists of global reach is a global enterprise of uncertain duration'. Its tone and posture mirror a particularly astute observation offered by Sir Michael Howard (2001: 101) the year before the publication of the NSS:

> American military supremacy over the rest of the world is now as great as that exercised by the European powers collectively a century ago. It provides the unchallengeable basis for a new world order. American elites remain very conscious of imperial responsibilities that are based on much the same combination of moral commitment and material interest that guided their European predecessors.

Overall, strategy is shaped to meet the new conditions, and strategic theories and doctrines are presented as vehicles for policy. Contrary to popular view, the NSS did not abandon deterrence in favour of pre-emption. Deterrence is still accorded a role, since 'forces will be strong enough to dissuade potential adversaries from pursuing a military build-up in hopes of surpassing, or equalling, the power of the United States'. Nonetheless, there is the realistic view that some new adversaries may be immune to deterrence. In this case, as Lawrence Freedman (2003: 105) suggests, 'it is difficult to argue with the principle that it is better to deal with threats as they develop rather than after they are realized'. It would have been more accurate, and also better public diplomacy, for the NSS to stress the strategic term 'prevention', rather than 'pre-emption', but it should be noted that 'to prevent' is used in the same paragraph as that which contains the most explicit commitment to pre-emption.

That the debate has been hindered and enflamed by the conflation of the two terms into pre-emption rather than prevention has been acknowledged (Gaddis 2005: 4–5). But the key message is that of adapting strategic postures to meet the demands of the real world where the crossover of transnational, fanatical terrorism, corrupt and collapsing rogue states and WMD is not improbable. However, the controversial practice of coercive counter-proliferation against Iraq in 2003 has distorted the image of the NSS. It is not a golf bag with a single club. Regarding the pre-emptive (preventive) use of force to counter proliferation, Colin Powell has urged that we 'see it as an elevation of one of the many tools that we've always had, but don't see it as a new doctrine that excludes or eliminates all the other tools of national security' (quoted in Litwak 2002–3: 59).

Often overlooked in the NSS is an entire chapter advancing strategic development aid as a core instrument of international security. Democratisation as a political instrument as well as an objective is also a theme which is woven into the fabric of the strategy. Other tools given prominence in the NSS include orthodox arms control, alliance formation, enhanced intelligence, coalitions of the willing, and mission-based coalitions. The recasting of US attitudes towards the utility of institutional multilateralism is a notable feature of the NSS. Even before the bruising experience with the United Nations over the Iraq war of 2003, the Bush administration seemed aware that flexibility in coalition-building would be a strategic requirement in a centrifugal world, as would having clear confidence in one's own national authority. The NSS marks a distinct change from its Clintonian predecessors, emphasising their implied failure to recognise the strategic and political realities of the twenty-first century. In the 1995 NSS there are 24 references to multilateralism; in 2002 there are ten (Toje 2005: 131). In 2000, before the selection of George W. Bush as the Republican candidate, Condoleezza Rice (2000: 62) gave a clear indication of the strategic approach of any Bush administration to multilateralism:

Foreign policy in a Republican administration will most certainly be internationalist; the leading contenders in the party's presidential race have strong credentials in that regard. But it will also proceed from the firm ground of the national interest, not from the interests of an illusory international community. America can exercise power without arrogance and pursue its interests without hectoring and bluster. When it does so in concert with those who share its core values, the world becomes more prosperous, democratic and peaceful. That has been America's special role in the past, and it should be again as we enter the next century.

The phrases 'coalitions of the willing' and 'mission-based coalitions' are used almost in passing in the NSS, but from the context the signal is clear. In matters of high national security, the United States will not be denied the utility of coalition support because of the institutional constraints of formal collective defence or security arrangements out of kilter with the realities of contemporary global threats. If denied any kind of meaningful coalition support, then the United States has the confidence of its own sovereign authority to act unilaterally. An important illustration of this strategic posture is the clear commitment in the NSS to permanent US military hegemony in order to allow the United States to exercise its own judgement as to the demands of global security and to apply the 'logic of force' as it decides. This commitment to overarching military superiority has created remarkably little political controversy within the US body politic (see Boot 2002). The same cannot be said in Europe, although some of the more experienced, strategically aware commentators recognise the merits of such a strategy for the United States:

> Since America is without equal and likely to remain so for some time, to act alone is a necessity and an expediency. It is a necessity because other powers, not least the allies in Europe, tend to wait for US leadership and are insufficiently united to pursue coherent world-order strategies of their own. US unilateralism is thus all too often the consequence of the passivity of other powers. It is an expediency because acting alone is often the most efficient way to respond to an emergency.
>
> (Bertram *et al.* 2002: 140)

The NSS is comprehensive, radical, pro-active and sceptical. It is sceptical about the contemporary value of the strategic status quo which emerged from the Cold War and continued through much of the 1990s. This order invested heavily in containment, deterrence, institutional collective consensus before action, and political stability and the avoidance of war at all costs. The NSS signals that such policies had value in a past strategic context, largely bipolar and nuclear, but that the new strategic environment is different in many ways. As the 1993 World Trade Center attack, the 1994 Rwanda massacres, the Balkan tragedies, the 1998 attacks on the US East African embassies, the Al Aqsa intifada, the Iraq/UN sanctions shambles, the *USS Cole* incident, and 9/11 amply demonstrated, the strategic orthodoxies had become deficient.

ESS: avoiding force

The European Council formally adopted the European Security Strategy in December 2003, 15 months after the NSS and in the wake of the shock of the intra-EU controversies over the 2003 Iraq war. From the early post-Cold War years the European Union had been slowly constructing the Common Foreign and Security Policy (CFSP) and the associated European Security and Defence Policy (ESDP), but the internal disputes over Iraq 'mocked the geopolitical vision of European unity' (Calleo 2004a: 32). At that time, political disunity was palpable. The United Kingdom and France were in dispute within the United Nations Security Council. The Terveuren initiative of France, Germany, Luxembourg and Belgium was a direct challenge not just to NATO but to the orthodox notion of ESDP (see Sloan 2005). France's President Chirac was questioning the value of EU enlargement if accession states were supportive of US strategies. The crisis of confidence within the European Union meant there were various ESS drafts from the spring of 2003 until its publication in December. The core purpose of the ESS was to define the European Union as a separate and coherent actor in world affairs (Blecher 2004: 345). However, the European Union is not a state, and the declaration by 15 heads of government of a text claiming to represent a common strategy for the European Union does not transform it into a single actor in high global politics. Reflecting the political context of its birth, the ESS addresses different priorities for different EU member states. For some the ESS is Europe's riposte to an overweening America. For others it is a reinforcement of a law-bound world order rooted in institutional multilateralism, and for others it is intended to be a European wake-up call about the dangers of the modern world (Everts 2004b: 1–2).

There are some points of contact with the NSS, but the ESS is a very different document, and demonstrates a very different strategic perspective. While the NSS has a dynamic character to it, and is constructed to accommodate change, the ESS has a 'final word' quality to it. In the ESS there is little sense of urgency and strategic awareness and, even in late 2003, an apparently grudging reluctance to accept the existence of a major threat:

> Taking these different elements together – terrorism committed to maximum violence, the availability of weapons of mass destruction, organised crime, the weakening of the state system and the privatisation of force – we *could be* confronted with a very radical threat indeed [emphasis added].

A check-list of key threats is presented in a truncated, hesitant manner. Which threats are the most salient, and which should be tackled first and with what degree of urgency, is not addressed. The answers to such questions could be divisive within the European Union and further damage consensus, but a viable strategy requires a focus. Terrorism is on the list, but no priority is implied until it is linked with WMD and then described simply as the 'most frightening scenario'. The relatively relaxed attitude to terrorism can probably be explained by Europe's experience, until the Madrid railway station bombings of March 2004 and the London tube and bus attacks of July 2005, of 'old' terrorism. Until very recently, the European experience has been of ethnic or nationalist terrorists, and not the mass terror attacks of the Bali 2002 and 2005 types. Against the 'old' terrorism, political and judicial capabilities played a major role and, despite the Madrid and London bombings, it may be argued that the orthodox view of the terrorist threat persists:

> Whereas US homeland security is now driven by potential consequences, European security tends to pivot on probabilities. Most European governments, accordingly, have continued to approach terrorism as predominantly a problem that can be assessed and dealt with on an emergent basis, after particular threats have arisen.
>
> (Stevenson 2003: 79)

European events with thousands, rather than tens, of casualties may be required to change such attitudes.

Strategy has been described as 'a process, a constant adaptation to shifting conditions and circumstances in a world where chance, uncertainty and ambiguity dominate' (Murray and Grimsley 1994: 1). The strategic culture manifest in the ESS is inflexibly rooted in the soft power, containment, deterrence, détente and multilateralism of late twentieth-century West European security. The ESS reflects the perception that this strategic medley delivered a 'long peace', and that it would be imprudent to move too far from the successful formula (Hyde-Price 2004: 328). However, as briefly acknowledged in the ESS, the formula was allowed to work only by virtue of the hard power foundation provided by the United States. But, of course, the strategic environment is now transformed from the last 30 or 40 years of the twentieth century. Illustrative of the inertial quality of the ESS is the deep commitment to institutional multilateralism, with its focus on international consensus rather than action. Indeed, it seems to deny the European Union authority to decide questions regarding the use of force, and defers to the United Nations. This stands in sharp contrast to the NSS which, while very internationalist in tone and content, retains absolute confidence in the authority of the United States to decide issues of war and peace. The ESS seeks to establish rules of international behaviour which are acceptable to the modern European political conscience, and which can – by choice or chance – limit the independent action of the world's only superpower. Even though much of 'new' Europe welcomes American strength, working for a 'rule-based international order' may be viewed as an astute asymmetrical strategy by the old European middle-range powers anxious to reduce the growing power disparities between themselves and their strongest ally. The European Union and the UN have been particularly valuable to France as mechanisms to sustain its declining global influence and prestige, especially in the post-Cold War world of German unification and the collapse of Moscow as a power balance to Washington (Longhurst and Zaborowski 2004: 387–8). Germany's ambition for a permanent seat on the UN Security Council is also driven by considerations of maximising relative influence in an international system dominated by one superpower. However, this posture only makes grand strategic sense if it is the United States which is the clear and present danger and not the matrix of anti-Western transnational terrorism, WMD proliferation, and rogue/failing states. As it is the aggregate of the latter which comprises the major threat, then maximum strategic flexibility unimpeded by anachronistic features of institutionalised multi-lateralism is essential. In this regard the ESS fails to alert the EU publics to the strategic realities of the twenty-first-century world.

Loyalty to institutional multilateralism is a core characteristic of the ESS, but the declaration also perpetuates other political premises of the last century into the new era. Asserting that the resolution of the Arab–Israeli conflict is required first before other Middle East problems can be addressed effectively, rather than considering, given the long-standing obscurantist policies of most local states hostile to Israel, that the reverse may be the case, suggests a disturbing attachment to old political shibboleths, whether they deliver or not. The ESS is fundamentally a document supporting the international status quo of a previous epoch. The ESS has something of the quality of a European security sermon, not daring to leave out any world problem, whether or not the use of force could be applicable. It could even be suggested that it 'gets carried away by its own language in calling optimistically for the coordination of almost everything under the sun' (Hill 2004: 6).

The ESS is not a strategy as defined earlier. It was written in direct reference to the NSS, but it does not really address questions as to when, where, for what reasons, and to what extent the European Union should use force (Toje 2005: 120–1). It is a political statement which attempts to be both a complement and a corrective to the NSS. The concept of security adopted is so wide as to be of marginal utility in the construction of a doctrine or the identification of strategic theories on which to build doctrine. Being prepared for the use of violence, and exploiting the outcome, is the role of strategy (Van Creveld 1991: 95–6). Yet military force and war are rarely mentioned. There is no modus operandi for military forces, and no sense of strategic direction except for multilateralism and broader institution-building. In the ESS the focus is clearly on what is deemed to be publicly acceptable – long term, cooperative political and economic means which avoid tough military actions. There is only one explicit mention of the use of armed force: 'In failed states, military instruments may be needed to restore order.' The controversial doctrine of anticipatory self-defence is, after agonised internal debate, called 'preventive action' and was presented as a pre- or post-conflict instrument, such was the desire not to be associated with actual coercion and violence. The assumption is that the European Union will possess the art of spotting crises before they arise and deploy largely non-military instruments to prevent such crises, or bring its unique capabilities to bear to resolve conflict after the conflict has stopped.

For the ESS, the notion of preventive action is couched in a markedly different strategic context from the NSS. In the ESS strategic doctrine is largely eschewed. The nearest it comes to a serious discussion of strategic instruments is actually in the final paragraph of the section entitled 'Addressing the Threats', most of which is a brief narrative describing EU behaviour in world affairs in recent years or making mild observations about the impact of globalisation on security. At the annual Munich Conference on security policy in 2005 an EU official was reported as arguing that 'the European Union is a peace process in itself' (Hoagland 2005: B08). The emphasis on 'soft power' diplomatic craft is evident in the ESS. The peaceful end to the Cold War further embedded the ethic of 'civilian power' in the receptive older members of the European Union, and none of the traumas in the post-Cold War Middle East, Balkans, Africa or Manhattan seems to have seriously shaken that faith. As a signal of what to expect militarily from the concert of states producing a quarter of the world's GDP in the inevitable turbulence of the twenty-first century, the ESS is not illuminating. Nowhere in the document is the EU rapid reaction force, theoretically declared operational at the Laeken EU summit of December 2001, mentioned. If one takes the ESS as a guide, then 'enemies' and 'rogue states' are not words in the European Council's strategic vocabulary (Bailes 2005: 5). Nor is the crucial issue of resources devoted to military power directly addressed beyond a short statement of the European Union's total defence spend of €160 billion, followed on the next page by a plea for 'more resources for defence'. As Michael Howard (2001: 101) notes, 'European states now spend no more on their armed forces than is necessary to persuade the United States that they are *bundnisfahig*; capable of functioning as useful allies.'

The NSS has a clear focus on external threats of a global nature, and addresses external origins and conditions; it signals a willingness to use military force, in many manifestations, to prevail over future adversaries. The ESS wishes to avoid future adversaries and the need to use military force. Regardless of some rhetoric about global issues, the ESS focus is largely regional and the concerns are internal. For the United States, 'internationalism' means a secure, liberal order of states with US power acting as referee. For the European Union, 'internationalism' actually means supranationalism, with states pooling sovereignty and abiding under common rules set by an overarching authority (Kagan 2002: 138). The European Union is the foremost model of this form of international organisation, and many of the leading capitals see security policy's primary role as that of reinforcing integration, while addressing external threats is a secondary function.

For these EU members, strategy looks inwards rather than outwards. Strategy is an instrument of a 'foreign policy' which is more anxious about domestic and intra-EU relations than about extra-European turbulence. Large Muslim populations, comprising about 12 million people and about 3.2 per cent of the EU population, complicate the political calculations of some leading European states about 'Atlanticism', and limit strategic options (Hoagland 2005; *The Economist* 2004). In contrast to the 2 per cent of the American population which is Muslim, European Muslims are 'only half-accepted socially and are politically underrepresented. This marginal status makes them susceptible to radicalisation – one factor that has helped prevent governments from taking steps that might seem anti-Muslim' (Stevenson 2003: 82). EU security strategy is primarily concerned about harmony and confidence within and amongst EU members, and not embedding an agenda which would make any member uncomfortable (Bailes 2005: 14). Essentially the ESS masquerades as a world strategy, but that does not mean that it has no value. For those who are 'Euro-introspective' (*The Economist* 2005: 48), it provides a political shelter where some debate can be conducted within clear parameters, and from which reassuring signals may be transmitted to interested elements of the European public. However, even measured as a political posture rather than one about the use of EU force, the ESS has its problems. For those new Central and East European members who have a real historically based reluctance to rely on a Franco-German security structure, the ESS offers little strategic guidance. For the United Kingdom, it is of little relevance to the inherent tensions between British enthusiasm for a robust European defence identity and the perceived strategic imperatives of an active global role in partnership with the United States. For 'West–West' relations, it would seem to confirm that Washington and the power-brokers of Brussels are separated by different, probably irreconcilable, strategic cultures.

Strategic disconnect: the Iraq war

It is unlikely that the collective security character of the ESS was intended, but that is what it projects. There is a marked reluctance to identify a clear enemy or to advance a distinct strategy or strategies. Consequently, the ESS is unsure how much emphasis to place on the use of military force or what kind and level of military power should be procured, and reliance is placed upon multilateral institutionalism. On the other hand, the NSS, which may be criticised as too bold and ambitious, concerns itself largely with issues about the use of force against distinct enemies and threats. Amidst the political rhetoric, which may have tempted the United States into a contro-versial, costly Middle Eastern adventure, the 'logic of force' is the clearest distinguishing feature.

Essentially, the ESS reflects the liberal concepts of international security and the limited utility of force which have come to dominate West European politics since détente with the Soviet Union in the 1970s. Meanwhile, the NSS is an expression of the largely realist understanding of strategy prevalent in US policy-making for decades – regardless of the political complexion of the administration. The ESS may be tinged by a modicum of realism, and the NSS may be tempered by elements of liberalism and idealism, not least the notion of the democratic peace (Snyder 2004: 57). But the two concepts of how states do and should secure themselves are far apart. Undeniably, the imbroglio of the Iraq war and its aftermath has provoked some debate in the United States amongst scholars and commentators, not least realists, about the nature and value of the NSS. However, much of the debate is actually about the strategic judgement of going to war in Iraq, not about the national security requirement for a strategy such as the NSS. In other words, the pre-emptive/preventive element of the NSS is appropriate for modern conditions and is applicable to necessary wars, but for some analysts Iraq 2003 was not a necessary war (Mearsheimer and Walt 2003). Pre-emptive war is a relatively simple strategic instrument, but making the strategic judgement as to when national security requires it to be used is not easy. The United States-led military intervention in Iraq may turn out to have been a 'strategic error' (Smith and Diamond 2004: 131), but that does not mean that the strategic tenets of the NSS are redundant. Regardless of how vociferous the debate may become, the character of the current security challenges to the advanced industrial democracies is beyond serious dispute and it is unlikely that the strategic mind-set which informs US national security will change radically. Undoubtedly, at some point soon, NSS 2002 will be replaced, but neither a Republican nor a Democrat administration will break from the 'logic of force' or abandon the long-standing commitment to democracy as a core national security interest.

Any juxtaposition of the NSS and the ESS must have a corrosive rather than a rehabilitative effect on the transatlantic relationship, particularly between the United States and the older continental members of the European Union. Given serious analysis, philosophical distinctions over the role of the military instrument and conceptual differences over the nature of the (in)security environment in the twenty-first century are clear. Also, any scrutiny of the ESS must also be discomforting for those EU actors, not least some of the new Central and East European members, who subscribe to notions of existential threats and the utility of hard power, and who attach value to a strategy, as commonly conceptualised, rather than a political statement. It may be argued that the ESS has perpetuated a security perspective which, regardless of a veneer of harmony, does little to repair the strategic disconnect which afflicts transatlantic relations.

12 Conclusion

Alliance dead or alive?

Roland Dannreuther and John Peterson

This volume began with a simple, honest premise: specifically, that caution is in order whenever the significance and import of any security strategy, including the two that are the central focus of this book, are assessed. Ultimately, the National Security Strategy (NSS) and its European counterpart (ESS) are mere paper documents, as opposed to statements with anything close to the power to bind. They are both outcomes of internal bureaucratic and political negotiation, complete with all the inevitable attendant compromises and obscuring of internal policy differences that such processes entail. They are also, by their very nature, statements of intent, expressing aspirations as to how the United States and the European Union *should* meet the challenges of a changing security environment. But they do not dictate particular policy outcomes or necessarily constrain the strategic autonomy of decision-makers on either side.

The strategies are also children (and prisoners) of the particular moment of their creation. Their continuing relevance is contingent on how they explain and justify subsequent developments, and the unexpected complexities and unintended outcomes the international world of the near future promises to feature. Few security strategies of the past, particularly those of the post-Cold war period, have stood the test of time and come to represent authoritative new doctrines about the nature and pursuit of security.

The NSS and the ESS are, at least in this sense, different. This conclusion emerges clearly from every contribution to this volume. Successfully or not, both strategies express clear ambitions to doctrinal innovation and strategic permanence. The NSS, as Asmus observes, seeks to encapsulate a 'Trumanesque moment' when the changing nature of security is revealed and the new rules for US foreign and military policy are cast for posterity. This ambition can be seen in the striking statement that we are now 'menaced less by fleets and armies than by catastrophic technologies in the hands of the embittered few'. It is a consequence of this conceptualisation of a radically changed security environment that the most significant strategic innovations of the NSS – the doctrine of military pre-emption, unilateral action and US primacy – are derived.

The ESS has a markedly different strategic ambition. Arguably, its principal purpose is more celebratory than foreboding: marking the ambitions of a European Union that has come of age as 'inevitably a global player', and thus is ready to 'share in the responsibility for global security and in building a better world'. The ESS argues that the great achievement of the European Union is in how 'the violence of the first half of the twentieth century has given way to a period of peace and stability unprecedented in European history'. The European Union itself can take much of the credit for this benign outcome. The strategic innovation of the ESS is, therefore, not so much what it says about the changed security environment but what it says about the European Union. The ESS is unique not just because it is the first substantive security strategy the European Union has ever had but also because it is the first attempt to give some concrete sense of what an autonomous European security actor might look like and what values it would seek to promote. Inevitably, the European Union's emergence as a 'global player' involves developing a degree of autonomy from the United States and NATO, and in asserting a distinctively European rather than trans-atlantic identity. The strong emphasis in the ESS on multilateralism, diplomacy and international law, which presents such a contrast from the NSS, is at least in part an assertion of Europe's strategic autonomy from the United States. The timing of this statement – within months of the 2003 attack on Iraq and after the unilateralism of the United States under George W. Bush had become impossible to deny (see Malone and Foong Khong 2003) – seemed ominous for transatlantic relations.

In fact, the NSS and ESS actually say rather little about transatlantic relations. Nevertheless, much can be learned about the health and prospects of the Atlantic Alliance in the early twenty-first century through close analysis of these documents. Both provide significant insights into transatlantic relations through what they say about each other's ambitions, goals and policies. As Asmus puts it, they 'shape expectations of each other in a time of strategic fluidity'.

Convergence or divergence?

A key question that all contributors to this volume were asked to address was the balance and evidence of convergence or divergence between the United States and European Union, especially as reflected in the two security strategies, in their respective topic areas. It would be fair to say that no simple answers have been provided, and that there is evidence of both rupture and renewal. The NSS and ESS do not definitively confirm the view, which appears to have gained adherents over time, that 'the Atlantic is growing wider' (Mazower 2005: 13; see also Calleo 2004b; Cox 2005). This conclusion *does* find support amongst our authors, including Molloy and Wyllie, who themselves start from almost diametrically opposed analytical positions. Others including Asmus, Bergman and Peterson, and even Cameron and

Howorth – despite remits that would seem to point towards the 'widening Atlantic' thesis – find considerable evidence to the contrary.

What does emerge is a general consensus that the United States and the European Union converge on the key ambition of promoting 'transformational diplomacy'. What marks out both the NSS and ESS is their ambition, and impatience, for change. Both documents see the outside world, particularly the conflict-ridden regions of the Middle East, Asia and Africa, as in desperate need of transformation. The United States and the European Union are also presented as both *models* of stability, freedom and prosperity and as *agents* of transformation with a vocation to change the world in their own images.

Perceptively, Howorth argues that the real strategic innovation of the NSS is the shift towards supporting democratic governments rather than propping up pro-Western authoritarian regimes. By this view, the shift signalled in the opening paragraph of the NSS – that 'these values of freedom are right and true for every person, in every society' – was confirmed (with much rhetorical flourish) in the 2005 inaugural address that followed George W. Bush's re-election:

> We have seen our vulnerability – and we have seen its deepest source. For as long as whole regions of the world simmer in resentment and tyranny – prone to ideologies that feed hatred and excuse murder – violence will gather, and multiply in destructive power, and cross the most defended borders, and raise a mortal threat. There is only one force of history that can break the reign of hatred and resentment, and expose the pretensions of tyrants, and reward the hope of the decent and tolerant, and that is the force of human freedom.
>
> (Bush 2005)

Bush's second term thus began with a dramatic foreign policy statement that combined breathtaking audacity, as in the claim that 'America's vital interests and our deepest beliefs are now one', with at least a fresh hint of modesty at how daunting and complicated the undertaking might be: 'This is not primarily the task of arms ... The difficulty of the task is no excuse for avoiding it. America's influence is not unlimited' (see also Fukuyama 2005). Still, there was little ambiguity in Bush's basic message:

> We are led, by events and common sense, to one conclusion: the survival of liberty in our land increasingly depends on the success of liberty in other lands ... So it is the policy of the United States to seek and support the growth of democratic movements and institutions in every nation and culture, with the ultimate goal of ending tyranny in our world.
>
> (Bush 2005)

It is impossible to imagine any spokesperson for the European Union delivering such a clear, confident and forceful new canon for EU foreign policy anytime soon. Yet, democratisation is an area where the European Union can justifiably claim special, accumulated expertise, as well as an exportable template based on its success in democratising and integrating East-Central Europe. Of course, there remains plenty of scope for charges of hypocrisy – not least from US policy-makers – in EU attempts to 'export' human rights, democracy and good governance to states such as Iran, Syria and Pakistan, particularly given the European Union's own lack of democratic and fiscal integrity credentials (see Smith 2003). Meanwhile, it is plausible to question the commitment of the United States under George W. Bush to democratisation, which has been mostly rhetorical and at times apparently forgotten in dealings with non-democratic governments in states of strategic interest, including Pakistan, Uzbekistan, China, Saudi Arabia, Egypt and others. Here we might heed the more general maxim that there is almost always more continuity than genuine change in US foreign policy when one administration replaces another (see Peterson and Pollack 2003), and remind ourselves that 'no US President has been willing to risk much blood or treasure solely to promote democracy or to advance human rights' (Walt 2005: 55).

Yet, these all could be viewed as reasons to see the United States and European security strategies as markers of basic forks in foreign policy roads, signalling the start of a long, evolutionary (far more than revolutionary), but shared sea change in an era of new and potentially catastrophic transnational security threats. Both the ESS and NSS signal that the United States and the European Union now view themselves as transformational and even revolutionary powers, impatient with and seeking to change the existing status quo. There is a clear convergence on basic goals, broadly reflecting the common, liberal democratic values that have traditionally cemented the transatlantic community. It is possible and even reasonable to think that these values are an increasingly weak glue holding the United States and Europe together in a true 'alliance', given their often sharp differences over actual policy on issues such as climate change, the treatment of suspected terrorist detainees, or Iraq. But it is also plausible to think that there will be more cases that resemble the recent ones of Ukraine, Georgia and Lebanon when the United States and the European Union (the latter often acting more through national capitals than Brussels) coaxed democratic movements into positions of actual power through both policy coordination and carefully calibrated divisions of labour (see European Commission 2005).

There is also a basic convergence on European and American assessments of the principal threats to their common values. Both the NSS and ESS converge on identifying terrorism, WMD proliferation, regional conflicts, and failing states as representing the major challenges. Where there are differences, they are more of emphasis and prioritisation than of substance. The European Union adds organised crime as a significant threat. The

United States places greater emphasis on the dangers of the conflation of WMD proliferation and international terrorism. The NSS is darker in tone, while the ESS more explicitly eulogises the benefits of the post-Cold War peace. But, in essence, they describe the same external world and provide similar strategic threat assessments.

Divergences emerge most clearly in the means and tools for implementing essentially common goals. In part, this is a relatively superficial issue of tone and style. As Howorth and Cameron highlight, Europeans were considerably taken aback by the tone of the NSS and how it appeared to reflect a sense of American triumphalism or neo-imperialism (see also Mann 2003; Ferguson 2004; Johnson 2004), where traditionally friendly allies would be marginalised and perhaps not even consulted. For many Americans, as Asmus makes clear, the ESS appeared to be unduly complacent, reflecting Europe's failure to galvanise the necessary urgency and the requisite support for a wounded America, thus feeding into a growing mood of Euroscepticism in Washington.

But there were also more substantial and deeper rooted sources of transatlantic divergence. Wyllie argues that the NSS and the ESS reflect differing paradigms or ideologies of international relations. The NSS is broadly a realist document, which above all seeks a 'balance of power that favours freedom', a goal mentioned no fewer than five times in the document. Such an outcome demands that preponderant power and military primacy be accorded to the United States so that it can fulfil its special responsibilities as the enlightened global hegemon. These realist foundations are then overlaid by a Wilsonian commitment to the expansion of freedom.

For its part, the ESS is imbued with a commitment to a progressive, some might say Panglossian, liberal internationalism, where socio-economic integration – essentially, attacking the economic roots of conflict between states and peoples – is the most critical force for change. Meanwhile, the model of European integration offers attractions, not least its commitment to transformation through persuasion rather than coercion. As one of the European Union's top diplomats, Robert Cooper (2005b), has suggested, the NSS and the ESS instantiate different conceptions of power and identity: the 'US is powerful for what it does ... the EU because of what it is'. These differences in ideology and conceptualisations of power feed into multiple transatlantic disputes over what constitutes acceptable international behaviour, variously discussed by our contributors. They include the frequency with which unilateralism must trump multilateralism; the value of international institutions as against 'coalitions of the willing'; the need for military pre-emption over and above diplomatic prevention; and very basic questions of the utility of the use of force as against the application of international law in dealing with the new security threats.

The fact that the United States and the European Union are very different sorts of actors is also a significant source of divergence. The reason why the NSS reads as a dynamic and focused document, with an enviable clarity in its goals and strategic objectives, is that it was written in the White House's National Security Council by a small group of Republican party faithfuls. As Cooper (2005b) notes, there are 'many different Americas' and the NSS does not necessarily reflect the interests and priorities of all of them. What it does do is to set out the strategic direction and ambitions of the George W. Bush administration, and to give a clear indication as to how this administration intended to utilise the many instruments of US power, not least the military, at its disposal.

The European Union's security strategy, in contrast, was the outcome of a complex inter-governmental agreement where consensus was achieved, typically for the EU, through greater blandness of content and more emphasis on aspirations than specific policies. Unlike the United States, the European Union has far more limited military tools and capabilities, which in part explains Europe's weakness in regions including the Middle East and Asia. To counter this weakness of military capacity, the ESS emphasises the unique selling point of the European Union: how political integration has helped Europe to transcend the tyranny of power politics and the ways in which this model can be potentially exported and applied elsewhere in the world. Unlike the NSS, it is considerably more reticent about what to do when more immediate threats and challenges are confronted.

Time and changing circumstances are also other critical elements in understanding the dynamics of divergence and convergence. Overall, time appears to have acted as a healer of division in transatlantic relations. As Howorth and Cameron note, originally starkly opposed positions, particularly as expressed during the 2003 Iraq war, have subsided over time, especially as the occupation of Iraq has proved to be more difficult than originally anticipated. The United States and Europe have converged significantly on the need for stability in Iraq and in prioritising the pursuit of a diplomatic solution to the challenges faced by potential WMD proliferation in Iran and North Korea. The sense that a storm has passed strengthens the argument that the ESS and the NSS should not be seen as intrinsically diverging or contradictory documents. In fact, one of the key purposes of the ESS was to make the European Union a more effective and capable strategic actor, an outcome which – if realised – stood to enhance transatlantic cooperation and power projection far more than to weaken it.

It should be remembered, in this context, that the ESS represented a significant advance on the tradition of Europe as a 'civilian power', which refused in principle to engage with the dirty business of threat assessments and strategic calculation (see Whitman 1998). For some in Europe, the problem of the ESS was that it moves too far towards the Americanisation and militarisation of European strategic culture. This concern has always been particularly acute among the non-aligned EU states although, as Bergman and Peterson argue, they have managed to keep their own priorities and aspirations for good relations with the United States at the centre of the European Union's foreign and defence policies. In any event, the ESS can be seen as a vehicle for convergence with, rather than divergence from, the United States and the NSS.

Finally, the issue of transatlantic divergence and convergence needs to be placed in its broader global context. Excessive attention to the minutiae of US and EU interaction, to what might be called the 'narcissism of minor difference', can obscure how both powers are either impotent towards or struggle with some of the most significant external challenges. March argues that neither the NSS nor the ESS meets the challenge of Russia's increasingly authoritarian direction under President Putin. Bailes argues similarly in relation to China that neither the US nor the EU strategy is capable of addressing the challenge of a China that emerges as a superpower by conquering markets rather than territories. The Doha development round of global trade talks have (at this writing) witnessed little transatlantic solidarity, let alone leadership. Europe's sluggish economic growth rates and looming demographic crisis, as well as America's massive budget and trade deficits, have made each side less attractive to the other as an economic partner and contrasted sharply with the galloping economic dynamism of China and India. And, as a number of contributors have noted, neither the United States nor Europe seems to have anything approaching a formula for defeating the threat from Al Qaeda or international terrorism more generally.

To be somewhat harsh, the basic problem of transatlantic relations may be precisely the convergence of doctrine signalled in the two security strategies: specifically, that 'a rational foreign policy cannot be compounded from a mix of oil-driven realpolitik and millenarian faith in the transforming power of democracy' (Gray 2006: 6). We might be somewhat more charitable and still conclude that transatlantic relations have evolved towards a 'businesslike, if sometimes sullen, accommodation' on the basis not of strength but rather of 'profound mutual weakness' in a world that 'is no longer a transatlantic world, if ever it was' (International Institute for Strategic Studies 2005: 1).

The NSS – a new doctrine for the twenty-first century?

A separate set of questions, only marginally related to the matter of whether the US and the EU security strategies signal convergence or divergence, surrounded the tangible impacts of the ESS and the NSS. Starting with the NSS, to what extent have its aspirations translated into effective policy? As noted earlier, the authors of the NSS were certainly not lacking in ambition, understood themselves as confronting a seismic shift in the post-9/11 strategic environment, and aspired to articulate a new strategic vision and set of doctrines to guide future generations (see Zelikow 2003).

Yet our contributors end up sharply divided in their assessment of whether the NSS fulfils these ambitions. Wyllie argues forcefully that the NSS is a timely and elegant strategy which sets out the dynamic and changing nature of contemporary international security and successfully identifies the appropriate tools and institutional frameworks required for forging an effective countervailing strategic response. For him, the NSS overturns the Cold War 'shibboleths' of 'containment, deterrence, institutional collective consensus before action, and political stability and the avoidance of war at all cost'. In contrast, Molloy criticises the NSS as signally failing to adapt a strategy to deal effectively with the viral, shadowy nature of modern international terrorist networks. Instead of a radical revision of US and international security strategy, he sees the United States depending on its own Cold War 'shibboleths' of attacking the states which purportedly sponsor terrorism rather than the terrorist viruses themselves. Moreover, Molloy argues that this misguided counter-terrorist strategic response has cynically served as a legitimation of *Machtpolitik*, with the United States assuming extraordinary prerogatives and 'recognising no legitimate brake on the exercise of its power in its interests'.

Of course, the 2003 Iraq war necessarily colours any substantive assessment of the NSS. Iconoclastically, Wyllie alone argues that the NSS should be evaluated independently from the Iraq war and that its intrinsic value is not linked to the relative success or failure of that policy. Other contributors are markedly less sanguine and see the success or failure of the NSS as linked directly to the ultimate success or failure of the intervention into Iraq. Although most of our contributors are broadly pessimistic about the prognosis for Iraq, Ehteshami reminds us that the problems of the Middle East are not limited to Iraq and that the United States and Europe will confront a whole range of security challenges over the next decade, such as Iran's continuing ambition to develop its nuclear capacity and the ever explosive Arab–Israeli conflict. It will also probably be a number of years before the contours of a post-Baathist Iraq will emerge.

In the meantime, according to Ehteshami, Iraq will 'continue to act as the security black hole of the region, with all the mysteries and uncertainties associated with a black hole'. A crucial and probably under-appreciated legacy of the NSS is the upturning of the Sunni-dominated order in Iraq, itself an inheritance of British imperial rule, with the extremely complex consequences and implications that this development has entailed for the region as a whole. The NSS's rhetoric of extending freedom and exporting democracy has translated, in practice, into a considerable strengthening of the Shia community in Iraq and the expansion of Iran's influence, and has greatly increased the fears of the Sunni-dominated Arab regimes, particularly Saudi Arabia and the Arab Gulf states. American strategy thus has embraced very high risks and unleashed powerful unintended consequences, which could possibly provide the impetus for the transformation of the region, as prefigured by the (arguably still very limited) evidence of political liberalisation in Lebanon and Egypt. If so, the value and success of the NSS will be assured. However, if the more pessimistic prognoses of most of our contributors prove correct, the NSS would be severely tarnished. One of the clearer conclusions of our volume is that its reputation, in many ways, will rise or fall in relation to the combustive and highly unpredictable politics of the Middle East.

The ESS – an exercise in wishful thinking?

The main significance of the ESS is not, as with the NSS, its intellectual contribution to particularly controversial policy outcomes. Rather, it is about whether the ESS can be seen to have any identifiable policy outcomes in the first place. As such, is the ESS merely an expression of intent, a set of pious aspirations, which does not actually result in any enhanced European capacity for strategic thinking and action? Much as the NSS has been coloured by the Iraq war, the ESS has been compromised by the French and Dutch rejections of the European Union's Constitutional Treaty, which envisaged an institutional strengthening of the European Union's foreign and security policy. The crisis arising from the European Union's failure to sell its policies to its own citizens hardly augurs well for a more dynamic and proactive European policy in countries and regions beyond Europe's borders.

Yet the question of the longer-term credibility of the ESS is an open one, with three significant dimensions. The first is whether the strategy represents something more than a lowest common denominator agreement between the various EU member states, which essentially papers over critical differences over strategic culture and outlook. As both the Cameron and Bergman/Peterson chapters highlight, the ESS is constrained, as is the ESDP, by different visions of Europe's security and defence role. Similarly, the ESS cannot simply transcend, with a flourish of the pen, the deep divisions which emerged during the 2003 Iraq war, between those in the pro- and the anti-war camps and between 'new' and 'old' Europe. As (especially) Bergman and Peterson argue, these relatively recent schisms overlay older divisions between large and small states, the original six EC states and the others, the budgetary net contributors v. the *demandeurs*. But these new and existing EU divisions do not necessarily mean paralysis. Peterson and Bergman illustrate how the ESDP and the ESS have been supported and even strengthened militarily and strategically by one of the more unlikely sources – the group of EU non-aligned states. Here we get insight into the peculiarly European method of integration where seemingly incommensurable positions can be overcome through the complex process of inter-state bargaining and negotiation. In this sense, despite all the multiple divisions and constraints, the ESS can be seen as something more than an aspirational document, reflecting a genuine internal convergence within the European Union in consolidating the Union's external role.

The real test – and a second dimension of credibility – comes with whether the ESS will actually translate into enhanced EU capabilities for action. Damro highlights how the European Union has shown no appetite thus far to close the growing military gaps with the United States. There is certainly some justification for the European Union not to seek to replicate the extremely expensive military transformation found in the United States (see Bacevich 2005), and some promise in its recent moves to institutionalise more efficient and effective military spending. Still, the absence of a credible European military capability certainly weakens the European Union's credibility in different non-European regional contexts. Ehteshami argues that it is this weakness that ultimately means that Europe's voice is always less powerful and influential in the Middle East than that of the United States. The same can be said in Asia. By 2007, on present trends, US military expenditure will be equal to the rest of the world combined (see Ikenberry 2004). Meanwhile, even in the most optimistic scenarios, European progress in the ESDP is likely to be modest. Necessarily, the effect is to provide a less grandiose context for the proclaimed global ambitions expressed in the ESS.

A third dimension of credibility arises from the implicit argument in the ESS that military prowess is not the only tool for change and that the European Union does possess its own secret weapon – specifically, a unique experience of integration. Cooper (2005b) calls this the European Union's 'highly developed system for mutual interference in each other's domestic affairs' which leads to an understanding of and capacity for engaging in the complex multilateral cooperation required for dealing with the far more complicated challenges of the post-Cold War era. Yet there is certainly debate, with sceptics able to cite the Union's unflattering track record, about whether this European model is transportable to other more conflict-ridden or pre-modern regions of the world (see Smith 2003). Can stability and prosperity, the fruits of integration, emerge through exporting European traditions of incessant meddling? Bailes argues perceptively that what is often seen as a non-existent EU policy towards China, which is sometimes less charitably viewed in Washington as a deliberate policy of appeasement, is at least as coherent and potentially effective as a US policy of great clarity, but arguably greater inconsistency, towards China. As Bailes concludes, 'the European approach is still far from a strategist's strategy. But that it will ultimately work cannot be excluded.' This observation is hardly, it must be admitted, a ringing endorsement for the strategic perspicacity of the ESS. But it does suggest that the United States does not necessarily have all the answers and the European Union's particular experiences might have resonance even in regions far from Europe.

Security strategies and global ambitions

What cannot be taken away from the NSS is that it articulates in a parsimonious and even elegant way the nature of the threats posed by international terrorism and the dangers of the proliferation of weapons of mass destruction. Clearly, the events of 9/11 were foremost in the minds of its drafters. But the ESS, which was written more than a year later and after the diversion of the war in Iraq, essentially accepted the NSS's conceptualisation of the core threats to international security: specifically, the convergence of international terrorism and WMD proliferation. This is a major change from the 1990s when terrorism and WMD proliferation were just two items on an unprioritised list of threats. After 9/11 and the publications of the NSS and the ESS, these threats have an unrivalled primacy.

Two questions arise from this process of refinement of threat assessments. The first is whether this significant reallocation of strategic priorities and resources has yielded positive results in the struggle or 'war' against international terrorism. Again, in the critical area of public diplomacy, of winning the information war or capturing the 'hearts and minds' in the Middle East and elsewhere in the Muslim world (see Lennon 2003), progress has been at best limited, and at worst something like the opposite of progress. Both Howorth and Ehteshami highlight the weaknesses and shortcomings of the US-sponsored Greater Middle East Initiative which had a short-lived and hardly very influential existence (see Walt 2005: 82).

The European Union does not, though, offer an obviously better alternative model, as the successive failures of the Euro-Mediterranean process to promote widespread economic growth and political liberalisation in the Middle East demonstrates. A stark reminder was the EU-hosted November 2005 EuroMed summit of 35 states in Barcelona, which none of the invited Arab heads of state attended, and which could only manage to agree a watered-down work plan on 'political pluralism' and a 'code of conduct' intended to increase police and judicial cooperation but which omitted a definition of terrorism on which the European Union had worked for months.[1] As such, neither the NSS nor the ESS provide a clear or definitive conception of how to deal with the deeply engrained roots of disaffection and alienation in the developing and especially Muslim world and thus 'drain the swamp' of international terrorism.

A second question is what the implications of priorities might have had on other potential challenges and threats to international security. One concern found in various places in this volume is the very limited attention given in both the NSS and the ESS to *strong* (instead of weak) developing states, such as Russia, China and India. There is little recognition that their emergence as great powers might create friction or provide challenges for either the United States or Europe or, more generally, for the management of the international system. Both security strategies document work on the assumption of a great power peace, where cooperation against the threats of aggressive sub-state groups and weak and failing states replaces traditional great power inter-state rivalry. But, as March argues perceptively, both the NSS and the ESS present an essentially false and inaccurate picture of Russia as a cooperative Western partner on the path of democratic consolidation, when the reality is of a growing authoritarianism and anti-Westernism in Russia under Putin's leadership. Similarly, Bailes argues that the traditional US debates over whether China is or is not a military threat fails to grasp the radically different challenge presented by a China which threatens to develop a financial and trading stranglehold on the United States. To its credit, the NSS does address directly the potential challenges of Russia and China. The ESS fails even to do this, ignoring even the possibility that these countries might be difficult partners for the Union or potentially represent challenges to EU strategic interests.

If history teaches one lesson, it is that future security challenges and threats are rarely the security obsessions which dominate the present. The danger is that the NSS and the ESS focus excessively on current priorities which might ultimately be less critical than our current fears and obsessions might suggest. In any case, it would seem unwise to work on the premise that a 'great power peace' is now firmly entrenched and that the age-old patterns of great power rivalries, and the conflicts and challenges that they present, can now be safely ignored. The failure of either the NSS or ESS to address these issues is, potentially, a major strategic weakness.

Conclusion: alliance dead or alive?

What does this volume tell us about the transatlantic alliance – that complex, difficult, but ultimately mutually advantageous set of relations which preserved the peace in Europe and successfully built a community of trust across the Atlantic? Addressing this question somewhat indirectly, it might be worthwhile revisiting some of the arguments which dominated the debates about the alliance during the 1990s. During this first post-Cold War decade, the focus of discussion was firmly on NATO and its future. Realists, for their part, argued that, in accordance with traditional alliance theory, NATO was bound to be severely weakened, or even disappear, in the absence of a common external threat and given that European and US strategic interests would naturally diverge (Mearsheimer 1990). Countering such realist pessimism, liberal institutionalists or constructivists valiantly came to NATO's defence, arguing that it was not a traditional realist alliance but represented a 'community of values' or a 'transatlantic security community' (Wendt 1999; Ikenberry 2000). Its value to both the United States and Europe was such that there would necessarily be a common interest in sustaining and transforming NATO to deal with the new and emerging security challenges and threats.

In the later half of the 1990s, it appeared that realist predictions had proved to be false. NATO expanded its membership to East Central Europe and demonstrated its continuing relevance through action in Bosnia and Kosovo. The continuing dynamic of transatlantic cooperation and coordination highlighted by liberal institutionalists and constructivists appeared to be holding true. However, developments in the new millennium have undoubtedly given new life and vitality to realist claims. It is particularly striking how little discussion there has been about NATO since the events of 9/11 amongst either analysts or the general public. It would have been inconceivable a few years ago for a book such as this on the transatlantic alliance to deal so marginally with NATO. But this emphasis, reflected above all by Cameron, merely confirms that there is a widespread recognition that NATO, though not dead, has a significantly more restricted and limited role, and that it cannot provide the institutional answer to the transatlantic relationship.

NATO's marginalisation is also a reflection of the fact that the disputes and divergences which emerged with the Bush administration and the 2003 Iraq war surpassed the expectations of even the more pessimistic exponents of fraying transatlantic ties. And no one, least of all our contributors, argues that the New Transatlantic Agenda structures for dialogue between the United States and the European Union form a robust institutional foundation for a strategic partnership. The reality is that even the most enthusiastic Atlanticist recognises that strategic dissonance will remain a key feature of US–European relations. The critical question now is whether this means definitive transatlantic rupture or whether renewal, on a more realistic and mutually cooperative basis, can be forged.

From the insights found in this book, it does not appear that Al Qaeda or China or other potential threats will replace the role played by the Soviet Union during the Cold War in ensuring strategic conformity across the Atlantic. As such, Europe and the United States are bound to have differing strategic views and priorities, driven by their differing geographical location, cultures and power capabilities. Strategic drift is, to a lesser or greater extent, inevitable. But, there is also no reason to believe that such drift will change partners and allies into strategic competitors who seek to counter-balance one another. The fact that, after the difficulties of the Iraq war, the United States and the European Union did make great efforts to reconstitute the transatlantic relationship highlights the continuing importance both sides accord to that relationship. The longer-term challenge is to provide a more effective and relevant institutional framework for this relationship that transcends the generally recognised limitations of NATO, and one which probably builds on and buttresses the existing US–EU dialogue while also making it a forum for strategic dialogue.

Yet, as has always been the case for cooperation on matters of grand strategy *within* the European Union, the most intractable obstacles to transatlantic foreign and security policy cooperation remain ones of identity and interest, not institutions (see Peterson and Sjursen 1998). On these fronts, there are at least signs that strategic drift is not inexorable or cumulative. The staggering economic ascent of India and China and the emergence of something like a developing country bloc during the Doha development round caused transatlantic divisions, as seen in the proposed lifting of the European Union's arms embargo on China or the mutual recriminations surrounding the 2005 Hong Kong WTO summit. But they have also focused American and European minds on areas where the West still has essentially common objectives. Some of the manifestations have remained well below the political radar, such as the first US–EU ministerial summit on deepening transatlantic economic cooperation in late 2005 that was nonetheless described by a leading industrialist as a 'small piece of history'.[2] Others, such as policy coordination on Afghanistan, Ukraine or the western Balkans, are part of a larger pattern of surprisingly vigorous US–EU foreign policy cooperation (see European Commission 2005).

Perhaps above all, it is in the area of Homeland Security and Justice and Home Affairs that the United States and the European Union find themselves engaged in the most intensive policy cooperation. Even the most unrepentant sceptics of 'transformational diplomacy' or transatlantic partnership (see Jervis 2005) find common ground with true believers in international institutions and liberal notions of progress on the idea that 'the transnational character of terrorism makes a national strategy impotent' (Ikenberry 2002a: 307). Again, shared strategic objectives cannot resolve basic differences of view on appropriate means in a war on terrorism, a point illustrated vibrantly by European outrage over allegations in late 2005 of 'secret CIA jails' run by the United States for interrogating suspected terrorists, purportedly including ones in Poland and Romania. Yet, in a sign that shared transatlantic values still apply to the most difficult disputes, the Bush administration quietly backed down on the treatment of alleged terrorist prisoners under pressure from Senator John McCain, a prominent member of George W. Bush's own Republican Party who had been tortured as a prisoner in Vietnam.

More generally, questions surrounding security strategy take on new meaning in an era when many of the best minds in the study of international politics concur that 'it is almost certain that the coming decade will see large terrorist attacks on the West, perhaps with WMD' (Jervis 2005: 375). The US and European security strategies arrived at a truly Trumanesque moment in 2002–3 when the strategic necessity of strenuous policy cooperation became clear if the transatlantic partners intended to, in George W. Bush's memorable phrase, 'save civilization itself' (Serfaty 2005: 65). Even the most hard-boiled American realist, while insisting that neither the United States nor Europe possessed any vision that could 'serve as a partnership of equals' and branding Europe's decline 'one of the oldest and best established trends in world politics', concedes that 'at the end of the day the necessities of international life will compel the two sides to keep overcoming their differences' (Mead 2005: 163–8). Ultimately, it will be such dynamics emanating from the ground up, not the top down, and reflecting those areas where day-to-day transatlantic cooperation is most needed, that a more durable and institutionalised alliance between the United States and Europe might be founded.

Notes

1 Daniel Dombey and Frederick Studemann, 'Middle East Tension Foils Final Euromed Declaration', *Financial Times*, 29 November 2005, p. 6.
2 See letter to the editor by Niall Ferguson, European chairman of the Transatlantic Business Dialogue, *Financial Times*, 6 December 2005. Online. Available: www.ft.com (accessed 10 December 2005).

Appendix 1

The National Security Strategy of
the United States*

THE NATIONAL
SECURITY STRATEGY

OF THE

UNITED STATES
OF AMERICA

SEPTEMBER 2002

* Source: US State Department

The great struggles of the twentieth century between liberty and totalitarianism ended with a decisive victory for the forces of freedom—and a single sustainable model for national success: freedom, democracy, and free enterprise. In the twenty-first century, only nations that share a commitment to protecting basic human rights and guaranteeing political and economic freedom will be able to unleash the potential of their people and assure their future prosperity. People everywhere want to be able to speak freely; choose who will govern them; worship as they please; educate their children—male and female; own property; and enjoy the benefits of their labor. These values of freedom are right and true for every person, in every society—and the duty of protecting these values against their enemies is the common calling of freedom-loving people across the globe and across the ages.

Today, the United States enjoys a position of unparalleled military strength and great economic and political influence. In keeping with our heritage and principles, we do not use our strength to press for unilateral advantage. We seek instead to create a balance of power that favors human freedom: conditions in which all nations and all societies can choose for themselves the rewards and challenges of political and economic liberty. In a world that is safe, people will be able to make their own lives better. We will defend the peace by fighting terrorists and tyrants. We will preserve the peace by building good relations among the great powers. We will extend the peace by encouraging free and open societies on every continent.

Defending our Nation against its enemies is the first and fundamental commitment of the Federal Government. Today, that task has changed dramatically. Enemies in the past needed great armies and great industrial capabilities to endanger America. Now, shadowy networks of individuals can bring great chaos and suffering to our shores for less than it costs to purchase a single tank. Terrorists are organized to penetrate open societies and to turn the power of modern technologies against us.

To defeat this threat we must make use of every tool in our arsenal—military power, better homeland defenses, law enforcement, intelligence, and vigorous efforts to cut off terrorist financing. The war against terrorists of global reach is a global enterprise of uncertain duration. America will help nations that need our assistance in combating terror. And America will hold to account nations that are compromised by terror, including those who harbor terrorists—because the allies of terror are the enemies of civilization. The United States and countries cooperating with us must not allow the terrorists to develop new home bases. Together, we will seek to deny them sanctuary at every turn.

The gravest danger our Nation faces lies at the crossroads of radicalism and technology. Our enemies have openly declared that they are seeking weapons of mass destruction, and evidence indicates that they are doing so with determination. The United States will not allow these efforts to succeed. We will build defenses against ballistic missiles and other means of delivery. We will cooperate with other nations to deny, contain, and curtail our enemies' efforts to acquire dangerous technologies. And, as a matter of common sense and self-defense, America will act against such emerging threats before they are fully formed. We cannot defend America and our friends by hoping for the best. So we must be prepared to defeat our enemies' plans, using the best intelligence and proceeding with deliberation. History will judge harshly those who saw this coming danger but failed to act. In the new world we have entered, the only path to peace and security is the path of action.

As we defend the peace, we will also take advantage of an historic opportunity to preserve the peace. Today, the international community has the best chance since the rise of the nation-state in the seventeenth century to build a world where great powers compete in peace instead of continually prepare for war. Today, the world's great powers find ourselves on the same side—united by common dangers of terrorist violence and chaos. The United States will build on these common interests to promote global security. We are also increasingly united by common values. Russia is in the midst of a hopeful transition, reaching for its democratic future and a partner in the war on terror. Chinese leaders are discovering that economic freedom is the only source of national wealth. In time, they will find that social and political freedom is the only source of national greatness. America will encourage the advancement of democracy and economic openness in both nations, because these are the best foundations for domestic stability and international order. We will strongly resist aggression from other great powers—even as we welcome their peaceful pursuit of prosperity, trade, and cultural advancement.

Finally, the United States will use this moment of opportunity to extend the benefits of freedom across the globe. We will actively work to bring the hope of democracy, development, free markets, and free trade to every corner of the world. The events of September 11, 2001, taught us that weak states, like Afghanistan, can pose as great a danger to our national interests as strong states. Poverty does not make poor people into terrorists and murderers. Yet poverty, weak institutions, and corruption can make weak states vulnerable to terrorist networks and drug cartels within their borders.

The United States will stand beside any nation determined to build a better future by seeking the rewards of liberty for its people. Free trade and free markets have proven their ability to lift whole societies out of poverty—so the United States will work with individual nations, entire regions, and the entire global trading community to build a world that trades in freedom and therefore grows in prosperity. The United States will deliver greater development assistance through the New Millennium Challenge Account to nations that govern justly, invest in their people, and encourage economic freedom. We will also continue to lead the world in efforts to reduce the terrible toll of HIV/AIDS and other infectious diseases.

In building a balance of power that favors freedom, the United States is guided by the conviction that all nations have important responsibilities. Nations that enjoy freedom must actively fight terror. Nations that depend on international stability must help prevent the spread of weapons of mass destruction. Nations that seek international aid must govern themselves wisely, so that aid is well spent. For freedom to thrive, accountability must be expected and required.

We are also guided by the conviction that no nation can build a safer, better world alone. Alliances and multilateral institutions can multiply the strength of freedom-loving nations. The United States is committed to lasting institutions like the United Nations, the World Trade Organization, the Organization of American States, and NATO as well as other long-standing alliances. Coalitions of the willing can augment these permanent institutions. In all cases, international obligations are to be taken seriously. They are not to be undertaken symbolically to rally support for an ideal without furthering its attainment.

Freedom is the non-negotiable demand of human dignity; the birthright of every person—in every civilization. Throughout history, freedom has been threatened by war and terror; it has been challenged by the clashing wills of powerful states and the evil designs of tyrants; and it has been tested by widespread poverty and disease. Today, humanity holds in its hands the opportunity to further freedom's triumph over all these foes. The United States welcomes our responsibility to lead in this great mission.

THE WHITE HOUSE,
September 17, 2002

Table of Contents

(the page that follows is blank in the original document)

I. OVERVIEW OF AMERICA'S INTERNATIONAL STRATEGY

"Our Nation's cause has always been larger than our Nation's defense.
We fight, as we always fight, for a just peace—a peace that favors liberty.
We will defend the peace against the threats from terrorists and tyrants.
We will preserve the peace by building good relations among the great powers.
And we will extend the peace by encouraging free and open societies on every continent."

PRESIDENT BUSH
WEST POINT, NEW YORK
JUNE 1, 2002

The United States possesses unprecedented—and unequaled—strength and influence in the world. Sustained by faith in the principles of liberty, and the value of a free society, this position comes with unparalleled responsibilities, obligations, and opportunity. The great strength of this nation must be used to promote a balance of power that favors freedom.

For most of the twentieth century, the world was divided by a great struggle over ideas: destructive totalitarian visions versus freedom and equality.

That great struggle is over. The militant visions of class, nation, and race which promised utopia and delivered misery have been defeated and discredited. America is now threatened less by conquering states than we are by failing ones. We are menaced less by fleets and armies than by catastrophic technologies in the hands of the embittered few. We must defeat these threats to our Nation, allies, and friends.

This is also a time of opportunity for America. We will work to translate this moment of influence into decades of peace, prosperity, and liberty.

The U.S. national security strategy will be based on a distinctly American internationalism that reflects the union of our values and our national interests. The aim of this strategy is to help make the world not just safer but better. Our goals on the path to progress are clear: political and economic freedom, peaceful relations with other states, and respect for human dignity.

And this path is not America's alone. It is open to all.

To achieve these goals, the United States will:

- champion aspirations for human dignity;

- strengthen alliances to defeat global terrorism and work to prevent attacks against us and our friends;

- work with others to defuse regional conflicts;

- prevent our enemies from threatening us, our allies, and our friends, with weapons of mass destruction;

- ignite a new era of global economic growth through free markets and free trade;

- expand the circle of development by opening societies and building the infrastructure of democracy;

- develop agendas for cooperative action with other main centers of global power; and

- transform America's national security institutions to meet the challenges and opportunities of the twenty-first century.

II. Champion Aspirations for Human Dignity

"Some worry that it is somehow undiplomatic or impolite to speak the language of right and wrong. I disagree. Different circumstances require different methods, but not different moralities."

President Bush
West Point, New York
June 1, 2002

In pursuit of our goals, our first imperative is to clarify what we stand for: the United States must defend liberty and justice because these principles are right and true for all people everywhere. No nation owns these aspirations, and no nation is exempt from them. Fathers and mothers in all societies want their children to be educated and to live free from poverty and violence. No people on earth yearn to be oppressed, aspire to servitude, or eagerly await the midnight knock of the secret police.

America must stand firmly for the nonnegotiable demands of human dignity: the rule of law; limits on the absolute power of the state; free speech; freedom of worship; equal justice; respect for women; religious and ethnic tolerance; and respect for private property.

These demands can be met in many ways. America's constitution has served us well. Many other nations, with different histories and cultures, facing different circumstances, have successfully incorporated these core principles into their own systems of governance. History has not been kind to those nations which ignored or flouted the rights and aspirations of their people.

America's experience as a great multi-ethnic democracy affirms our conviction that people of many heritages and faiths can live and prosper in peace. Our own history is a long struggle to live up to our ideals. But even in our worst moments, the principles enshrined in the Declaration of Independence were there to guide us. As a result, America is not just a stronger, but is a freer and more just society.

Today, these ideals are a lifeline to lonely defenders of liberty. And when openings arrive, we can encourage change—as we did in central and eastern Europe between 1989 and 1991, or in Belgrade in 2000. When we see democratic processes take hold among our friends in Taiwan or in the Republic of Korea, and see elected leaders replace generals in Latin America and Africa, we see examples of how authoritarian systems can evolve, marrying local history and traditions with the principles we all cherish.

Embodying lessons from our past and using the opportunity we have today, the national security strategy of the United States must start from these core beliefs and look outward for possibilities to expand liberty.

Our principles will guide our government's decisions about international cooperation, the character of our foreign assistance, and the allocation of resources. They will guide our actions and our words in international bodies.

We will:

- speak out honestly about violations of the nonnegotiable demands of human dignity using our voice and vote in international institutions to advance freedom;

- use our foreign aid to promote freedom and support those who struggle non-violently for it, ensuring that nations moving toward democracy are rewarded for the steps they take;

- make freedom and the development of democratic institutions key themes in our bilateral relations, seeking solidarity and cooperation from other democracies while we press governments that deny human rights to move toward a better future; and

- take special efforts to promote freedom of religion and conscience and defend it from encroachment by repressive governments.

We will champion the cause of human dignity and oppose those who resist it.

III. STRENGTHEN ALLIANCES TO DEFEAT GLOBAL TERRORISM AND WORK TO PREVENT ATTACKS AGAINST US AND OUR FRIENDS

"Just three days removed from these events, Americans do not yet have
the distance of history. But our responsibility to history is already clear:
to answer these attacks and rid the world of evil. War has been
waged against us by stealth and deceit and murder. This nation is peaceful,
but fierce when stirred to anger. The conflict was begun on the timing and terms
of others. It will end in a way, and at an hour, of our choosing."

PRESIDENT BUSH
WASHINGTON, D.C. (THE NATIONAL CATHEDRAL)
SEPTEMBER 14, 2001

The United States of America is fighting a war against terrorists of global reach. The enemy is not a single political regime or person or religion or ideology. The enemy is terrorism—premeditated, politically motivated violence perpetrated against innocents.

In many regions, legitimate grievances prevent the emergence of a lasting peace. Such grievances deserve to be, and must be, addressed within a political process. But no cause justifies terror. The United States will make no concessions to terrorist demands and strike no deals with them. We make no distinction between terrorists and those who knowingly harbor or provide aid to them.

The struggle against global terrorism is different from any other war in our history. It will be fought on many fronts against a particularly elusive enemy over an extended period of time. Progress will come through the persistent accumulation of successes—some seen, some unseen.

Today our enemies have seen the results of what civilized nations can, and will, do against regimes that harbor, support, and use terrorism to achieve their political goals. Afghanistan has been liberated; coalition forces continue to hunt down the Taliban and al-Qaida. But it is not only this battlefield on which we will engage terrorists. Thousands of trained terrorists remain at large with cells in North America, South America, Europe, Africa, the Middle East, and across Asia.

Our priority will be first to disrupt and destroy terrorist organizations of global reach and attack their leadership; command, control, and communications; material support; and finances. This will have a disabling effect upon the terrorists' ability to plan and operate.

We will continue to encourage our regional partners to take up a coordinated effort that isolates the terrorists. Once the regional campaign localizes the threat to a particular state, we will help ensure the state has the military, law enforcement, political, and financial tools necessary to finish the task.

The United States will continue to work with our allies to disrupt the financing of terrorism. We will identify and block the sources of funding for terrorism, freeze the assets of terrorists and those who support them, deny terrorists access to the international financial system, protect legitimate charities from being abused by terrorists, and prevent the movement of terrorists' assets through alternative financial networks.

However, this campaign need not be sequential to be effective, the cumulative effect across all regions will help achieve the results we seek.

We will disrupt and destroy terrorist organizations by:

- direct and continuous action using all the elements of national and international power. Our immediate focus will be those terrorist organizations of global reach and any terrorist or state sponsor of terrorism which attempts to gain or use weapons of mass destruction (WMD) or their precursors;

- defending the United States, the American people, and our interests at home and abroad by identifying and destroying the threat before it reaches our borders. While the United States will constantly strive to enlist the support of the international community, we will not hesitate to act alone, if necessary, to exercise our right of self-defense by acting preemptively against such terrorists, to prevent them from doing harm against our people and our country; and

- denying further sponsorship, support, and sanctuary to terrorists by convincing or compelling states to accept their sovereign responsibilities.

We will also wage a war of ideas to win the battle against international terrorism. This includes:

- using the full influence of the United States, and working closely with allies and friends, to make clear that all acts of terrorism are illegitimate so that terrorism will be viewed in the same light as slavery, piracy, or genocide: behavior that no respectable government can condone or support and all must oppose;

- supporting moderate and modern government, especially in the Muslim world, to ensure that the conditions and ideologies that promote terrorism do not find fertile ground in any nation;

- diminishing the underlying conditions that spawn terrorism by enlisting the international community to focus its efforts and resources on areas most at risk; and

- using effective public diplomacy to promote the free flow of information and ideas to kindle the hopes and aspirations of freedom of those in societies ruled by the sponsors of global terrorism.

While we recognize that our best defense is a good offense, we are also strengthening America's homeland security to protect against and deter attack.

This Administration has proposed the largest government reorganization since the Truman Administration created the National Security Council and the Department of Defense. Centered on a new Department of Homeland Security and including a new unified military command and a fundamental reordering of the FBI, our comprehensive plan to secure the homeland encompasses every level of government and the cooperation of the public and the private sector.

This strategy will turn adversity into opportunity. For example, emergency management systems will be better able to cope not just with terrorism but with all hazards. Our medical system will be strengthened to manage not just bioterror, but all infectious diseases and mass-casualty dangers. Our border controls will not just stop terrorists, but improve the efficient movement of legitimate traffic.

While our focus is protecting America, we know that to defeat terrorism in today's globalized world we need support from our allies and friends. Wherever possible, the United States will rely on regional organizations and state powers to meet their obligations to fight terrorism. Where governments find the fight against terrorism beyond their capacities, we will match their willpower and their resources with whatever help we and our allies can provide.

As we pursue the terrorists in Afghanistan, we will continue to work with international organizations such as the United Nations, as well as non-governmental organizations, and other countries to provide the humanitarian, political, economic, and security assistance necessary to rebuild Afghanistan so that it will never again abuse its people, threaten its neighbors, and provide a haven for terrorists.

In the war against global terrorism, we will never forget that we are ultimately fighting for our democratic values and way of life. Freedom and fear are at war, and there will be no quick or easy end to this conflict. In leading the campaign against terrorism, we are forging new, productive international relationships and redefining existing ones in ways that meet the challenges of the twenty-first century.

(the page that follows is blank in the original document)

iv. Work with others to
Defuse Regional Conflicts

"We build a world of justice, or we will live in a world of coercion.
The magnitude of our shared responsibilities makes our disagreements look so small."

PRESIDENT BUSH
BERLIN, GERMANY
MAY 23, 2002

Concerned nations must remain actively engaged in critical regional disputes to avoid explosive escalation and minimize human suffering. In an increasingly interconnected world, regional crisis can strain our alliances, rekindle rivalries among the major powers, and create horrifying affronts to human dignity. When violence erupts and states falter, the United States will work with friends and partners to alleviate suffering and restore stability.

No doctrine can anticipate every circumstance in which U.S. action—direct or indirect—is warranted. We have finite political, economic, and military resources to meet our global priorities. The United States will approach each case with these strategic principles in mind:

- The United States should invest time and resources into building international relationships and institutions that can help manage local crises when they emerge.

- The United States should be realistic about its ability to help those who are unwilling or unready to help themselves. Where and when people are ready to do their part, we will be willing to move decisively.

The Israeli-Palestinian conflict is critical because of the toll of human suffering, because of America's close relationship with the state of Israel and key Arab states, and because of that region's importance to other global priorities of the United States. There can be no peace for either side without freedom for both sides. America stands committed to an independent and democratic Palestine, living beside Israel in peace and security. Like all other people, Palestinians deserve a government that serves their interests and listens to their voices. The United States will continue to encourage all parties to step up to their responsibilities as we seek a just and comprehensive settlement to the conflict.

The United States, the international donor community, and the World Bank stand ready to work with a reformed Palestinian government on economic development, increased humanitarian assistance, and a program to establish, finance, and monitor a truly independent judiciary. If Palestinians embrace democracy, and the rule of law, confront corruption, and firmly reject terror, they can count on American support for the creation of a Palestinian state.

Israel also has a large stake in the success of a democratic Palestine. Permanent occupation threatens Israel's identity and democracy. So the United States continues to challenge Israeli leaders to take concrete steps to support the emergence of a viable, credible Palestinian state. As there is progress towards security, Israel forces need to withdraw fully to positions they held prior to September 28, 2000. And consistent with the recommendations of the Mitchell Committee, Israeli settlement activity in the occupied territories must stop. As violence subsides, freedom of movement should be restored, permitting innocent Palestinians to resume work and normal life. The United States can play a crucial role but, ultimately, lasting peace can only come when Israelis and Palestinians resolve the issues and end the conflict between them.

In South Asia, the United States has also emphasized the need for India and Pakistan to resolve their disputes. This Administration invested time and resources building strong bilateral relations with India and Pakistan. These strong relations then gave us leverage to play a constructive role when tensions in the region became acute. With Pakistan, our bilateral relations have been bolstered by Pakistan's choice to join the war against terror and move toward building a more open and tolerant society. The Administration sees India's potential to become one of the great democratic powers of the twenty-first century and has worked hard to transform our relationship accordingly. Our involvement in this regional dispute, building on earlier investments in bilateral relations, looks first to concrete steps by India and Pakistan that can help defuse military confrontation.

Indonesia took courageous steps to create a working democracy and respect for the rule of law. By tolerating ethnic minorities, respecting the rule of law, and accepting open markets, Indonesia may be able to employ the engine of opportunity that has helped lift some of its neighbors out of poverty and desperation. It is the initiative by Indonesia that allows U.S. assistance to make a difference.

In the Western Hemisphere we have formed flexible coalitions with countries that share our priorities, particularly Mexico, Brazil, Canada, Chile, and Colombia. Together we will promote a truly democratic hemisphere where our integration advances security, prosperity, opportunity, and hope. We will work with regional institutions, such as the Summit of the Americas process, the Organization of American States (OAS), and the Defense Ministerial of the Americas for the benefit of the entire hemisphere.

Parts of Latin America confront regional conflict, especially arising from the violence of drug cartels and their accomplices. This conflict and unrestrained narcotics trafficking could imperil the health and security of the United States. Therefore we have developed an active strategy to help the Andean nations adjust their economies, enforce their laws, defeat terrorist organizations, and cut off the supply of drugs, while—as important—we work to reduce the demand for drugs in our own country.

In Colombia, we recognize the link between terrorist and extremist groups that challenge the security of the state and drug trafficking activities that help finance the operations of such groups. We are working to help Colombia defend its democratic institutions and defeat illegal armed groups of both the left and right by extending effective sovereignty over the entire national territory and provide basic security to the Colombian people.

In Africa, promise and opportunity sit side by side with disease, war, and desperate poverty. This threatens both a core value of the United States—preserving human dignity—and our strategic priority—combating global terror. American interests and American principles, therefore, lead in the same direction: we will work with others for an African continent that lives in liberty, peace, and growing prosperity. Together with our European allies, we must help strengthen Africa's fragile states, help build indigenous capability to secure porous borders, and help build up the law enforcement and intelligence infrastructure to deny havens for terrorists.

An ever more lethal environment exists in Africa as local civil wars spread beyond borders to create regional war zones. Forming coalitions of the willing and cooperative security arrangements are key to confronting these emerging transnational threats.

Africa's great size and diversity requires a security strategy that focuses on bilateral engagement and builds coalitions of the willing. This Administration will focus on three interlocking strategies for the region:

- countries with major impact on their neighborhood such as South Africa, Nigeria, Kenya, and Ethiopia are anchors for regional engagement and require focused attention;

- coordination with European allies and international institutions is essential for constructive conflict mediation and successful peace operations; and

- Africa's capable reforming states and sub-regional organizations must be strengthened as the primary means to address transnational threats on a sustained basis.

Ultimately the path of political and economic freedom presents the surest route to progress in sub-Saharan Africa, where most wars are conflicts over material resources and political access often tragically waged on the basis of ethnic and religious difference. The transition to the African Union with its stated commitment to good governance and a common responsibility for democratic political systems offers opportunities to strengthen democracy on the continent.

(the page that follows is blank in the original document)

v. Prevent Our Enemies from Threatening Us, Our Allies, and Our Friends with Weapons of Mass Destruction

*"The gravest danger to freedom lies at the crossroads of radicalism and technology.
When the spread of chemical and biological and nuclear weapons,
along with ballistic missile technology—when that occurs, even weak states
and small groups could attain a catastrophic power to strike great nations.
Our enemies have declared this very intention, and have been caught seeking
these terrible weapons. They want the capability to blackmail us, or to harm us,
or to harm our friends—and we will oppose them with all our power."*

President Bush
West Point, New York
June 1, 2002

The nature of the Cold War threat required the United States—with our allies and friends—to emphasize deterrence of the enemy's use of force, producing a grim strategy of mutual assured destruction. With the collapse of the Soviet Union and the end of the Cold War, our security environment has undergone profound transformation.

Having moved from confrontation to cooperation as the hallmark of our relationship with Russia, the dividends are evident: an end to the balance of terror that divided us; an historic reduction in the nuclear arsenals on both sides; and cooperation in areas such as counterterrorism and missile defense that until recently were inconceivable.

But new deadly challenges have emerged from rogue states and terrorists. None of these contemporary threats rival the sheer destructive power that was arrayed against us by the Soviet Union. However, the nature and motivations of these new adversaries, their determination to obtain destructive powers hitherto available only to the world's strongest states, and the greater likelihood that they will use weapons of mass destruction against us, make today's security environment more complex and dangerous.

In the 1990s we witnessed the emergence of a small number of rogue states that, while different in important ways, share a number of attributes. These states:

- brutalize their own people and squander their national resources for the personal gain of the rulers;

- display no regard for international law, threaten their neighbors, and callously violate international treaties to which they are party;

- are determined to acquire weapons of mass destruction, along with other advanced military technology, to be used as threats or offensively to achieve the aggressive designs of these regimes;

- sponsor terrorism around the globe; and

- reject basic human values and hate the United States and everything for which it stands.

At the time of the Gulf War, we acquired irrefutable proof that Iraq's designs were not limited to the chemical weapons it had used against Iran and its own people, but also extended to the acquisition of nuclear weapons and biological agents. In the past decade North Korea has become the world's principal purveyor of ballistic missiles, and has tested increasingly capable missiles while developing its own WMD arsenal. Other rogue regimes seek nuclear, biological, and chemical weapons as well. These states' pursuit of, and global trade in, such weapons has become a looming threat to all nations.

We must be prepared to stop rogue states and their terrorist clients before they are able to threaten or use weapons of mass destruction against the United States and our allies and friends. Our response must take full advantage of strengthened alliances, the establishment of new partnerships with former adversaries, innovation in the use of military forces, modern technologies, including the development of an effective missile defense system, and increased emphasis on intelligence collection and analysis.

Our comprehensive strategy to combat WMD includes:

- *Proactive counterproliferation efforts.* We must deter and defend against the threat before it is unleashed. We must ensure that key capabilities—detection, active and passive defenses, and counterforce capabilities—are integrated into our defense transformation and our homeland security systems. Counterproliferation must also be integrated into the doctrine, training, and equipping of our forces and those of our allies to ensure that we can prevail in any conflict with WMD-armed adversaries.

- *Strengthened nonproliferation efforts to prevent rogue states and terrorists from acquiring the materials, technologies, and expertise necessary for weapons of mass destruction.* We will enhance diplomacy, arms control, multilateral export controls, and threat reduction assistance that impede states and terrorists seeking WMD, and when necessary, interdict enabling technologies and materials. We will continue to build coalitions to support these efforts, encouraging their increased political and financial support for nonproliferation and threat reduction programs. The recent G-8 agreement to commit up to $20 billion to a global partnership against proliferation marks a major step forward.

- *Effective consequence management to respond to the effects of WMD use, whether by terrorists or hostile states.* Minimizing the effects of WMD use against our people will help deter those who possess such weapons and dissuade those who seek to acquire them by persuading enemies that they cannot attain their desired ends. The United States must also be prepared to respond to the effects of WMD use against our forces abroad, and to help friends and allies if they are attacked.

It has taken almost a decade for us to comprehend the true nature of this new threat. Given the goals of rogue states and terrorists, the United States can no longer solely rely on a reactive posture as we have in the past. The inability to deter a potential attacker, the immediacy of today's threats, and the magnitude of potential harm that could be caused by our adversaries' choice of weapons, do not permit that option. We cannot let our enemies strike first.

- In the Cold War, especially following the Cuban missile crisis, we faced a generally status quo, risk-averse adversary. Deterrence was an effective defense. But deterrence based only upon the threat of retaliation is less likely to work against leaders of rogue states more willing to take risks, gambling with the lives of their people, and the wealth of their nations.

- In the Cold War, weapons of mass destruction were considered weapons of last resort whose use risked the destruction of those who used them. Today, our enemies see weapons of mass destruction as weapons of choice. For rogue states these weapons are tools of intimidation and military aggression against their neighbors. These weapons may also allow these states to attempt to blackmail the United States and our allies to prevent us from deterring or repelling the aggressive behavior of rogue states. Such states also see these weapons as their best means of overcoming the conventional superiority of the United States.

- Traditional concepts of deterrence will not work against a terrorist enemy whose avowed tactics are wanton destruction and the targeting of innocents; whose so-called soldiers seek martyrdom in death and whose most potent protection is statelessness. The overlap between states that sponsor terror and those that pursue WMD compels us to action.

For centuries, international law recognized that nations need not suffer an attack before they can lawfully take action to defend themselves against forces that present an imminent danger of attack. Legal scholars and international jurists often conditioned the legitimacy of preemption on the existence of an imminent threat—most often a visible mobilization of armies, navies, and air forces preparing to attack.

We must adapt the concept of imminent threat to the capabilities and objectives of today's adversaries. Rogue states and terrorists do not seek to attack us using conventional means. They know such attacks would fail. Instead, they rely on acts of terror and, potentially, the use of weapons of mass destruction—weapons that can be easily concealed, delivered covertly, and used without warning.

The targets of these attacks are our military forces and our civilian population, in direct violation of one of the principal norms of the law of warfare. As was demonstrated by the losses on September 11, 2001, mass civilian casualties is the specific objective of terrorists and these losses would be exponentially more severe if terrorists acquired and used weapons of mass destruction.

The United States has long maintained the option of preemptive actions to counter a sufficient threat to our national security. The greater the threat, the greater is the risk of inaction—and the more compelling the case for taking anticipatory action to defend ourselves, even if uncertainty remains as to the time and place of the enemy's attack. To forestall or prevent such hostile acts by our adversaries, the United States will, if necessary, act preemptively.

The United States will not use force in all cases to preempt emerging threats, nor should nations use preemption as a pretext for aggression. Yet in an age where the enemies of civilization openly and actively seek the world's most destructive technologies, the United States cannot remain idle while dangers gather.

We will always proceed deliberately, weighing the consequences of our actions. To support preemptive options, we will:

- build better, more integrated intelligence capabilities to provide timely, accurate information on threats, wherever they may emerge;

- coordinate closely with allies to form a common assessment of the most dangerous threats; and

- continue to transform our military forces to ensure our ability to conduct rapid and precise operations to achieve decisive results.

The purpose of our actions will always be to eliminate a specific threat to the United States or our allies and friends. The reasons for our actions will be clear, the force measured, and the cause just.

VI. IGNITE A NEW ERA OF GLOBAL ECONOMIC GROWTH THROUGH FREE MARKETS AND FREE TRADE

"When nations close their markets and opportunity is hoarded by a privileged few, no amount—no amount—of development aid is ever enough. When nations respect their people, open markets, invest in better health and education, every dollar of aid, every dollar of trade revenue and domestic capital is used more effectively."

PRESIDENT BUSH
MONTERREY, MEXICO
MARCH 22, 2002

A strong world economy enhances our national security by advancing prosperity and freedom in the rest of the world. Economic growth supported by free trade and free markets creates new jobs and higher incomes. It allows people to lift their lives out of poverty, spurs economic and legal reform, and the fight against corruption, and it reinforces the habits of liberty.

We will promote economic growth and economic freedom beyond America's shores. All governments are responsible for creating their own economic policies and responding to their own economic challenges. We will use our economic engagement with other countries to underscore the benefits of policies that generate higher productivity and sustained economic growth, including:

- pro-growth legal and regulatory policies to encourage business investment, innovation, and entrepreneurial activity;

- tax policies—particularly lower marginal tax rates—that improve incentives for work and investment;

- rule of law and intolerance of corruption so that people are confident that they will be able to enjoy the fruits of their economic endeavors;

- strong financial systems that allow capital to be put to its most efficient use;

- sound fiscal policies to support business activity;

- investments in health and education that improve the well-being and skills of the labor force and population as a whole; and

- free trade that provides new avenues for growth and fosters the diffusion of technologies and ideas that increase productivity and opportunity.

The lessons of history are clear: market economies, not command-and-control economies with the heavy hand of government, are the best way to promote prosperity and reduce poverty. Policies that further strengthen market incentives and market institutions are relevant for all economies—industrialized countries, emerging markets, and the developing world.

A return to strong economic growth in Europe and Japan is vital to U.S. national security interests. We want our allies to have strong economies for their own sake, for the sake of the global economy, and for the sake of global security. European efforts to remove structural barriers in their economies are particularly important in this regard, as are Japan's efforts to end deflation and address the problems of non-performing loans in the Japanese banking system. We will continue to use our regular consultations with Japan and our European partners—including through the Group of Seven (G-7)—to discuss policies they are adopting to promote growth in their economies and support higher global economic growth.

Improving stability in emerging markets is also key to global economic growth. International flows of investment capital are needed to expand the productive potential of these economies. These flows allow emerging markets and developing countries to make the investments that raise living standards and reduce poverty. Our long-term objective should be a world in which all countries have investment-grade credit ratings that allow them access to international capital markets and to invest in their future.

We are committed to policies that will help emerging markets achieve access to larger capital flows at lower cost. To this end, we will continue to pursue reforms aimed at reducing uncertainty in financial markets. We will work actively with other countries, the International Monetary Fund (IMF), and the private sector to implement the G-7 Action Plan negotiated earlier this year for preventing financial crises and more effectively resolving them when they occur.

The best way to deal with financial crises is to prevent them from occurring, and we have encouraged the IMF to improve its efforts doing so. We will continue to work with the IMF to streamline the policy conditions for its lending and to focus its lending strategy on achieving economic growth through sound fiscal and monetary policy, exchange rate policy, and financial sector policy.

The concept of "free trade" arose as a moral principle even before it became a pillar of economics. If you can make something that others value, you should be able to sell it to them. If others make something that you value, you should be able to buy it. This is real freedom, the freedom for a person—or a nation—to make a living. To promote free trade, the Unites States has developed a comprehensive strategy:

- *Seize the global initiative.* The new global trade negotiations we helped launch at Doha in November 2001 will have an ambitious agenda, especially in agriculture, manufacturing, and services, targeted for completion in 2005. The United States has led the way in completing the accession of China and a democratic Taiwan to the World Trade Organization. We will assist Russia's preparations to join the WTO.

- *Press regional initiatives.* The United States and other democracies in the Western Hemisphere have agreed to create the Free Trade Area of the Americas, targeted for completion in 2005. This year the United States will advocate market-access negotiations with its partners, targeted on agriculture, industrial goods, services, investment, and government procurement. We will also offer more opportunity to the poorest continent, Africa, starting with full use of the preferences allowed in the African Growth and Opportunity Act, and leading to free trade.

- *Move ahead with bilateral free trade agreements.* Building on the free trade agreement with Jordan enacted in 2001, the Administration will work this year to complete free trade agreements with Chile and Singapore. Our aim is to achieve free trade agreements with a mix of developed and developing countries in all regions of the world. Initially, Central America, Southern Africa, Morocco, and Australia will be our principal focal points.

- *Renew the executive-congressional partnership.* Every administration's trade strategy depends on a productive partnership with Congress. After a gap of 8 years, the Administration reestablished majority support in the Congress for trade liberalization by passing Trade Promotion Authority and the other market opening measures for developing countries in the Trade Act of 2002. This Administration will work with Congress to enact new bilateral, regional, and global trade agreements that will be concluded under the recently passed Trade Promotion Authority.

- *Promote the connection between trade and development.* Trade policies can help developing countries strengthen property rights, competition, the rule of law, investment, the spread of knowledge, open societies, the efficient allocation of resources, and regional integration—all leading to growth, opportunity, and confidence in developing countries. The United States is implementing The Africa Growth and Opportunity Act to provide market-access for nearly all goods produced in the 35 countries of sub-Saharan Africa. We will make more use of this act and its equivalent for the Caribbean Basin and continue to work with multilateral and regional institutions to help poorer countries take advantage of these opportunities. Beyond market access, the most important area where trade intersects with poverty is in public health. We will ensure that the WTO intellectual property rules are flexible enough to allow developing nations to gain access to critical medicines for extraordinary dangers like HIV/AIDS, tuberculosis, and malaria.

- *Enforce trade agreements and laws against unfair practices.* Commerce depends on the rule of law; international trade depends on enforceable agreements. Our top priorities are to resolve ongoing disputes with the European Union, Canada, and Mexico and to make a global effort to address new technology, science, and health regulations that needlessly impede farm exports and improved agriculture. Laws against unfair trade practices are often abused, but the international community must be able to address genuine concerns about government subsidies and dumping. International industrial espionage which undermines fair competition must be detected and deterred.

- *Help domestic industries and workers adjust.* There is a sound statutory framework for these transitional safeguards which we have used in the agricultural sector and which we are using this year to help the American steel industry. The benefits of free trade depend upon the enforcement of fair trading practices. These safeguards help ensure that the benefits of free trade do not come at the expense of American workers. Trade adjustment assistance will help workers adapt to the change and dynamism of open markets.

- *Protect the environment and workers.* The United States must foster economic growth in ways that will provide a better life along with widening prosperity. We will incorporate labor and environmental concerns into U.S. trade negotiations, creating a healthy "network" between multilateral environmental agreements with the WTO, and use the International Labor Organization, trade preference programs, and trade talks to improve working conditions in conjunction with freer trade.

- *Enhance energy security.* We will strengthen our own energy security and the shared prosperity of the global economy by working with our allies, trading partners, and energy producers to expand the sources and types of global energy supplied, especially in the Western Hemisphere, Africa, Central Asia, and the Caspian region. We will also continue to work with our partners to develop cleaner and more energy efficient technologies.

Economic growth should be accompanied by global efforts to stabilize greenhouse gas concentrations associated with this growth, containing them at a level that prevents dangerous human interference with the global climate. Our overall objective is to reduce America's greenhouse gas emissions relative to the size of our economy, cutting such emissions per unit of economic activity by 18 percent over the next 10 years, by the year 2012. Our strategies for attaining this goal will be to:

- remain committed to the basic U.N. Framework Convention for international cooperation;

- obtain agreements with key industries to cut emissions of some of the most potent greenhouse gases and give transferable credits to companies that can show real cuts;

- develop improved standards for measuring and registering emission reductions;

- promote renewable energy production and clean coal technology, as well as nuclear power—which produces no greenhouse gas emissions, while also improving fuel economy for U.S. cars and trucks;

- increase spending on research and new conservation technologies, to a total of $4.5 billion—the largest sum being spent on climate change by any country in the world and a $700 million increase over last year's budget; and

- assist developing countries, especially the major greenhouse gas emitters such as China and India, so that they will have the tools and resources to join this effort and be able to grow along a cleaner and better path.

VII. Expand the Circle of Development by Opening Societies and Building the Infrastructure of Democracy

"In World War II we fought to make the world safer, then worked to rebuild it. As we wage war today to keep the world safe from terror, we must also work to make the world a better place for all its citizens."

President Bush
Washington, D.C. (Inter-American Development Bank)
March 14, 2002

A world where some live in comfort and plenty, while half of the human race lives on less than $2 a day, is neither just nor stable. Including all of the world's poor in an expanding circle of development—and opportunity—is a moral imperative and one of the top priorities of U.S. international policy.

Decades of massive development assistance have failed to spur economic growth in the poorest countries. Worse, development aid has often served to prop up failed policies, relieving the pressure for reform and perpetuating misery. Results of aid are typically measured in dollars spent by donors, not in the rates of growth and poverty reduction achieved by recipients. These are the indicators of a failed strategy.

Working with other nations, the United States is confronting this failure. We forged a new consensus at the U.N. Conference on Financing for Development in Monterrey that the objectives of assistance—and the strategies to achieve those objectives—must change.

This Administration's goal is to help unleash the productive potential of individuals in all nations. Sustained growth and poverty reduction is impossible without the right national policies. Where governments have implemented real policy changes, we will provide significant new levels of assistance. The United States and other developed countries should set an ambitious and specific target: to double the size of the world's poorest economies within a decade.

The United States Government will pursue these major strategies to achieve this goal:

- *Provide resources to aid countries that have met the challenge of national reform.* We propose a 50 percent increase in the core development assistance given by the United States. While continuing our present programs, including humanitarian assistance based on need alone, these billions of new dollars will form a new Millennium Challenge Account for projects in countries whose governments rule justly, invest in their people, and encourage economic freedom. Governments must fight corruption, respect basic human rights, embrace the rule of law, invest in health care and education, follow responsible economic policies, and enable entrepreneurship. The Millennium Challenge Account will reward countries that have demonstrated real policy change and challenge those that have not to implement reforms.

- *Improve the effectiveness of the World Bank and other development banks in raising living standards.* The United States is committed to a comprehensive reform agenda for making the World Bank and the other multilateral development banks more effective in improving the lives of the world's poor. We have reversed the downward trend in U.S. contributions and proposed an 18 percent increase in the U.S. contributions to the International Development Association (IDA)—the World Bank's fund for the poorest countries—and the African Development Fund. The key to raising living standards and reducing poverty around the world is increasing productivity growth, especially in the poorest countries. We will continue to press the multilateral development banks to focus on activities that increase economic productivity, such as improvements in education, health, rule of law, and private sector development. Every project, every loan, every grant must be judged by how much it will increase productivity growth in developing countries.

- *Insist upon measurable results to ensure that development assistance is actually making a difference in the lives of the world's poor.* When it comes to economic development, what really matters is that more children are getting a better education, more people have access to health care and clean water, or more workers can find jobs to make a better future for their families. We have a moral obligation to measure the success of our development assistance by whether it is delivering results. For this reason, we will continue to demand that our own development assistance as well as assistance from the multilateral development banks has measurable goals and concrete benchmarks for achieving those goals. Thanks to U.S. leadership, the recent IDA replenishment agreement will establish a monitoring and evaluation system that measures recipient countries' progress. For the first time, donors can link a portion of their contributions to IDA to the achievement of actual development results, and part of the U.S. contribution is linked in this way. We will strive to make sure that the World Bank and other multilateral development banks build on this progress so that a focus on results is an integral part of everything that these institutions do.

- *Increase the amount of development assistance that is provided in the form of grants instead of loans.* Greater use of results-based grants is the best way to help poor countries make productive investments, particularly in the social sectors, without saddling them with ever-larger debt burdens. As a result of U.S. leadership, the recent IDA agreement provided for significant increases in grant funding for the poorest countries for education, HIV/AIDS, health, nutrition, water, sanitation, and other human needs. Our goal is to build on that progress by increasing the use of grants at the other multilateral development banks. We will also challenge universities, nonprofits, and the private sector to match government efforts by using grants to support development projects that show results.

- *Open societies to commerce and investment.* Trade and investment are the real engines of economic growth. Even if government aid increases, most money for development must come from trade, domestic capital, and foreign investment. An effective strategy must try to expand these flows as well. Free markets and free trade are key priorities of our national security strategy.

- *Secure public health.* The scale of the public health crisis in poor countries is enormous. In countries afflicted by epidemics and pandemics like HIV/AIDS, malaria, and tuberculosis, growth and development will be threatened until these scourges can be contained. Resources from the developed world are necessary but will be effective only with honest governance, which supports prevention programs and provides effective local infrastructure. The United States has strongly backed the new global fund for HIV/AIDS organized by U.N. Secretary General Kofi Annan and its focus on combining prevention with a broad strategy for treatment and care. The United States already contributes more than twice as much money to such efforts as the next largest donor. If the global fund demonstrates its promise, we will be ready to give even more.

- *Emphasize education.* Literacy and learning are the foundation of democracy and development. Only about 7 percent of World Bank resources are devoted to education. This proportion should grow. The United States will increase its own funding for education assistance by at least 20 percent with an emphasis on improving basic education and teacher training in Africa. The United States can also bring information technology to these societies, many of whose education systems have been devastated by HIV/AIDS.

- *Continue to aid agricultural development.* New technologies, including biotechnology, have enormous potential to improve crop yields in developing countries while using fewer pesticides and less water. Using sound science, the United States should help bring these benefits to the 800 million people, including 300 million children, who still suffer from hunger and malnutrition.

(the page that follows is blank in the original document)

VIII. DEVELOP AGENDAS FOR COOPERATIVE ACTION WITH THE OTHER MAIN CENTERS OF GLOBAL POWER

*"We have our best chance since the rise of the nation-state in the 17th century
to build a world where the great powers compete in peace instead of prepare for war."*

PRESIDENT BUSH
WEST POINT, NEW YORK
JUNE 1, 2002

America will implement its strategies by organizing coalitions—as broad as practicable—of states able and willing to promote a balance of power that favors freedom. Effective coalition leadership requires clear priorities, an appreciation of others' interests, and consistent consultations among partners with a spirit of humility.

There is little of lasting consequence that the United States can accomplish in the world without the sustained cooperation of its allies and friends in Canada and Europe. Europe is also the seat of two of the strongest and most able international institutions in the world: the North Atlantic Treaty Organization (NATO), which has, since its inception, been the fulcrum of transatlantic and inter-European security, and the European Union (EU), our partner in opening world trade.

The attacks of September 11 were also an attack on NATO, as NATO itself recognized when it invoked its Article V self-defense clause for the first time. NATO's core mission—collective defense of the transatlantic alliance of democracies—remains, but NATO must develop new structures and capabilities to carry out that mission under new circumstances. NATO must

build a capability to field, at short notice, highly mobile, specially trained forces whenever they are needed to respond to a threat against any member of the alliance.

The alliance must be able to act wherever our interests are threatened, creating coalitions under NATO's own mandate, as well as contributing to mission-based coalitions. To achieve this, we must:

- expand NATO's membership to those democratic nations willing and able to share the burden of defending and advancing our common interests;

- ensure that the military forces of NATO nations have appropriate combat contributions to make in coalition warfare;

- develop planning processes to enable those contributions to become effective multinational fighting forces;

- take advantage of the technological opportunities and economies of scale in our defense spending to transform NATO military forces so that they dominate potential aggressors and diminish our vulnerabilities;

- streamline and increase the flexibility of command structures to meet new operational demands and the associated requirements of training, integrating, and experimenting with new force configurations; and

- maintain the ability to work and fight together as allies even as we take the necessary steps to transform and modernize our forces.

If NATO succeeds in enacting these changes, the rewards will be a partnership as central to the security and interests of its member states as was the case during the Cold War. We will sustain a common perspective on the threats to our societies and improve our ability to take common action in defense of our nations and their interests. At the same time, we welcome our European allies' efforts to forge a greater foreign policy and defense identity with the EU, and commit ourselves to close consultations to ensure that these developments work with NATO. We cannot afford to lose this opportunity to better prepare the family of transatlantic democracies for the challenges to come.

The attacks of September 11 energized America's Asian alliances. Australia invoked the ANZUS Treaty to declare the September 11 was an attack on Australia itself, following that historic decision with the dispatch of some of the world's finest combat forces for Operation Enduring Freedom. Japan and the Republic of Korea provided unprecedented levels of military logistical support within weeks of the terrorist attack. We have deepened cooperation on counterterrorism with our alliance partners in Thailand and the Philippines and received invaluable assistance from close friends like Singapore and New Zealand.

The war against terrorism has proven that America's alliances in Asia not only underpin regional peace and stability, but are flexible and ready to deal with new challenges. To enhance our Asian alliances and friendships, we will:

- look to Japan to continue forging a leading role in regional and global affairs based on our common interests, our common values, and our close defense and diplomatic cooperation;

- work with South Korea to maintain vigilance towards the North while preparing our alliance to make contributions to the broader stability of the region over the longer term;

- build on 50 years of U.S.-Australian alliance cooperation as we continue working together to resolve regional and global problems—as we have so many times from the Battle of the Coral Sea to Tora Bora;

- maintain forces in the region that reflect our commitments to our allies, our requirements, our technological advances, and the strategic environment; and

- build on stability provided by these alliances, as well as with institutions such as ASEAN and the Asia-Pacific Economic Cooperation forum, to develop a mix of regional and bilateral strategies to manage change in this dynamic region.

We are attentive to the possible renewal of old patterns of great power competition. Several potential great powers are now in the midst of internal transition—most importantly Russia, India, and China. In all three cases, recent developments have encouraged our hope that a truly global consensus about basic principles is slowly taking shape.

With Russia, we are already building a new strategic relationship based on a central reality of the twenty-first century: the United States and Russia are no longer strategic adversaries. The Moscow Treaty on Strategic Reductions is emblematic of this new reality and reflects a critical change in Russian thinking that promises to lead to productive, long-term relations with the Euro-Atlantic community and the United States. Russia's top leaders have a realistic assessment of their country's current weakness and the policies—internal and external—needed to reverse those weaknesses. They understand, increasingly, that Cold War approaches do not serve their national interests and that Russian and American strategic interests overlap in many areas.

United States policy seeks to use this turn in Russian thinking to refocus our relationship on emerging and potential common interests and challenges. We are broadening our already extensive cooperation in the global war on terrorism. We are facilitating Russia's entry into the World Trade Organization, without lowering standards for accession, to promote beneficial bilateral trade and investment relations. We have created the NATO-Russia Council with the goal of deepening security cooperation among Russia, our European allies, and ourselves. We will continue to bolster the independence and stability of the states of the former Soviet Union in the belief that a prosperous and stable neighborhood will reinforce Russia's growing commitment to integration into the Euro-Atlantic community.

At the same time, we are realistic about the differences that still divide us from Russia and about the time and effort it will take to build an enduring strategic partnership. Lingering distrust of our motives and policies by key Russian elites slows improvement in our relations. Russia's uneven commitment to the basic values of free-market democracy and dubious record in combating the proliferation of weapons of mass destruction remain matters of great concern. Russia's very weakness limits the opportunities for cooperation. Nevertheless, those opportunities are vastly greater now than in recent years—or even decades.

The United States has undertaken a transformation in its bilateral relationship with India based on a conviction that U.S. interests require a strong relationship with India. We are the two largest democracies, committed to political freedom protected by representative government. India is moving toward greater economic freedom

as well. We have a common interest in the free flow of commerce, including through the vital sea lanes of the Indian Ocean. Finally, we share an interest in fighting terrorism and in creating a strategically stable Asia.

Differences remain, including over the development of India's nuclear and missile programs, and the pace of India's economic reforms. But while in the past these concerns may have dominated our thinking about India, today we start with a view of India as a growing world power with which we have common strategic interests. Through a strong partnership with India, we can best address any differences and shape a dynamic future.

The United States relationship with China is an important part of our strategy to promote a stable, peaceful, and prosperous Asia-Pacific region. We welcome the emergence of a strong, peaceful, and prosperous China. The democratic development of China is crucial to that future. Yet, a quarter century after beginning the process of shedding the worst features of the Communist legacy, China's leaders have not yet made the next series of fundamental choices about the character of their state. In pursuing advanced military capabilities that can threaten its neighbors in the Asia-Pacific region, China is following an outdated path that, in the end, will hamper its own pursuit of national greatness. In time, China will find that social and political freedom is the only source of that greatness.

The United States seeks a constructive relationship with a changing China. We already cooperate well where our interests overlap, including the current war on terrorism and in promoting stability on the Korean peninsula. Likewise, we have coordinated on the future of Afghanistan and have initiated a comprehensive dialogue on counterterrorism and similar transitional concerns. Shared health and environmental threats, such as the spread of HIV/AIDS, challenge us to promote jointly the welfare of our citizens.

Addressing these transnational threats will challenge China to become more open with information, promote the development of civil society, and enhance individual human rights. China has begun to take the road to political openness, permitting many personal freedoms and conducting village-level elections, yet remains strongly committed to national one-party rule by the Communist Party. To make that nation truly accountable to its citizen's needs and aspirations, however, much work remains to be done. Only by allowing the Chinese people to think, assemble, and worship freely can China reach its full potential.

Our important trade relationship will benefit from China's entry into the World Trade Organization, which will create more export opportunities and ultimately more jobs for American farmers, workers, and companies. China is our fourth largest trading partner, with over $100 billion in annual two-way trade. The power of market principles and the WTO's requirements for transparency and accountability will advance openness and the rule of law in China to help establish basic protections for commerce and for citizens. There are, however, other areas in which we have profound disagreements. Our commitment to the self-defense of Taiwan under the Taiwan Relations Act is one. Human rights is another. We expect China to adhere to its nonproliferation commitments. We will work to narrow differences where they exist, but not allow them to preclude cooperation where we agree.

The events of September 11, 2001, fundamentally changed the context for relations between the United States and other main centers of global power, and opened vast, new opportunities. With our long-standing allies in Europe and Asia, and with leaders in Russia, India, and China, we must develop active agendas of cooperation lest these relationships become routine and unproductive.

Every agency of the United States Government shares the challenge. We can build fruitful habits of consultation, quiet argument, sober analysis, and common action. In the long-term, these are the practices that will sustain the supremacy of our common principles and keep open the path of progress.

ix. Transform America's National Security Institutions to Meet the Challenges and Opportunities of the Twenty-First Century

"Terrorists attacked a symbol of American prosperity. They did not touch its source. America is successful because of the hard work, creativity, and enterprise of our people."

President Bush
Washington, D.C. (Joint Session of Congress)
September 20, 2001

The major institutions of American national security were designed in a different era to meet different requirements. All of them must be transformed.

It is time to reaffirm the essential role of American military strength. We must build and maintain our defenses beyond challenge. Our military's highest priority is to defend the United States. To do so effectively, our military must:

- assure our allies and friends;

- dissuade future military competition;

- deter threats against U.S. interests, allies, and friends; and

- decisively defeat any adversary if deterrence fails.

The unparalleled strength of the United States armed forces, and their forward presence, have maintained the peace in some of the world's most strategically vital regions. However, the threats and enemies we must confront have changed, and so must our forces. A military structured to deter massive Cold War-era armies must be transformed

to focus more on how an adversary might fight rather than where and when a war might occur. We will channel our energies to overcome a host of operational challenges.

The presence of American forces overseas is one of the most profound symbols of the U.S. commitments to allies and friends. Through our willingness to use force in our own defense and in defense of others, the United States demonstrates its resolve to maintain a balance of power that favors freedom. To contend with uncertainty and to meet the many security challenges we face, the United States will require bases and stations within and beyond Western Europe and Northeast Asia, as well as temporary access arrangements for the long-distance deployment of U.S. forces.

Before the war in Afghanistan, that area was low on the list of major planning contingencies. Yet, in a very short time, we had to operate across the length and breadth of that remote nation, using every branch of the armed forces. We must prepare for more such deployments by developing assets such as advanced remote sensing, long-range precision strike capabilities, and transformed maneuver and expeditionary forces. This broad portfolio of military capabilities must also include the ability to defend the homeland, conduct information operations, ensure U.S. access to distant theaters, and protect critical U.S. infrastructure and assets in outer space.

Innovation within the armed forces will rest on experimentation with new approaches to warfare, strengthening joint operations, exploiting U.S. intelligence advantages, and taking full advantage of science and technology. We must also transform the way the Department of Defense is run, especially in financial management and recruitment and retention. Finally, while maintaining near-term readiness and the ability to fight the war on terrorism, the goal must be to provide the President with a wider range of military options to discourage aggression or any form of coercion against the United States, our allies, and our friends.

We know from history that deterrence can fail; and we know from experience that some enemies cannot be deterred. The United States must and will maintain the capability to defeat any attempt by an enemy—whether a state or non-state actor—to impose its will on the United States, our allies, or our friends. We will maintain the forces sufficient to support our obligations, and to defend freedom. Our forces will be strong enough to dissuade potential adversaries from pursuing a military build-up in hopes of surpassing, or equaling, the power of the United States.

Intelligence—and how we use it—is our first line of defense against terrorists and the threat posed by hostile states. Designed around the priority of gathering enormous information about a massive, fixed object—the Soviet bloc—the intelligence community is coping with the challenge of following a far more complex and elusive set of targets.

We must transform our intelligence capabilities and build new ones to keep pace with the nature of these threats. Intelligence must be appropriately integrated with our defense and law enforcement

systems and coordinated with our allies and friends. We need to protect the capabilities we have so that we do not arm our enemies with the knowledge of how best to surprise us. Those who would harm us also seek the benefit of surprise to limit our prevention and response options and to maximize injury.

We must strengthen intelligence warning and analysis to provide integrated threat assessments for national and homeland security. Since the threats inspired by foreign governments and groups may be conducted inside the United States, we must also ensure the proper fusion of information between intelligence and law enforcement.

Initiatives in this area will include:

- strengthening the authority of the Director of Central Intelligence to lead the development and actions of the Nation's foreign intelligence capabilities;

- establishing a new framework for intelligence warning that provides seamless and integrated warning across the spectrum of threats facing the nation and our allies;

- continuing to develop new methods of collecting information to sustain our intelligence advantage;

- investing in future capabilities while working to protect them through a more vigorous effort to prevent the compromise of intelligence capabilities; and

- collecting intelligence against the terrorist danger across the government with all-source analysis.

As the United States Government relies on the armed forces to defend America's interests, it must rely on diplomacy to interact with other nations. We will ensure that the Department of State receives funding sufficient to ensure the success of American diplomacy. The State Department takes the lead in managing our bilateral relationships with other governments. And in this new era, its people and institutions must be able to interact equally adroitly with non-governmental organizations and international institutions. Officials trained mainly in international politics must also extend their reach to understand complex issues of domestic governance around the world, including public health, education, law enforcement, the judiciary, and public diplomacy.

Our diplomats serve at the front line of complex negotiations, civil wars, and other humanitarian catastrophes. As humanitarian relief requirements are better understood, we must also be able to help build police forces, court systems, and legal codes, local and provincial government institutions, and electoral systems. Effective international cooperation is needed to accomplish these goals, backed by American readiness to play our part.

Just as our diplomatic institutions must adapt so that we can reach out to others, we also need a different and more comprehensive approach to public information efforts that can help people around the world learn about and understand America. The war on terrorism is not a clash of civilizations. It does, however, reveal the clash inside a civilization, a battle for the future of the Muslim world. This is a struggle of ideas and this is an area where America must excel.

We will take the actions necessary to ensure that our efforts to meet our global security commitments and protect Americans are not impaired by the potential for investigations, inquiry, or prosecution by the International Criminal Court (ICC), whose jurisdiction does not extend to Americans and which we do not accept. We will work together with other nations to avoid complications in our military operations and cooperation, through such mechanisms as multilateral and bilateral agreements that will protect U.S. nationals from the ICC. We will implement fully the American Servicemembers Protection Act, whose provisions are intended to ensure and enhance the protection of U.S. personnel and officials.

We will make hard choices in the coming year and beyond to ensure the right level and allocation of government spending on national security. The United States Government must strengthen its defenses to win this war. At home, our most important priority is to protect the homeland for the American people.

Today, the distinction between domestic and foreign affairs is diminishing. In a globalized world, events beyond America's borders have a greater impact inside them. Our society must be open to people, ideas, and goods from across the globe. The characteristics we most cherish—our freedom, our cities, our systems of movement, and modern life—are vulnerable to terrorism. This vulnerability will persist long after we bring to justice those responsible for the September 11 attacks. As time passes, individuals may gain access to means of destruction that until now could be wielded only by armies, fleets, and squadrons. This is a new condition of life. We will adjust to it and thrive—in spite of it.

In exercising our leadership, we will respect the values, judgment, and interests of our friends and partners. Still, we will be prepared to act apart when our interests and unique responsibilities require. When we disagree on particulars, we will explain forthrightly the grounds for our concerns and strive to forge viable alternatives. We will not allow such disagreements to obscure our determination to secure together, with our allies and our friends, our shared fundamental interests and values.

Ultimately, the foundation of American strength is at home. It is in the skills of our people, the dynamism of our economy, and the resilience of our institutions. A diverse, modern society has inherent, ambitious, entrepreneurial energy. Our strength comes from what we do with that energy. That is where our national security begins.

Appendix 2
The European Security Strategy*

A SECURE EUROPE IN A BETTER WORLD

EUROPEAN SECURITY STRATEGY

Brussels, 12 December 2003

EN

* Source: The Council of the European Union

Introduction

Europe has never been so prosperous, so secure nor so free. The violence of the first half of the 20th Century has given way to a period of peace and stability unprecedented in European history.

The creation of the European Union has been central to this development. It has transformed the relations between our states, and the lives of our citizens. European countries are committed to dealing peacefully with disputes and to co-operating through common institutions. Over this period, the progressive spread of the rule of law and democracy has seen authoritarian regimes change into secure, stable and dynamic democracies. Successive enlargements are making a reality of the vision of a united and peaceful continent.

No single country is able to tackle today's complex problems on its own

The United States has played a critical role in European integration and European security, in particular through NATO. The end of the Cold War has left the United States in a dominant position as a military actor. However, no single country is able to tackle today's complex problems on its own.

Europe still faces security threats and challenges. The outbreak of conflict in the Balkans was a reminder that war has not disappeared from our continent. Over the last decade, no region of the world has been untouched by armed conflict. Most of these conflicts have been within rather than between states, and most of the victims have been civilians.

As a union of 25 states with over 450 million people producing a quarter of the world's Gross National Product (GNP), and with a wide range of instruments at its disposal, the European Union is inevitably a global player. In the last decade European forces have been deployed abroad to

As a union of 25 states with over 450 million people producing a quarter of the world's Gross National Product (GNP), the European Union is inevitably a global player... it should be ready to share in the responsibility for global security and in building a better world.

places as distant as Afghanistan, East Timor and the DRC. The increasing convergence of European interests and the strengthening of mutual solidarity of the EU makes us a more credible and effective actor. Europe should be ready to share in the responsibility for global security and in building a better world.

I.   THE SECURITY ENVIRONMENT: GLOBAL CHALLENGES AND KEY THREATS

Global Challenges

The post Cold War environment is one of increasingly open borders in which the internal and external aspects of security are indissolubly linked. Flows of trade and investment, the development of technology and the spread of democracy have brought freedom and prosperity to many people. Others have perceived globalisation as a cause of frustration and injustice. These developments have also increased the scope for non-state groups to play a part in international affairs. And they have increased European dependence – and so vulnerability – on an interconnected infrastructure in transport, energy, information and other fields.

Since 1990, almost 4 million people have died in wars, 90% of them civilians. Over 18 million people world-wide have left their homes as a result of conflict.

45 million people die every year of hunger and malnutrition... Aids contributes to the breakdown of societies... Security is a precondition of development

In much of the developing world, poverty and disease cause untold suffering and give rise to pressing security concerns. Almost 3 billion people, half the world's population, live on less than 2 Euros a day. 45 million die every year of hunger and malnutrition. AIDS is now one of the most devastating pandemics in human history and contributes to the breakdown of societies. New diseases can spread rapidly and become global threats. Sub-Saharan Africa is poorer now than it was 10 years ago. In many cases, economic failure is linked to political problems and violent conflict.

Security is a precondition of development. Conflict not only destroys infrastructure, including social infrastructure; it also encourages criminality, deters investment and makes normal economic activity impossible. A number of countries and regions are caught in a cycle of conflict, insecurity and poverty.

Competition for natural resources - notably water - which will be aggravated by global warming over the next decades, is likely to create further turbulence and migratory movements in various regions.

Energy dependence is a special concern for Europe. Europe is the world's largest importer of oil and gas. Imports account for about 50% of energy consumption today. This will rise to 70% in 2030. Most energy imports come from the Gulf, Russia and North Africa.

<u>Key Threats</u>

Large-scale aggression against any Member State is now improbable. Instead, Europe faces new threats which are more diverse, less visible and less predictable.

Terrorism: Terrorism puts lives at risk; it imposes large costs; it seeks to undermine the openness and tolerance of our societies, and it poses a growing strategic threat to the whole of Europe. Increasingly, terrorist movements are well-resourced, connected by electronic networks, and are willing to use unlimited violence to cause massive casualties.

The most recent wave of terrorism is global in its scope and is linked to violent religious extremism. It arises out of complex causes. These include the pressures of modernisation, cultural, social and political crises, and the alienation of young people living in foreign societies. This phenomenon is also a part of our own society.

Europe is both a target and a base for such terrorism: European countries are targets and have been attacked. Logistical bases for Al Qaeda cells have been uncovered in the UK, Italy, Germany, Spain and Belgium. Concerted European action is indispensable.

Proliferation of Weapons of Mass Destruction is potentially the greatest threat to our security. The international treaty regimes and export control arrangements have slowed the spread of WMD and delivery systems. We are now, however, entering a new and dangerous period that raises the possibility of a WMD arms race, especially in the Middle East. Advances in the biological sciences may increase the potency of biological weapons in the coming

The last use of WMD was by the Aum terrorist sect in the Tokyo underground in 1995, using sarin gas. 12 people were killed and several thousand injured. Two years earlier, Aum had sprayed anthrax spores on a Tokyo street.

years; attacks with chemical and radiological materials are also a serious possibility. The spread of missile technology adds a further element of instability and could put Europe at increasing risk.

The most frightening scenario is one in which terrorist groups acquire weapons of mass destruction. In this event, a small group would be able to inflict damage on a scale previously possible only for States and armies.

Regional Conflicts: Problems such as those in Kashmir, the Great Lakes Region and the Korean Peninsula impact on European interests directly and indirectly, as do conflicts nearer to home, above all in the Middle East. Violent or frozen conflicts, which also persist on our borders, threaten regional stability. They destroy human lives and social and physical infrastructures; they threaten minorities, fundamental freedoms and human rights. Conflict can lead to extremism, terrorism and state failure; it provides opportunities for organised crime. Regional insecurity can fuel the demand for WMD. The most practical way to tackle the often elusive new threats will sometimes be to deal with the older problems of regional conflict.

State Failure: Bad governance – corruption, abuse of power, weak institutions and lack of accountability - and civil conflict corrode States from within. In some cases, this has brought about the collapse of State institutions. Somalia, Liberia and Afghanistan under the Taliban are the best known recent examples. Collapse of the State can be associated with obvious threats, such as organised crime or terrorism. State failure is an alarming phenomenon, that undermines global governance, and adds to regional instability.

Organised Crime: Europe is a prime target for organised crime. This internal threat to our security has an important external dimension: cross-border trafficking in drugs, women, illegal migrants and weapons accounts for a large part of the activities of criminal gangs. It can have links with terrorism.

Such criminal activities are often associated with weak or failing states. Revenues from drugs have fuelled the weakening of state structures in several drug-producing countries. Revenues from trade in gemstones, timber and small arms, fuel conflict in other parts of the world. All these activities undermine both the rule of law and social order itself. In extreme cases, organised crime can come to dominate the state. 90% of the heroin in Europe comes from poppies grown in Afghanistan – where the drugs trade pays for private armies. Most of it is distributed through Balkan criminal networks which are also responsible for some 200,000 of the 700,000 women victims of the sex trade world wide. A new dimension to organised crime which will merit further attention is the growth in maritime piracy.

Taking these different elements together – terrorism committed to maximum violence, the availability of weapons of mass destruction, organised crime, the weakening of the state system and the privatisation of force – we could be confronted with a very radical threat indeed.

II.   STRATEGIC OBJECTIVES

We live in a world that holds brighter prospects but also greater threats than we have known. The future will depend partly on our actions. We need both to think globally and to act locally. To defend its security and to promote its values, the EU has three strategic objectives:

Addressing the Threats

The European Union has been active in tackling the key threats.

- It has responded after 11 September with measures that included the adoption of a European Arrest Warrant, steps to attack terrorist financing and an agreement on mutual legal assistance with the U.S.A. The EU continues to develop cooperation in this area and to improve its defences.

- It has pursued policies against proliferation over many years. The Union has just agreed a further programme of action which foresees steps to strengthen the International Atomic Energy Agency, measures to tighten export controls and to deal with illegal shipments and illicit procurement. The EU is committed to achieving universal adherence to multilateral treaty regimes, as well as to strengthening the treaties and their verification provisions.

- The European Union and Member States have intervened to help deal with regional conflicts and to put failed states back on their feet, including in the Balkans, Afghanistan, and in the DRC. Restoring good government to the Balkans, fostering democracy and enabling the authorities there to tackle organised crime is one of the most effective ways of dealing with organised crime within the EU.

In an era of globalisation, distant threats may be as much a concern as those that are near at hand. Nuclear activities in North Korea, nuclear risks in South Asia, and proliferation in the Middle East are all of concern to Europe.

> *In an era of globalisation, distant threats may be as much a concern as those that are near at hand... The first line of defence will be often be abroad. The new threats are dynamic...*
>
> *Conflict prevention and threat prevention cannot start too early.*

Terrorists and criminals are now able to operate world-wide: their activities in central or south-east Asia may be a threat to European countries or their citizens. Meanwhile, global communication increases awareness in Europe of regional conflicts or humanitarian tragedies anywhere in the world.

Our traditional concept of self- defence – up to and including the Cold War – was based on the threat of invasion. With the new threats, the first line of defence will often be abroad. The new threats are dynamic. The risks of proliferation grow over time; left alone, terrorist networks will become ever more dangerous. State failure and organised crime spread if they are neglected – as we have seen in West Africa. This implies that we should be ready to act before a crisis occurs. Conflict prevention and threat prevention cannot start too early.

In contrast to the massive visible threat in the Cold War, none of the new threats is purely military; nor can any be tackled by purely military means. Each requires a mixture of instruments. Proliferation may be contained through export controls and attacked through political, economic and other pressures while the underlying political causes are also tackled. Dealing with terrorism may require a mixture of intelligence, police, judicial, military and other means. In failed states, military instruments may be needed to restore order, humanitarian means to tackle the immediate crisis. Regional conflicts need political solutions but military assets and effective policing may be needed in the post conflict phase. Economic instruments serve reconstruction, and civilian crisis management helps restore civil government. The European Union is particularly well equipped to respond to such multi-faceted situations.

Building Security in our Neighbourhood

Even in an era of globalisation, geography is still important. It is in the European interest that countries on our borders are well-governed. Neighbours who are engaged in violent conflict, weak states where organised crime flourishes, dysfunctional societies or exploding population growth on its borders all pose problems for Europe.

Enlargement should not create new dividing lines in Europe.
Resolution of the Arab/Israeli conflict is a strategic priority for Europe

The integration of acceding states increases our security but also brings the EU closer to troubled areas. Our task is to promote a ring of well governed countries to the East of the European Union and on the borders of the Mediterranean with whom we can enjoy close and cooperative relations.

The importance of this is best illustrated in the Balkans. Through our concerted efforts with the US, Russia, NATO and other international partners, the stability of the region is no longer threatened by the outbreak of major conflict. The credibility of our foreign policy depends on the consolidation of our achievements there. The European perspective offers both a strategic objective and an incentive for reform.

It is not in our interest that enlargement should create new dividing lines in Europe. We need to extend the benefits of economic and political cooperation to our neighbours in the East while tackling political problems there. We should now take a stronger and more active interest in the problems of the Southern Caucasus, which will in due course also be a neighbouring region.

Resolution of the Arab/Israeli conflict is a strategic priority for Europe. Without this, there will be little chance of dealing with other problems in the Middle East. The European Union must remain engaged and ready to commit resources to the problem until it is solved. The two state solution - which Europe has long supported- is now widely accepted. Implementing it will require a united and cooperative effort by the European Union, the United States, the United Nations and Russia, and the countries of the region, but above all by the Israelis and the Palestinians themselves.

The Mediterranean area generally continues to undergo serious problems of economic stagnation, social unrest and unresolved conflicts. The European Union's interests require a continued engagement with Mediterranean partners, through more effective economic, security and cultural cooperation in the framework of the Barcelona Process. A broader engagement with the Arab World should also be considered.

AN INTERNATIONAL ORDER BASED ON EFFECTIVE MULTILATERALISM

In a world of global threats, global markets and global media, our security and prosperity increasingly depend on an effective multilateral system. The development of a stronger international society, well functioning international institutions and a rule-based international order is our objective.

We are committed to upholding and developing International Law. The fundamental framework for international relations is the United Nations Charter. The United Nations Security Council has the primary responsibility for the maintenance of international peace and security. Strengthening the United Nations, equipping it to fulfil its responsibilities and to act effectively, is a European priority.

Our security and prosperity increasingly depend on an effective multilateral system. We are committed to upholding and developing International Law. The fundamental framework for international relations is the United Nations Charter.

We want international organisations, regimes and treaties to be effective in confronting threats to international peace and security, and must therefore be ready to act when their rules are broken.

Key institutions in the international system, such as the World Trade Organisation (WTO) and the International Financial Institutions, have extended their membership. China has joined the WTO and Russia is negotiating its entry. It should be an objective for us to widen the membership of such bodies while maintaining their high standards.

One of the core elements of the international system is the transatlantic relationship. This is not only in our bilateral interest but strengthens the international community as a whole. NATO is an important expression of this relationship.

Regional organisations also strengthen global governance. For the European Union, the strength and effectiveness of the OSCE and the Council of Europe has a particular significance. Other regional organisations such as ASEAN, MERCOSUR and the African Union make an important contribution to a more orderly world.

It is a condition of a rule-based international order that law evolves in response to developments such as proliferation, terrorism and global warming. We have an interest in further developing existing institutions such as the World Trade Organisation and in supporting new ones such as the International Criminal Court. Our own experience in Europe demonstrates that security can be increased through confidence building and arms control regimes. Such instruments can also make an important contribution to security and stability in our neighbourhood and beyond.

The quality of international society depends on the quality of the governments that are its foundation. The best protection for our security is a world of well-governed democratic states. Spreading good governance, supporting social and political reform, dealing with corruption and abuse of power, establishing the rule of law and protecting human rights are the best means of strengthening the international order.

Trade and development policies can be powerful tools for promoting reform. As the world's largest provider of official assistance and its largest trading entity, the European Union and its Member States are well placed to pursue these goals.

Contributing to better governance through assistance programmes, conditionality and targeted trade measures remains an important feature in our policy that we should further reinforce. A world seen as offering justice and opportunity for everyone will be more secure for the European Union and its citizens.

A number of countries have placed themselves outside the bounds of international society. Some have sought isolation; others persistently violate international norms. It is desirable that such countries should rejoin the international community, and the EU should be ready to provide assistance. Those who are unwilling to do so should understand that there is a price to be paid, including in their relationship with the European Union.

III. POLICY IMPLICATIONS FOR EUROPE

The European Union has made progress towards a coherent foreign policy and effective crisis management. We have instruments in place that can be used effectively, as we have demonstrated in the Balkans and beyond. But if we are to make a contribution that matches our potential, we need to be more active, more coherent and more capable. And we need to work with others.

We need to develop a strategic culture that fosters early, rapid and when necessary, robust intervention.

More active in pursuing our strategic objectives. This applies to the full spectrum of instruments for crisis management and conflict prevention at our disposal, including political, diplomatic, military and civilian, trade and development activities. Active policies are needed to counter the new dynamic threats. We need to develop a strategic culture that fosters early, rapid, and when necessary, robust intervention.

As a Union of 25 members, spending more than 160 billion Euros on defence, we should be able to sustain several operations simultaneously. We could add particular value by developing operations involving both military and civilian capabilities.

The EU should support the United Nations as it responds to threats to international peace and security. The EU is committed to reinforcing its cooperation with the UN to assist countries emerging from conflicts, and to enhancing its support for the UN in short-term crisis management situations.

We need to be able to act before countries around us deteriorate, when signs of proliferation are detected, and before humanitarian emergencies arise. Preventive engagement can avoid more serious problems in the future. A European Union which takes greater responsibility and which is more active will be one which carries greater political weight.

More Capable. A more capable Europe is within our grasp, though it will take time to realise our full potential. Actions underway – notably the establishment of a defence agency – take us in the right direction.

To transform our militaries into more flexible, mobile forces, and to enable them to address the new threats, more resources for defence and more effective use of resources are necessary.

Systematic use of pooled and shared assets would reduce duplications, overheads and, in the medium-term, increase capabilities.

In almost every major intervention, military efficiency has been followed by civilian chaos. We need greater capacity to bring all necessary civilian resources to bear in crisis and post crisis situations.

Stronger diplomatic capability: we need a system that combines the resources of Member States with those of EU institutions. Dealing with problems that are more distant and more foreign requires better understanding and communication.

Common threat assessments are the best basis for common actions. This requires improved sharing of intelligence among Member States and with partners.

As we increase capabilities in the different areas, we should think in terms of a wider spectrum of missions. This might include joint disarmament operations, support for third countries in combating terrorism and security sector reform. The last of these would be part of broader institution building.

The EU-NATO permanent arrangements, in particular Berlin Plus, enhance the operational capability of the EU and provide the framework for the strategic partnership between the two organisations in crisis management. This reflects our common determination to tackle the challenges of the new century.

More Coherent. The point of the Common Foreign and Security Policy and European Security and Defence Policy is that we are stronger when we act together. Over recent years we have created a number of different instruments, each of which has its own structure and rationale.

The challenge now is to bring together the different instruments and capabilities: European assistance programmes and the European Development Fund, military and civilian capabilities from Member States and other instruments. All of these can have an impact on our security and on that of third countries. Security is the first condition for development.

Diplomatic efforts, development, trade and environmental policies, should follow the same agenda. In a crisis there is no substitute for unity of command.

Better co-ordination between external action and Justice and Home Affairs policies is crucial in the fight both against terrorism and organised crime.

Greater coherence is needed not only among EU instruments but also embracing the external activities of the individual member states.

Coherent policies are also needed regionally, especially in dealing with conflict. Problems are rarely solved on a single country basis, or without regional support, as in different ways experience in both the Balkans and West Africa shows.

Working with partners There are few if any problems we can deal with on our own. The threats described above are common threats, shared with all our closest partners. International cooperation is a necessity. We need to pursue our objectives both through multilateral cooperation in international organisations and through partnerships with key actors.

Acting together, the European Union and the United States can be a formidable force for good in the world.

The transatlantic relationship is irreplaceable. Acting together, the European Union and the United States can be a formidable force for good in the world. Our aim should be an effective and balanced partnership with the USA. This is an additional reason for the EU to build up further its capabilities and increase its coherence.

We should continue to work for closer relations with Russia, a major factor in our security and prosperity. Respect for common values will reinforce progress towards a strategic partnership.

Our history, geography and cultural ties give us links with every part of the world: our neighbours in the Middle East, our partners in Africa, in Latin America, and in Asia. These relationships are an important asset to build on. In particular we should look to develop strategic partnerships, with Japan, China, Canada and India as well as with all those who share our goals and values, and are prepared to act in their support.

Conclusion

This is a world of new dangers but also of new opportunities. The European Union has the potential to make a major contribution, both in dealing with the threats and in helping realise the opportunities. An active and capable European Union would make an impact on a global scale. In doing so, it would contribute to an effective multilateral system leading to a fairer, safer and more united world.

Bibliography

Achcar, G. (2004) 'Fantasy of a Region that Doesn't Exist', *Le Monde Diplomatique*, April. Online. Available: http://mondediplo.com/2004/04/04world (accessed 8 December 2005).

Adams, G., Cornu, C. and James, A. D. (2001) *Between Cooperation and Competition: the transatlantic defence market*, Chaillot Paper (January), Paris: Institute for Security Studies-WEU.

Ahern, B. (2003) 'Statement by the Taoiseach', in *Debates of the Houses of the Oireachtas*, 16 December. Online. Available: http://www.gov.ie/debates-03/16Dec/Sect3.htm (accessed 8 December 2005).

Ahern, B. (2004a) Address by Minister Ahern Introducing Mr Kofi Annan, UNSG, in the Forum on Europe (14 October). Online. Available: http://foreign affairs.gov.ie/information/display.asp?ID=1604 (accessed 8 December 2005).

Ahern, B. (2004b) 'European Council to Focus on Fight Against Terrorism', Remarks as the President of the European Council (16 March). Online. Available: http://www.eu2004.ie/templates/news.asp?sNavlocator=66&list_id=420 (accessed 7 December 2005).

Ahlström, C. (2005) 'The EU Strategy against Proliferation of Weapons of Mass Destruction', in A. Kile (ed.), *Europe and Iran: perspectives on non-proliferation*, Stockholm International Peace Research Institute Report no. 21, Oxford: Oxford University Press.

Aldrich, R. J. (2004) 'Transatlantic Intelligence and Security Cooperation', *International Affairs*, 80 (4): 731–53.

Anderson, S., Bennis, P., Cavanagh, J. and Leaver, E. (2003) *Coalition of the Willing or Coalition of the Coerced?*, Washington DC: Institute for Policy Studies. Online. Available: http://www.ips-dc.org/iraq/COERCED2.pdf (accessed 8 December 2005).

Andréani, G. (2004–5) 'The "War on Terror": good cause; wrong concept', *Survival*, 46 (4): 31–50.

Anthony, I. (2005) 'Militarily Relevant EU–China Trade and Technology Transfers: issues and problems', paper for the Chinese Military Modernization: East Asian Political, Economic, and Defense Industrial Responses Conference, Center for Strategic and International Studies (19–20 May). Online. Available: http://www.sipri.org/contents/expcon/euchinapaper (accessed 7 December 2005).

Applebaum, A. (2003) 'Here Comes the new Europe', *Washington Post*, 29 January: A21.

Arend, A. C. (2003) 'International Law and the Pre-emptive Use of Military Force', *Washington Quarterly*, 26 (2): 89–103.

Asmus, R. D. (2002) *Opening NATO's Door: how the Alliance remade itself for a new era*, New York: Columbia University Press.

Asmus, R. D. (2005) 'Rethinking the EU: why Washington needs to support European integration', *Survival*, 47 (3): 93–102.

Asmus, R. D. and Pollack, K. M. (2002) 'The New Transatlantic Project: a response to Robert Kagan', *Policy Review*, October–November: 3–18.

Asmus, R. D., Everts, P. and Isernia, P. (2004) 'Power, War and Public Opinion', *Policy Review*, February–March: 73–89.

Averre, D. (2005) 'Russia and the European Union: convergence or divergence?', *European Security*, 14 (2): 175–202.

Bacevich, A. J. (2005) *The New American Militarism*, Oxford: Oxford University Press.

Bacon, E., Renz, B. and Cooper, J. (forthcoming) *Securitising Russia: the domestic politics of Putin*, Manchester: Manchester University Press.

Bailes, A. J. K. (1990) 'Eastern Europe II: the Chinese connection', *The World Today*, 46 (7): 134–5.

Bailes, A. J. K. (2003) 'European Security from a Northern Perspective: the roles for Finland and Sweden', in B. Huldt, T. Ries, J. Mörtberg and E. Davidson (eds), *The New Northern Security Agenda: perspectives from Finland and Sweden*, Strategic Yearbook 2004, Stockholm: Swedish National Defence College.

Bailes, A. J. K. (2004) 'US and EU Strategic Concept: a mirror for partnership and difference?', *International Spectator*, 39 (1): 17–32.

Bailes, A. J. K. (2005) *The European Security Strategy: an evolutionary history*, Policy Paper no. 10, Stockholm: Stockholm International Peace Research Institute. Online. Available: http://www.sipri.org (accessed 7 December 2005).

Barysch, K. (2005) *Embracing the Dragon: the EU's relationship with China*, London: Centre for European Reform.

Bauer, S. and Bromley, M. (2004) *The European Code of Conduct on Arms Export*, Policy Paper no. 8, Stockholm: Stockholm International Peace Research Institute. Online. Available: http://www.sipri.org (accessed 7 December 2005).

Baylis, J. and Wirtz, J. (2002) 'Introduction', in J. Baylis, J. Wirtz, E. Cohen and C. Gray (eds), *Strategy in the Contemporary World*, Oxford: Oxford University Press.

Berenskoetter, F. (2005) 'US and European Security Strategies', *Security Dialogue*, 36 (1): 71–92.

Bergman, A. (2004) 'The Nordic Militaries – Forces for Good?', in L. Elliot and G. Cheeseman (eds), *Forces for Good? Cosmopolitan militaries in the 21st Century*, Manchester: Manchester University Press.

Bergman, A. (2006) 'Adjacent Internationalism: the concept of solidarity and post-Cold War Nordic–Baltic Relations', *Cooperation and Conflict*, 41: forthcoming.

Bertram, C. *et al.* (2002) 'One Year After: a grand strategy for the West', *Survival*, 44 (4): 135–56.

Bildt, C. (1998) *Peace Journey: the struggle for peace in Bosnia,* London: Weidenfeld and Nicolson.

Biscop, S. (2004a) 'Able and Willing? Assessing the EU's capacity for military action', *European Foreign Affairs Review*, 9(2): 509–27.

Biscop, S. (2004b) *The European Security Strategy: implementing a distinctive approach to security*, Paper no. 82 (March), Brussels: Royal Defence College.

Biscop, S. (2005) *The European Security Strategy: a global agenda for positive power*, Abingdon: Ashgate.

Bitzinger, R. A. (2003) *Towards a Brave New Arms Industry?*, Adelphi Paper no. 356, Oxford: Oxford University Press/International Institute for Strategic Studies.

Blecher, K. (2004) 'Has-Been, Wannabe or Leader: Europe's role in the world after the 2003 European Security Strategy', *European Security*, 13 (4): 345–59.

Blinken, A. J. (2003–4) 'From Pre-emption to Engagement', *Survival*, 45 (4): 33–60.

Boot, M. (2002) 'Doctrine of the Big Enchilada', *Washington Post*, 14 October: A29.

Brodie, B. (1959) *Strategy in the Missile Age*, Princeton, NJ: Princeton University Press.

Broughton, P. D. (2003) 'France and Germany Plan Alliance to Dilute US Power', *Daily Telegraph*, 13 November: 18.

Brzezinski, Z. (2003) 'Where Do We Go From Here?', *Internationale Politik*, 4 (3): 3–10.

Bull, H. (1968) 'Strategic Studies and its Critics', *World Politics*, 20 (4): 593–605.

Bull, H. (1978) *The Anarchical Society*, London: Macmillan.

Bush, G. H. W. (1991a) 'Address to a Joint Session of the Congress on the State of the Union', Washington, DC, 22 January. Online. Available: http://bushlibrary. tamu.edu/research/papers/1991/91012902.html (accessed 8 December 2005).

Bush, G. H. W. (1991b) *National Security Strategy of the United States*, Washington, DC: Brassey's.

Bush, G. H. W. (1991c) 'Endorsement of European Sanctions and Security Council Measures', The Hague, 9 November. Online. Available: http://bushlibrary.tamu. edu/research/papers/1991/91110902.html (accessed 8 December 2005).

Bush, G. H. W. (1992) 'Address to the Nation on the Situation in Somalia', Washington, DC, 4 December. Online. Available: http://bushlibrary.tamu.edu/ research/papers/1992/92120400.html (accessed 8 December 2005).

Bush, G. W. (2005) 'President Sworn into Second Term'. Presidential inaugural address, delivered 20 January 2005. Online. Available: http://www.whitehouse.gov/ news/releases/2005/01/20050120-1.html (accessed 7 January 2006).

Buzan, B. (1991) 'Is International Security Possible?', in K. Booth (ed.), *New Thinking about Strategy and International Security*, London: HarperCollins Academic.

Buzan, B. and Waever. O. (2003) *Regions and Powers: the structure of international security*, Cambridge: Cambridge University Press.

Buzan, B., Waever, O. and de Wilde, J. (1998) *Security: a new framework for analysis*, London: Lynne Rienner.

Calleo, D. P. (2004a) 'For an End to Arrogance', *Internationale Politik*, 5 (1): 25–32.

Calleo, D. P. (2004b) 'The Broken West', *Survival*, 46 (3): 29–38.

Cameron, F. (2002; 2nd edn 2005) *US Foreign Policy After the Cold War: global hegemon or reluctant sheriff?*, London and New York: Routledge.

Cameron, F. and Quille, G. (2004) 'ESDP: The state of play', European Policy Centre Working Paper no. 11, Brussels: European Policy Centre.

Cameron, F., Berkofsky, A. and Crossick, S. (2005) 'EU–China relations – towards a strategic partnership', European Policy Centre Working Paper no. 19. Online. Available: http://www.isn.ethz.ch/pubs/ph/details.cfm?id=13588 (accessed 7 December 2005).

Capuano, M.-J. (2005) 'Cooperation: OCCAR is going on', *EuroFuture*, Spring: 70–3.

Center for Strategic and International Studies (2003) *The Future of the Transatlantic Defense Community*, CSIS Panel Report (January), Washington, DC: CSIS Press.

Center for Strategic and International Studies (2004) *The Transatlantic Dialogue on Terrorism: initial findings*, Washington, DC: CSIS Press, August.

Centre for Defence Studies (2005) 'Terrorist Attacks in Britain: the next phase', CDS Briefing Paper, London: King's College London, August.

Centre for the Study of Global Governance (2004) *A Human Security Doctrine for Europe: the Barcelona report of the Study Group on Europe's capabilities*, London: London School of Economics and Political Science. Online. Available: http://www.lse.ac.uk/Depts/global/5publications3.htm (accessed 7 December 2005).

Cheney, R. (2004) 'Special Address by Dick Cheney, Vice-President of the United States of America', Speech at the World Economic Forum at Davos. Online. Available: http://www.weforum.org/site/homepublic.nsf/Content/Special+Addre ss+by+Dick+Cheney%2C+Vice-President+of+the+United+States+of+America (accessed 8 December 2005).

Chesterman, S. (2005) *You, the People: the United Nations, transitional administrations and state-building*, Oxford: Oxford University Press.

Chomsky, N. (1999) *The New Military Humanism: lessons from Kosovo*, Monroe, ME: Common Courage Press.

Cimbalo, J. L. (2004) 'Saving NATO from Europe', *Foreign Affairs*, 83 (6) November–December: 111–20.

Clark, W. K. (2001) *Waging Modern War*, New York: Public Affairs.

Clarke, R. (2004) *Against All Enemies: inside America's war on terror*, London: Free Press.

Clinton, W. J. (1993) 'A Strategic Alliance with Russian Reform', Annapolis, MD, 1 April. Online. Available: http://clinton6.nara.gov/1993/04/1993-04-01-prepared-text-for-speech-on-russia.html (accessed 8 December 2005).

Cohen, S. F. (1999) 'Russian Studies Without Russia', *Post-Soviet Affairs*, 15 (1): 37–55.

Cooper, R. (2004a) 'The Goals of Diplomacy, Hard Power, and Soft Power', in D. Held and M. Koenig-Archibugi (eds), *American Power in the Twenty-First Century*, Cambridge: Polity Press, pp. 167–80.

Cooper, R. (2004b) [untitled commentary] in N. Gnesotto (ed.), *EU Security and Defence Policy: the first five years (1999–2004)*, Paris: European Union Institute for Security Studies, pp. 189–93.

Cooper, R. (2005a) 'Imperial Liberalism', *The National Interest*, 79 (Spring): 25–34.

Cooper, R. (2005b) 'Security Strategy: is Europe from Venus, America from Mars?', the First Annual John Erickson Memorial Lecture, Old College, University of Edinburgh, 25 February.

Cornish, P. and Edwards, G. (2001) 'Identifying the Development of an EU "Strategic Culture"', *International Affairs*, 77 (3): 587–604.

Cornish, P. and Edwards, G. (2005) 'The Strategic Culture of the European Union: a progress report', *International Affairs*, 81 (4): 801–20.

Council on Foreign Relations (2004) *Renewing the Atlantic Partnership*, Task Force Report no. 51, Washington, DC: CFR.

Cowen, B. (2003a) 'Minister Cowen Announces Joint Irish, Finnish, Swedish and Austrian Proposal on EU Defence', Irish Department of Foreign Affairs

Press Release (5 December). Online. Available: http://foreignaffairs.gov.ie/information/display.asp?ID=1388 (accessed on 7 December 2005).

Cowen, B. (2003b) 'Remarks by the Irish Minister for Foreign Affairs', at the Center for Strategic and International Studies, Washington, DC, 2 March.

Cox, M. (2005) 'Beyond the West: terrors in Transatlantia', *European Journal of International Relations*, 11 (2): 203–33.

Daalder, I. H. and Kagan, R. (2004) 'The Allies Must Step Up', *Washington Post*, 20 June: B07.

Daalder, I. H. and Lindsay, J. M. (2003) *America Unbound: the Bush revolution in foreign policy*, Washington, DC: Brookings Institution Press.

Daalder, I. H. and O'Hanlon, M. E. (2001) *Winning Ugly: NATO's wars to save Kosovo*, Washington, DC: Brookings Institution Press.

Daalder, I. H. and Steinberg, J. (2005) 'The Future of Preemption', *The American Interest*, 1 (2) Winter. Online. Available: http://www.the-american-interest.com/cms/abstract.cfm?Id=26 (accessed 15 December 2005).

Dannreuther, R. (ed.) (2004) *European Union Foreign and Security Policy: towards a neighbourhood strategy*, London: Routledge.

Delegation of the European Commission in Russia, *Russia's Middle-Term Strategy towards the European Union (2000–2010)*, unofficial translation of Russia's response to the European Union's Common Strategy, 2000. Online. Available: http://www.delrus.cec.eu.int/en/p_245.htm (accessed 6 December 2005).

Delpech, T. (2002) *International Terrorism and Europe*, Chaillot Paper no. 56, Paris: European Union Institute for Security Studies. Online. Available: http://www.iss-eu.org/chaillot/chai56e.pdf (accessed 8 December 2005).

Dempsey, J. (2005a) 'US Rebuffs Germany on Plan for NATO', *International Herald Tribune*, 15 February. Online. Available: http://www.iht.com/articles/2005/02/14/news/munich.php (accessed 14 December 2005).

Dempsey, J. (2005b) 'For EU and NATO, a race for influence', *International Herald Tribune*, 18 February. Online. Available: http://www.forum-europe.com/index.html?http://www.forum-europe.com/news_detail.asp?ID=339&frame=yes~main (accessed 14 December 2005).

den Boer, M. (2003) '9/11 and the Europeanisation of Anti-Terrorism Policy: a critical assessment', Policy Paper no. 6, Paris: Notre Europe.

Diamond, L. (2005) *Squandered Victory: the American occupation and the bungled effort to bring democracy to Iraq*, New York: Holt.

Dittrich, M. (2005) 'Facing the Global Terrorist Threat: a European response', EPC Working Paper no. 14, Brussels: European Policy Centre.

Dodge, T. (2004) 'A Sovereign Iraq?', *Survival*, 46 (3): 39–58.

Dombey, D. (2005) 'Bush Fails to Heal Rift with Europeans', *Financial Times*, 26 February. Online. Available: http://www.ft.com (accessed 14 December 2005).

Donovan, J. (2005) 'Moscow Clashes with OSCE', *RFE/RL Russian Political Weekly*, 5 (13) 1 April.

Duke, S. (2004) 'The European Security Strategy in a Comparative Framework: does it make for secure alliances in a better world?' *European Foreign Affairs Review*, 9 (4): 459–81.

The Economist (2004) 'A Growing Band of Brothers', 6 March: 41–2.

The Economist (2005) 'Let's Talk – But Where?', 26 February: 48.

Edwards, G. (2005) 'The Pattern of the EU's Global Activity', in C. Hill and M. Smith (eds), *International Relations and the European Union*, Oxford: Oxford University Press.

Eliasson, J. (2004) 'Traditions, Identity and Security: the legacy of neutrality in Finnish and Swedish policies in light of European integration', *European Integration online Papers* (EIoP), 8 (6). Online. Available: eiop.or.at/eiop/pdf/2004-006.pdf (accessed 7 December 2005).

Eriksson, A. (2003) 'Sweden and the Europeanisation of Security and Defence Policy', in B. Huldt, T. Ries, J. Mörtberg, and E. Davidson (eds), *The New Northern Security Agenda: perspectives from Finland and Sweden*, Strategic Yearbook 2004, Stockholm: Swedish National Defence College.

Errera, P. (2005) 'Three Circles of Threat', *Survival*, 47 (1): 71–88.

European Commission (2002) 'Russia Country Strategy Paper 2002–2006 and National Indicative Programme 2002–2003', Brussels: DG External Relations. Online. Available: http://europa.eu.int/comm/external_relations/russia/csp/index.htm (accessed 12 December 2005).

European Commission (2005) 'Review of the Framework for Relations Between the European Union and United States: an independent study', April, Brussels: DG External Relations. Online. Available: http://europa.eu.int/comm/external_relations/us/revamping/final_report_260405.pdf (accessed 7 December 2005).

Everts, S. (2004a) *Engaging Iran: a test case for EU foreign policy*, London: Centre for European Reform.

Everts, S. (2004b) 'The EU's New Security Strategy Is an Important Step Forward'. Online. Available: http://www.europeanaffairs.org/current_issue/2004_winter/2004_winter_92.php4 (accessed 23 August 2005).

Fahim, A. (2004) 'Liberating Saudi Shi'ites (and their Oil)', *Middle East International*, 722: 29–30.

Farrell, T. (2002) 'Constructivist Security Studies: portrait of a research program', *International Studies Review*, 4 (1): 49–72.

Felgenhauer, P. (2005) 'Conceptual Indecisiveness', *Moscow Times.com*, 26 July. Online. Available: http://www.themoscowtimes.com (accessed 1 February 2006).

Ferguson, N. (2004) *Colossus: the price of America's empire*, New York: Penguin Press.

Ferreira-Pereira, L. C. (2005) 'Swedish Military Neutrality in the Post-Cold War: "old habits die hard"', *Perspectives on European Politics and Society*, 6 (3): 463–90.

Ferrero-Waldner, B. (2003) 'Keeping to our Course in a Changing World', Address delivered by the Federal Minister for Foreign Affairs to the Austrian Association of Foreign Policy and IR on 20 May.

Ferrero-Waldner, B. (2004) 'Statement by Federal Minister for Foreign Affairs of the Republic of Austria at the 59th Session of the United Nations General Assembly', New York, 23 September. Online. Available: www.un.org/webcast/ga/59/statements/auseng040923.pdf (accessed 7 December 2005).

Finnish Minister for Foreign Affairs (2003) *Summary of Annual Report*, Helsinki: Ministry for Foreign Affairs.

Finnish Permanent Representation (to the EU) (1996) 'Memorandum Finland and Sweden: the IGC and the security and defence dimension – towards an enhanced EU role in crisis management', 25 April. Online. Available: http://europa.eu.int/en/agenda/igc-home/ms-doc/state-fi/finlswed.htm (accessed 10 December 2005).

Finnish Prime Minister's Office (2004) *Finnish Security and Defence Policy 2004*, Government Report 6/2004, Helsinki: Prime Minister's Office.

Fischer, J. (2004) 'Speech at the 40th Munich Conference on Security Policy', 2 July. Online. Available: http://www.securityconference.de/konferenzen/rede.php?menu_2004=&menu_konferenzen=&sprache=en&id=123& (accessed 8 December 2005).

Fitzwater, M. (1991) 'Statement by Press Secretary Fitzwater on Yugoslavia', 2 July. Online. Available: http://bushlibrary.tamu.edu/research/papers/1991/91070201.htm (accessed 8 December 2005).

Fox, R. (2005) 'GWOT is History. Now for SAVE', *New Statesman*, 8 August. Online. Available: http://www.newstatesman.com/200508080007 (accessed 8 December 2005).

Freedman, L. (2003) 'Prevention, Not Pre-emption', *Washington Quarterly*, 26 (2): 105–14. Online. Available: http://www.twq.com/03spring/docs/03spring_freedman.pdf (accessed 8 December 2005).

Freivalds, L. and Tuomioja, E. (2003) 'Vi vill stärka EU: säkerhetspolitik', *Dagens Nyheter*, 11 November.

Frum, D. and Perle, R. (2003) *An End to Evil: how to win the war on terror*, New York: Random House.

Fukuyama, F. (2005) 'The Bush Doctrine, Before and After', *Financial Times*, 11 October. Online. Available: www.sais-jhu.edu/insider/pdf/2005_articles/fukuyama_ft_101105.pdf (accessed 15 December 2005).

G-8 Summit (2004) 'Partnership for Progress and a Common Future with the Region of the Broader Middle East and North Africa', Sea Island, GA, 9 June. Online. Available: http://www.whitehouse.gov/news/releases/2004/06/20040609-30.html (accessed 8 December 2005).

Gaddis, J. L. (2004) *Surprise, Security and the American Experience*, Cambridge, MA: Harvard University Press.

Gaddis, J. L. (2005) 'Grand Strategy in the Second Term', *Foreign Affairs*, 84 (1): 2–15.

Gill, B. (2004) 'China's New Security Multilateralism and its Implications for the Asia-Pacific region', in *SIPRI Yearbook 2004: armament, disarmament and international security*, Oxford: Oxford University Press.

Gill, B. (2005) 'Testimony to the Senate Foreign Relations Committee on 16 March'. Online. Available: http://Foreign.senate.gov/hearings/2005/hrg050316p2.html (accessed 8 December 2005).

Glain, S. (2003) *Dreaming of Damascus: merchants, mullahs, and militants in the new Middle East*, London: John Murray.

Gnesotto, N. (2004a) 'A quoi sert le "Grand Moyen-Orient"?', *Le Figaro*, 10 February. Online. Available: http://www.iss-eu.org/new/analysis/analy074.html (accessed 8 December 2005).

Gnesotto, N. (ed.) (2004b) *EU Security and Defence Policy: the first five years*, Paris: European Union Institute for Security Studies.

Gnesotto, N. et al. (2004) *European Defence: a proposal for a white paper*, Paris: European Union Institute for Security Studies.

Gompert, D. C., Godement, F., Medeiros, E. S. and Mulvenon, J. C. (2005) *China on the Move: a Franco-American analysis of emerging Chinese strategic policies and their consequences for transatlantic relations*, Santa Monica, CA: RAND Corporation.

Gordon, P. H. and Shapiro, J. (2004) *Allies at War: America, Europe and the crisis over Iraq*, New York: McGraw-Hill.

Gowan, R. (2004) 'The EU, Regional Organizations and Security: strategic partners or convenient alibis?', in S. Biscop (ed.), *Audit of European Strategy*, Egmont Paper no. 3, Brussels: Royal Institute of International Relations, pp. 8–17.

Gray, C. (1999) *Modern Strategy*, Oxford: Oxford University Press.

Gray, J. (2006) 'The Mirage of Empire', *New York Review of Books*, LIII (1), 12 January: 4–8.

Greenwood, C. (2002) 'International Law and the "War against Terrorism"', *International Affairs*, 78 (2): 301–17.

Grendstad, G. (2001) 'Nordic Cultural Baselines: accounting for domestic convergence and foreign policy divergence', *Journal of Comparative Policy Analysis*, 3 (1): 5–29.

Guay, T. and Callum, R. (2002) 'The Transformation and Future Prospects of Europe's Defence Industry', *International Affairs*, 78 (4): 757–76.

Haas, R. N. (1999) *Intervention: the uses of American military force in the post-Cold War world*, Washington, DC: Carnegie Endowment for Peace.

Hagel, C. (2004) 'The United States, NATO, and the Greater Middle East', Speech to US Mission to NATO, Brussels, 23 January. Online. Available: http://www.kas.de/db_files/dokumente/7_dokument_dok_pdf_3929_2.pdf (accessed 8 December 2005).

Haine, J.-Y. and Lindstrom, G. (2002) 'An Analysis of the National Security Strategy of the United States of America', Paris: European Union Institute for Security Studies, October. Online. Available: http://www.iss-eu.org/new/analysis/analy 034.html (accessed 8 December 2005).

Hajnoczi, T. (2005) 'Comments on the Austrian Position', in E. Munro (ed.), *Challenges to Neutral and Non-Aligned Countries in Europe and Beyond*, July, Geneva: Geneva Centre for Security Policy. Online. Available: http://www.gcsp.ch/e/publications/Conf-Proceedings/2004/neutrality.htm (accessed 7 December 2005).

Halliday, F. (1997) 'The Middle East, the Great Powers, and the Cold War', in Y. Sayigh and A. Shlaim (eds), *The Cold War and the Middle East*, Oxford: Oxford University Press.

Hamilton, D. (ed.) (2004) *Transatlantic Transformation: equipping NATO for the 21st century*, Washington, DC: Center for Transatlantic Relations.

Hansen, F. (2004) 'In the Transatlantic Gap', *Russia in Global Affairs*, 4 (October–December). Online. Available: http://eng.globalaffairs.ru (accessed 6 December 2005).

Hassner, P. (2002) *The United States: the empire of force or the force of empire?*, Chaillot Paper no. 54, Paris: European Union Institute for Security Studies. Online. Available: http://www.iss-eu.org/chaillot/chai54e.pdf (accessed 8 December 2005).

Havel, V. (1999) 'Kosovo and the End of the Nation-State', *New York Review of Books*, 46 (10). Online. Available: http://www.nybooks.com/articles/article-preview?article_id=455 (accessed 28 November 2005).

Heisbourg, F. (2003) 'A Work in Progress: the Bush doctrine and its consequences', *Washington Quarterly*, 26 (2). Online. Available: http://www.twq.com/03spring/docs/03spring_heisbourg.pdf (accessed 8 December 2005).

Heisbourg, F. (2004) 'The "European Security Strategy" Is Not a Security Strategy', in S. Everts, L. Freedman, C. Grant, F. Heisbourg, D. Keohane and M. O'Hanlon, *A European Way of War*, London: Centre for Economic Reform.

Hellman, C. and Baker, S. H. (2002) 'Bush Budget Stalls Transformation Drive', Center for Defense Information. Online. Available: http://www.cdi.org/issues/budget/transformation-stalls-pr.cfm (accessed 19 October 2005).

Hersch, S. (2003) 'Who Lied to Whom?', *New Yorker*, 31 March. Online. Available: http://www.newyorker.com/fact/content/?030331fa_fact1 (accessed 7 December 2005).

Hill, C. (2004) 'Britain and the European Security Strategy.' Online. Available: http://www.fornet.info/documents/Working%20Paper20no%206.pdf (accessed 8 July 2005).

Hill, C. and Smith, M. (eds) (2005) *International Relations and the European Union*, Oxford: Oxford University Press.

Hironaka, A. (2005) *Never-ending Wars: the international community, weak states and the perpetuation of conflict*, Cambridge, MA: Harvard University Press.

Hjelm-Wallén, L. (2003) *Svenska perspektiv pa EUs framtidskonvent, Vagval for Europa-En rapportserie om EUs framtid* (Swedish Perspectives on the Future of the EU, Choice for Europe: a series of reports), Stockholm: Utrikespolitiska Institutet.

Hoagland, J. (2005) 'The Limits of Reconciliation', *Washington Post*, 20 February: B08.

Hoffmann, S. (2003) *L'Amérique vraiment impériale? Entretiens sur le vif avec Frédéric Bozo*, Paris: Audibert.

Holbrooke, R. (1999) *To End a War*, New York: The Modern Library.

Hollis, R. (2005) 'Europe in the Middle East', in L. Fawcett (ed.), *International Relations of the Middle East*, Oxford: Oxford University Press.

Howard, M. (2001) *The Invention of Peace*, London: Profile Books.

Howard, M. (2002) 'What's in a Name? How to fight terrorism', *Foreign Affairs*, 81(1): 8–13.

Howlett, D. (2005) 'Strategic Culture: reviewing recent literature', *Strategic Insights*, 4–10 October. Online. Available: http://www.ccc.nps.navy.mil/si/2005/Oct/howlettOct05.asp#references (accessed 7 December 2005).

Howorth, J. (2005) 'From Security to Defence: the evolution of the CFSP', in C. Hill and M. Smith (eds), *International Relations and the European Union*, Oxford: Oxford University Press.

Howorth, J. *et al.* (2004) 'L'impact sur les organisations de défense du concept de "coalition de circonstance"', IFRI/DAS Report to French Ministry of Defence, Paris.

Huband, M. (2005) 'Call to Act on US Arms Lead', *Financial Times*, 27 April: 6.

Hudson, M. C. (2005) 'The United States in the Middle East', in L. Fawcett (ed.), *International Relations of the Middle East*, Oxford: Oxford University Press.

Huldt, B. (2003) 'Introduction', in B. Huldt, T. Ries, J. Mörtberg and E. Davidson (eds), *The New Northern Security Agenda: perspectives from Finland and Sweden*, Strategic Yearbook 2004, Stockholm: Swedish National Defence College.

Hunter, R. E. (2004) 'The US and the European Union: bridging the strategic gap?', *International Spectator*, 39 (1), January–March: 35–50.

Hyde-Price, A. (2004) 'European Security, Strategic Culture, and the Use of Force', *European Security*, 13 (4): 323–43.

Ignatieff, M. (ed.) (2005) *American Exceptionalism and Human Rights*, Princeton, NJ: Princeton University Press.

Ikenberry, G. J. (2000) *After Victory: institutions, strategic restraint, and the rebuilding of order after major wars*, Princeton, NJ: Princeton University Press.

Ikenberry, G. J. (ed.) (2002a) *America Unrivaled: the Future of the Balance of Power*. Ithaca, NY: Cornell University Press.

Ikenberry, G. J. (2002b) 'America's Imperial Ambition', *Foreign Affairs*, 81 (5), September–October: 44–60.

Ikenberry, G. J. (2004). 'Liberal Hegemony or Empire? American power in the age of unipolarity', in D. Held and M. Koenig-Archibugi, *American Power in the 21st Century*, Cambridge: Polity Press.

International Institute for Strategic Studies (2002) 'The Bush National Security Strategy: what does "pre-emption" mean?', *Strategic Comments*, 8 (8) October. Online. Available: http://www.iiss.org/newsite/showsubpdfsarchive.php?scID=239&type=iiss.pdf (accessed 8 December 2005).

International Institute for Strategic Studies (2005) 'Transatlantic Relations: persistent predicaments', *Strategic Comments*, 11 (7), September. Online. Available: http://www.iiss.org/newsite/showsubpdfsarchive.php?scID=239&type=iiss.pdf (accessed 4 January 2006).

Jervis, R. (2002) 'Theories of War in an Era of Leading-Power Peace', *American Political Science Review*, 96 (1): 1–14.

Jervis, R. (2005) 'Why the Bush Doctrine Cannot Be Sustained', *Political Science Quarterly*, 120 (3): 351–77.

Johnson, C. (2004) *The Sorrows of Empire: militarism, secrecy and the end of the republic*, New York: Metropolitan Books.

Kagan, R. (2002) 'Power and Weakness', *Policy Review*, 113 (June–July): 1–16.

Kagan, R. (2003) *Of Paradise and Power: America and Europe in the New World Order*, London: Atlantic Books.

Kagan, R. *et al.* (2002) 'One Year After: a grand strategy for the West', *Survival*, 44 (4): 135–56.

Kamp, K.-H. (2003) 'Prevention in US Security Strategy', *Internationale Politik*, Spring: 17–20.

Kaplan, F. (2005) 'Say G-WOT?', *The Slate*, 26 July.

Kapstein, E. (2004) 'Capturing Fortress Europe: international collaboration and the joint strike fighter', *Survival*, 46 (3): 137–60.

Keohane, D. (2004) 'EU on Offensive about Defence', *EuropeanVoice.com*, 22–28 July. Online. Available: http://www.cer.org.uk/articles/keohane_europeanvoice_jul04.html (accessed 16 August 2005).

Keohane, D. (2005) *The EU and Counter-Terrorism*, London: Centre for European Reform.

Keohane, R. O. (2002) 'Ironies of Sovereignty: the European Union and the United States', *Journal of Common Market Studies*, 40 (4): 743–65.

Kile, A. (ed.) (2005) *Europe and Iran: perspectives on non-proliferation*, Stockholm International Peace Research Institute, Report no. 21, Oxford: Oxford University Press.

Kissinger, H. (1994) *Diplomacy*, New York: Simon and Schuster.

Koch, C. and Neugart, F. (2004) 'Introduction', in C. Koch and F. Neugart (eds), *A Window of Opportunity: Europe, Gulf security and the aftermath of the Iraq War*, Dubai: Gulf Research Center.

Koenig-Archibugi, M. (2004) 'Explaining Government Preferences for Institutional Change in EU Foreign and Security Policy', *International Organization*, 58 (1): 137–74.

Kuchins, A., Nikonov, V. and Trenin, D. (2005) 'US–Russian Relations: the case for an upgrade', Washington: Carnegie Endowment for International Peace, January.

Larrabee, S. (2004) 'ESDP and NATO: assuring complementarity', *International Spectator*, 39 (1): 51–70.

Lennon, A. T. J. (ed.) (2003) *The Battle for Hearts and Minds*, Cambridge, MA: MIT Press.

Leonard, D. (2005) 'Is the Single Defence Market a Flight of Fancy?', *European Voice*, 4–11 May: 15.

Leonard, M. and Gowan, R. (2004) *Global Europe: implementing the European Security Strategy*, Brussels: Foreign Policy Centre and British Council.

Levite, A. E. and Sherwood-Randall, E. (2002–3) 'The Case for Discriminate Force', *Survival*, 44 (4): 81–97.

Levy, D., Pensky, M. and Torpey, J. (eds) (2005) *Old Europe, New Europe, Core Europe: transatlantic relations after the Iraq War*, London: Verso.

Light, M. (2003) 'US and European Perspectives on Russia', in J. Peterson and M. A. Pollack (eds), *Europe, America, Bush: transatlantic relations in the twenty-first century*, London: Routledge.

Lindberg, T. (ed.) (2005) *Beyond Paradise and Power: Europe, America and the future of a troubled partnership*, London: Routledge.

Lindh, A. and Tuomioja, E. (2000) 'Katastrofhjalpen duger inte artikel av utrikes-minister Anna Lindh och finske utrikesministern Erkki Tuomioja på DN Debatt', *Dagens Nyheter*, Sunday, 30 April. Online. Available: http://www.dn.se/ (accessed 15 December 2005).

Lindh, A. and Tuomioja, E. (2002) 'Combating New Threats with Deeper Solidarity', Stockholm: Regeringskansliet. Online. Available: http://regeringen.se/galactica/service=irnews=obj_show?c_obj_id=47956 (accessed 23 March 2003).

Lindstrom, G. (2005) *EU–US Burdensharing: who does what?*, Chaillot Paper no. 82 (September), Paris: European Union Institute for Security Studies.

Litwak, R. S. (2002–3) 'The New Calculus of Pre-emption', *Survival*, 44 (4): 53–79.

Lo, B. (2003) *Vladimir Putin and the Evolution of Russian Foreign Policy*, London: Royal Institute of International Affairs.

Longhurst, K. and Zaborowski, M. (2004) 'The Future of European Security', *European Security*, 13 (4): 381–91.

Lugar, R. G. (2004) 'NATO and the Greater Middle East', Speech at the 40th Munich Conference on Security Policy. Online. Available: http://www.securityconference.de/konferenzen/rede.php?menu_2004=&menu_konferenzen=&sprache=de&id=134& (accessed 8 December 2005).

Lundestad, G. (2003) *The United States and Western Europe since 1945: from empire by invitation to transatlantic drift*, Oxford: Oxford University Press.

Lynch, D. (2003) *Russia Faces Europe*, Chaillot Paper no. 65, Paris: European Union Institute for Security Studies.

Lynch, D. (2004) 'Russia's Strategic Partnership with Europe', *Washington Quarterly*, 27 (2): 99–118.

Lynch, D. (2005) '"The Enemy is at the Gate": Russia after Beslan', *International Affairs*, 81 (1): 141–61.

McBean, K. (2005) 'Comments on the Irish Position', in E. Munro (ed.), *Challenges to Neutral and Non-Aligned Countries in Europe and Beyond*, July, Geneva: Geneva Centre for Security Policy. Online. Available: http://www.gcsp.ch/e/publications/Conf-Proceedings/2004/neutrality.htm (accessed 7 December 2005).

MccGwire, M. (2000) 'Why Did We Bomb Belgrade?', *International Affairs*, 76 (1): 1–23.

Mahbubani, K. (2005) 'Understanding China', *Foreign Affairs*, 'China edition', 84 (5): 49–60.

Malone, D. M. and Foong Khong, Y. (eds) (2003) *Unilateralism and US Foreign Policy: international perspectives*, Boulder, CO: Lynne Rienner.

Manigart, P. (ed.) (2001) *Public Opinion and European Defence: convergence or divergence?*, Brussels: Belgian Ministry of Defence.

Mann, J. (2004) *Rise of the Vulcans: the history of Bush's war cabinet*, New York: Viking.

Mann, M. (2003) *Incoherent Empire*, New York: Verso.

Manners, I. (2002) 'Normative Power Europe: a contradiction in terms?', *Journal of Common Market Studies*, 40 (2): 235–58.

Mastanduno, M. (1997) 'Preserving the Unipolar Moment: realist theories and US grand strategy after the Cold War', *International Security*, 21 (4): 123–62.

Mathews, J. (1989) 'Redefining Security', *Foreign Affairs*, 68 (2): 162–77.

Mazaar, M. J. (2002–3) 'Acting like a Leader', *Survival*, 44 (4): 107–20.

Mazower, M. (2005) 'A World Order Gone Wobbly', *Financial Times*, 27 December: 13.

Mead, W. R. (2002) *Special Providence: American foreign policy and how it changed the world*, London: Routledge.

Mead, W. R. (2005) 'American Endurance', in T. Lindberg (ed.), *Beyond Paradise and Power: Europe, America and the future of a troubled partnership*, London: Routledge.

Mearsheimer, J. J. (1990) 'Back to the Future: instability in Europe after the Cold War', *International Security*, 15 (1): 5–56.

Mearsheimer, J. J. (2001) *The Tragedy of Great Power Politics*, New York: Norton.

Mearsheimer, J. J. and Walt, S. M. (2003) 'An Unnecessary War', *Foreign Policy*, 134: 50–9.

Mendelson, S. E. (2004) 'Wanted: a new US policy on Russia', Program on New Approaches to Russian Security (PONARS) Policy Memo 324, January.

Menon, A. and Lipkin, J. (2003) 'European Attitudes Towards Transatlantic Relations 2000–2003: an analytical survey', prepared for the informal meeting of EU Foreign Ministers 2–4 May, Rhodes and Kastelloizo, Birmingham: University of Birmingham European Research Institute.

Missiroli, A. (ed.) (2005) *Disasters, Diseases, Disruptions: a new D-drive for the EU*, Chaillot Paper no. 83 (September), Paris: European Union Institute for Security Studies.

Monaghan, A. (2005) 'Russian Perspectives of Russia–EU Security Relations', *Conflict Studies Research Centre Russia Series*, no. 5/38 (August). Online. Available: http://www.da.mod.uk/CSRC/documents/Russian/ (accessed 15 December 2005).

Monar, J. (2004) 'The EU as an International Actor in the Domain of Justice and Home Affairs', *European Foreign Affairs Review*, 9 (3): 395–415.

Moran, D. (2002) 'Strategic Theory and the History of War', in J. Baylis, J. Wirtz,

E. Cohen and C. Gray (eds), *Strategy in the Contemporary World*, Oxford: Oxford University Press.

Moravcsik, A. (1998) *The Choice for Europe: social purpose and state power from Messina to Maastricht*, London: UCL Press.

Morozov, V. (2003) 'V poiskakh Evropy: rossiiskii politicheskii diskurs i okruzhay-ushchii mir' ('In Search of Europe: Russian political discourse and the surrounding world'), *Neprikosnovennii Zapas* (NZ), 30 (4). Online. Available: http://www.eurozine.com/journals/nz/issue/2003-09-16.html (accessed 16 December 2005).

Mörth, U. (2003) 'Framing an American Threat: the European Commission and the technology gap', in M. Knodt and S. Princen (eds), *Understanding the European Union's External Relations*, London: Routledge.

Muller, H. (2003) *Terrorism, Proliferation: a European threat assessment*, Chaillot Paper no. 58, Paris: European Union Institute for Security Studies. Online. Available: http://www.iss-eu.org/chaillot/chai58e.pdf (accessed 8 December 2005).

Munro, E. (ed.) (2005) *Challenges to Neutral and Non-Aligned Countries in Europe and Beyond*, Geneva: Centre for Security Policy.

Murray, W. and Grimsley, M. (1994) 'Introduction: on strategy', in W. Murray, M. Knox and A. Bernstein (eds), *The Making of Strategy: rulers, states and wars*, Cambridge: Cambridge University Press.

Nasr, V. (2004) 'Regional Implications of Shi'a Revival in Iraq', *Washington Quarterly*, 27 (3): 7–24.

National Commission on Terrorist Attacks (2003) *The 9-11 Commission Report: final report of the National Commission on Terrorist Attacks Upon the United States*, Washington, DC: US Government Printing Office. Online. Available: http://www.gpoaccess.gov/911/ (accessed 1 December 2005).

National Intelligence Council (2005) *Mapping the Global Future: report of the National Intelligence Council's 2020 project*, Washington, DC: CIA. Online. Available: http://www.foia.cia.gov/2020/2020.pdf (accessed 8 December 2005).

Neuhold, H. (2003) 'Comments on the Austrian Positions', in H. Ojanen (ed.), *Neutrality and Non-Alignment in Europe Today*, Helsinki: Finnish Institute of International Affairs Report, p. 6.

Neumann, I. B. and Heikka, H. (2005) 'Grand Strategy, Strategic Culture, Practice: the social roots of Nordic defence', *Cooperation and Conflict*, 40 (1): 5–23.

Newman, A. (2004) 'Arms Control, Proliferation and Terrorism: the Bush administration's post-September 11 security strategy', *Journal of Strategic Studies*, 27 (1): 59–88.

Nielsen, A. D. and Hamilton, D. (2005) *Transatlantic Homeland Security*, London: Routledge.

Nilsson, A. S. (1991) *Den Solidariska Stormakten*, Stockholm: Timbro.

Nye, J. S. Jr. (2003) 'US Power and Strategy after Iraq', *Foreign Affairs*, 82 (4): 60–73.

Nye, J. S. Jr. (2004) *Soft Power: the means to success in world politics*, New York: Public Affairs.

O'Loughlin, J., Tuathail, G. O. and Kolossov, V. (2004) 'A "Risky Westward Turn"? Putin's 9-11 script and ordinary Russians', *Europe–Asia Studies*, 56 (1): 3–34.

Ojanen, H. (ed.) (2003) *Neutrality and Non-Alignment in Europe Today*, Finnish Institute of International Affairs Report, 6/2003, Helsinki: FIIA.

Owen, D. (1995) *Balkan Odyssey*, London: Victor Gollancz.

Oxford Analytica (2004) 'Middle East: Arab reform plan is long-term project', *Oxford Analytica Daily Brief*, 15 June. Online. Available: http://www.oxweb.com/daily_brief.asp?NewsItemID=100560&Link=FALSE (accessed 8 December 2005).

Paarlberg, R. L. (2004) 'Knowledge as Power: science, military dominance, and US security', *International Security*, 29 (1): 122–25.

Patten, C. (2001) *Barcelona: five years later*, Brussels: European Commission.

Patten, C. (2004a) 'Islam and the West – at the Crossroads', speech at the Oxford Centre for Islamic Studies, 24 May. Online. Available: http://europa.eu.int/comm/external_relations/news/patten/sp04_256.htm (accessed 8 December 2005).

Patten, C. (2004b) Speech to the European Parliament, 14 September.

Peel, Q. (2004) 'Europe Won't Buy Big Idea', *Financial Times*, 4 February: 13.

Persson, G. (2004) 'Contribution by Prime Minister of Sweden to Debate in the Riksdag', *Snabbprotokoll*, 30 January: 61.

Peterson, J. (2003) 'The US and Europe in the Balkans', in J. Peterson and M. A. Pollack (eds), *Europe, America, Bush*, London: Routledge.

Peterson, J. (2006) 'The College of Commissioners', in J. Peterson and M. Shackleton (eds), *The Institutions of the European Union*, 2nd edition, Oxford: Oxford University Press.

Peterson, J. and Bomberg, E. (1998) 'Northern Enlargement and EU Decision-making', in P. H. Laurent and M. Maresceau (eds), *The State of the European Union*, vol. 4, Boulder, CO: Lynne Rienner.

Peterson, J. and Bomberg, E. (1999) *Decision-Making in the European Union*, Basingstoke: Palgrave.

Peterson, J. and Pollack, M. A. (eds) (2003) *Europe, America, Bush*, London: Routledge.

Peterson, J. and Sjursen, H. (eds) (1998) *A Common Foreign Policy for Europe? Competing visions of the CFSP*, London: Routledge.

Petrov, N. (2004) 'Putin's Anti-Federal Reform 2: back to the USSR', Program on New Approaches to Russian Security (PONARS) Policy Memo 339.

Phillips, D. L. (2005) *Losing Iraq: inside the post-war reconstruction fiasco*, New York: Westview.

Pletka, D. (2005) 'Europe is Starting to Dance to the Bush Tune', American Enterprise Institute for Public Policy Research. Online. Available: http://www.aei.org/publications/filter.all,pubID.21922/pub_detail.asp (accessed 2 December 2005).

Pond, E. (2004) *Friendly Fire: the near death of the transatlantic alliance*, Washington, DC: Brookings Institution Press.

Putin, V. (2000) 'Russia at the Turn of the Millennium', in V. Putin, *First Person: an astonishingly frank self-portrait by Russia's President Vladimir Putin*, London: Hutchinson.

Raik, K. (2004) 'European Security Strategy from the Finnish Perspective: the fading away of non-alignment?', in M. Overhaus, H. W. Maull, and S. Harnisch (eds), 'The European Security Strategy: paper tiger or catalyst for joint action?', *German Foreign Policy in Dialogue* (Newsletter), 5 (14): 22–8. Online. Available: www.deutsche-aussenpolitik.de/newsletter/issue14.pdf (accessed 10 December 2005).

Rees, G. W. (1998) *The Western European Union at the Crossroads*, Oxford: Westview Press.

Reiter, E. and Frank, J. (2004) 'The European Security Strategy from the Austrian Perspective: a valuable contribution to the further Europeanization of Austria's security policy', in M. Overhaus, H. W. Maull and S. Harnisch (eds), 'The European Security Strategy: paper tiger or catalyst for joint action?', *German Foreign Policy in Dialogue* (Newsletter), 5 (14): 16–21. Online. Available: www. deutsche-aussenpolitik.de/newsletter/issue14.pdf (accessed 10 December 2005).

Rice, C. (2000) 'Campaign 2000: promoting the national interest', *Foreign Affairs*, 79 (1): 45–62.

Rice, C. (2003) 'Speech to the IISS', London, 26 June. Online. Available: http://www.iiss.org/conferencepage.php?confID=60 (accessed 8 December 2005).

Risse, T. (2003) 'For a New Transatlantic – and European – Bargain', *Internationale Politik*, Fall: 22–30.

Risse, T. (2004) 'Beyond Iraq: the crisis of the transatlantic security community', in D. Held and M. Koenig-Archibugi (eds), *American Power in the 21st Century*, Cambridge: Polity Press.

Roberts, A. (2003) 'Law and the Use of Force after Iraq', *Survival*, 45 (2): 31–56.

Robertson, G. (2001) 'European Defence: challenges and prospects', *Journal of Common Market Studies*, 39 (4): 791–800.

Ronin, V. (2001) 'Russia: Outside Europe?', in K. Malfliet and L. Verpoest (eds), *Russia and Europe in a Changing International Environment*, Leuven: Leuven University Press, pp. 117–32.

Royal Institute of International Affairs (2004) *Iraq in Transition: vortex or catalyst?*, Chatham House Middle East Programme Report, London: RIIA, September. Online. Available: http://www.riia.org/pdf/research/mep/BP0904.pdf (accessed 8 December 2005).

Ruhala, K. (2003) 'Alliance and Non-Alignment at the Onset of the 21st Century', in B. Huldt, T. Ries, J. Mörtberg and E. Davidson (eds), *The New Northern Security Agenda: perspectives from Finland and Sweden*, Strategic Yearbook 2004, Stockholm: Swedish National Defence College.

Rumsfeld, D. (2002) '"21st Century Transformation" of U.S. Armed Forces', speech at National Defense University, Fort McNair, Washington, DC, 31 January. Online. Available: http://www.defenselink.mil/speeches/2002/s20020131-secdef. html (accessed 7 January 2006).

Rupp, R. E. (2006) *NATO After 9/11: an alliance in decline*, New York: Palgrave.

Salminen, P. (2003) '"Nordic Power Projection" and International Operations: aspects from the past and new opportunities', in B. Huldt, T. Ries, J. Mörtberg and E. Davidson (eds), *The New Northern Security Agenda: perspectives from Finland and Sweden*, Strategic Yearbook 2004, Stockholm: Swedish National Defence College.

Salmon, T. and Shepherd, A. J. K. (2003) *Toward a European Army: a military power in the making?*, Boulder, CO: Lynne Rienner.

Scannell, D. (2004) 'Financing ESDP Military Operations', *European Foreign Affairs Review*, 9: 529–49.

Schmitt, B. (2003) *The European Union and Armaments: getting a bigger bang for the euro*, Chaillot Paper no. 63 (August), Paris: European Union Institute for Security Studies.

Schmitt, B. (2005) 'Defense Procurement in the European Union: the current debate', Report of an EUISS Task Force (May), Paris: European Union Institute for Security Studies.

Schmitt, E. and Shanker, T. (2005) 'New Name for "War on Terror" Reflects Wider US Campaign', *New York Times*, 26 July.

Schuette, R. (2004) *EU–Russia Relations: Interests and Values – A European Perspective*, Washington, DC: Carnegie Endowment for International Peace.

Serfaty, S. (2005) *The Vital Partnership – Power and Order: America and Europe beyond Iraq*, Boulder, CO: Rowman and Littlefield.

Shambaugh, D. (2005) 'The New Strategic Triangle: US and European reactions to China's rise', *Washington Quarterly*, 28 (3): 7–25.

Sivonen, P. (2003) 'Finland's Security and Defence Policy in the Post Post-Cold War World', in B. Huldt, T. Ries, J. Mörtberg and E. Davidson (eds), *The New Northern Security Agenda: perspectives from Finland and Sweden*, Strategic Yearbook 2004, Stockholm: Swedish National Defence College.

Sjursen, H. (1998) 'Missed Opportunity or Eternal Fantasy? The idea of a European security and defence policy', in J. Peterson and H. Sjursen (eds), *A Common Foreign Policy for Europe? Competing visions of the CFSP*, London: Routledge.

Sköns, E., Omitoogun, W., Perdomo, C. and Stålenheim, P. (2005) 'Military Expenditure', in *SIPRI Yearbook 2005: armaments, disarmament and international security*, Oxford: Oxford University Press.

Sloan, S. R. (2003; 2nd edn 2005) *NATO, the European Union, and the Atlantic Community: the transatlantic bargain reconsidered*, Lanham, MD: Rowman and Littlefield.

Slocombe, W. B. (2003) 'Force, Pre-emption and Legitimacy', *Survival*, 45 (1): 117–30.

Smith, K. E. (2003) *European Union Foreign Policy in a Changing World*, Cambridge and Malden, MA: Polity Press.

Smith, K. E. (2005) 'Enlargement and the European Order', in C. Hill and M. Smith (eds), *The International Relations of the European Union*, Oxford: Oxford University Press.

Smith, M. (2004) *Europe's Foreign and Security Policy: the institutionalisation of cooperation*, Cambridge: Cambridge University Press.

Smith, S. (2002) 'The End of the Unipolar Moment? September 11 and the future of world order', *International Relations*, 16 (2): 171–83.

Smith, T. and Diamond, L. (2004) 'Was Iraq a Fool's Errand?', *Foreign Affairs*, 83 (6): 130–3.

Snyder, J. (2004) 'One World, Rival Theories', *Foreign Policy*, 145: 53–62.

Solana, J. (2003) 'The Voice of Europe on Security Matters', Royal Institute for International Relations (IRRI-KIIB), Palais d'Egmont, 26 November 2003. Online. Available: http://ue.eu.int/cms3_applications/applications/solana/list.asp?cmsid=246&bid=107&page=arch&archDate=2003&archMonth=11 (accessed 1 December 2005).

Spears, J. (2003) 'The Emergence of a European "Strategic Personality"', *Arms Control Today*, November. Online. Available: http://www.armscontrol.org/act/2003_11/Spear.asp?print (accessed 8 December 2005).

Stålvant, C.-E. (2003) 'Interests, Loyalties, and the Lures of Power: the Baltic Sea states in future European governance', in B. Huldt, T. Ries, J. Mörtberg and E. Davidson (eds), *The New Northern Security Agenda: perspectives from Finland and Sweden*, Strategic Yearbook 2004, Stockholm: Swedish National Defence College.

Steffenson, R. (2005) *Managing EU–US Relations*, Manchester: Manchester University Press.

Stephens, P. (2005) 'An American Map of the Future Bush Cannot Ignore', *Financial*

Times, 21 January. Online. Available: http://www.ft.com (accessed 15 December 2005).

Stevenson, J. (2003) 'How Europe and America Defend Themselves', *Foreign Affairs*, 82 (2): 75–90.

Strömvik, M. (2005) 'To Act as a Union: explaining the development of the EU's collective foreign policy', unpublished thesis, University of Lund.

Susser, A. (2003) 'The Decline of the Arabs', *Middle East Quarterly*, 10 (4): 3–16.

Swedish Government (2004) *Vart Framtida Forsvar – forsvarspolitisk inriktning 2005–2007*, Stockholm: Regeringskansliet.

Swedish Ministry for Foreign Affairs (2003) 'Questions and Answers on the Swedish Rapid Reaction Force in the Democratic Republic of Congo', http://www.ud.se/inenglish/frontpage/030701_congo.htm (accessed 21 August 2003).

Tallberg, J. and Elgström, O. (2001) 'Avslutning', in J. Tallberg, *Nar Europa kom till Sverige*, Stockholm: SNS Forlag.

Tewes, H. (2002) *Germany, Civilian Power and the New Europe*, Basingstoke: Palgrave.

Toje, A. (2005) 'The 2003 European Security Strategy: a critical appraisal', *European Foreign Affairs Review*, 10: 117–33.

Tonra, B. (2001) *The Europeanisation of National Foreign Policy*, Aldershot: Ashgate.

Tuomioja, E. (2004) 'Shaping the EU's Future Role in the World', address by the Finnish Foreign Minister at Global Europe 2020 Seminar in Helsinki, 26 October.

United Nations (2004) *A More Secure World: our shared responsibility*, New York: report of the UN Secretary General's High Level Panel.

US Department of Defense (2001) *Network Centric Warfare*, Report to Congress, Washington, DC, 27 July.

US Department of Defense (2005) 'Annual Report to Congress: the military power of the People's Republic of China'. Online. Available: http://www.defenselink.mil/news/Jul2005/20050720_2163.html (accessed 7 December 2005).

Valásek, T. (2005) 'New EU Members in Europe's Security Policy', *Cambridge Review of International Affairs*, 18 (2): 217–28.

Van Creveld, M. (1991) *The Transformation of War*, New York: Free Press.

Venusberg Group (2004) *A European Defence Strategy*, Gütersloh: Bertelsmann. Online. Available: http://www.cap.uni-muenchen.de/download/2004/2004_Venusberg_Report.pdf (accessed 8 December 2005).

Walt, S. M. (1997) 'Why Alliances Endure or Collapse', *Survival*, 39 (1): 156–79.

Walt, S. M. (2005) *Taming American Power: the global response to US primacy*, London: W. W. Norton.

Waltz, K. (1979) *Theory of International Politics*, Reading, MA: Addison-Wesley.

Wang, J. (2005) 'China's Search for Stability With America', *Foreign Affairs*, 'China edition', 84 (5): 39–48.

Wendt, A. (1999) *Social Theory of International Politics*, Cambridge: Cambridge University Press.

White House (2003) *National Strategy for Combating Terrorism*. Online. Available: http://www.whitehouse.gov/news/releases/2003/02/counter_terrorism/counter_terrorism_strategy.pdf (accessed 8 December 2005).

Whitman, R. G. (1998) *From Civilian Power to Superpower? The international identity of the European Union*, Basingstoke: Palgrave.

Wilhelmsen, J. and Flikke, G. (2005) '"Copy That . . . " A Russian "Bush Doctrine" in the CIS?', Oslo: Norwegian Institute of International Affairs.

Wohlforth, W. (2004) 'The Transatlantic Dimension', in R. Dannreuther (ed.), *European Union Foreign and Security Policy*, London: Routledge.

Wolfowitz, P. (2002) 'Speech to International Institute for Strategic Studies', 2 December. Online. Available: http://www.iiss.org/conferencepage.php?confID =42 (accessed 8 December 2005).

Wong, R. (2005) 'The Europeanization of Foreign Policy', in C. Hill and M. Smith (eds), *International Relations and the European Union*, Oxford: Oxford University Press.

Woodward, B. (2004) *Plan of Attack*, London: Simon and Schuster.

Working Group VIII-Defence (2002) *Report from the Chairman of the Working Group VIII-Defence Convention*, Brussels: European Convention Secretariat.

Zelikow, P. (2003) 'The Transformation of National Security', *The National Interest*, 71 (Spring): 17–28.

Zelikow, P. and Rice, C. (1997) *Germany Unified and Europe Transformed: a study in statecraft*, Cambridge, MA: Harvard University Press.

Zheng, B. (2005) 'China's "Peaceful Rise" to Great-Power Status', *Foreign Affairs*, 'China edition', 84 (5): 18–24.

Zweig, D. and Bi, J. (2005) 'China's Global Hunt for Energy', *Foreign Affairs*, 'China edition', 84 (5): 25–38.

Index